AF594167

“Bill, you will love this camera.”

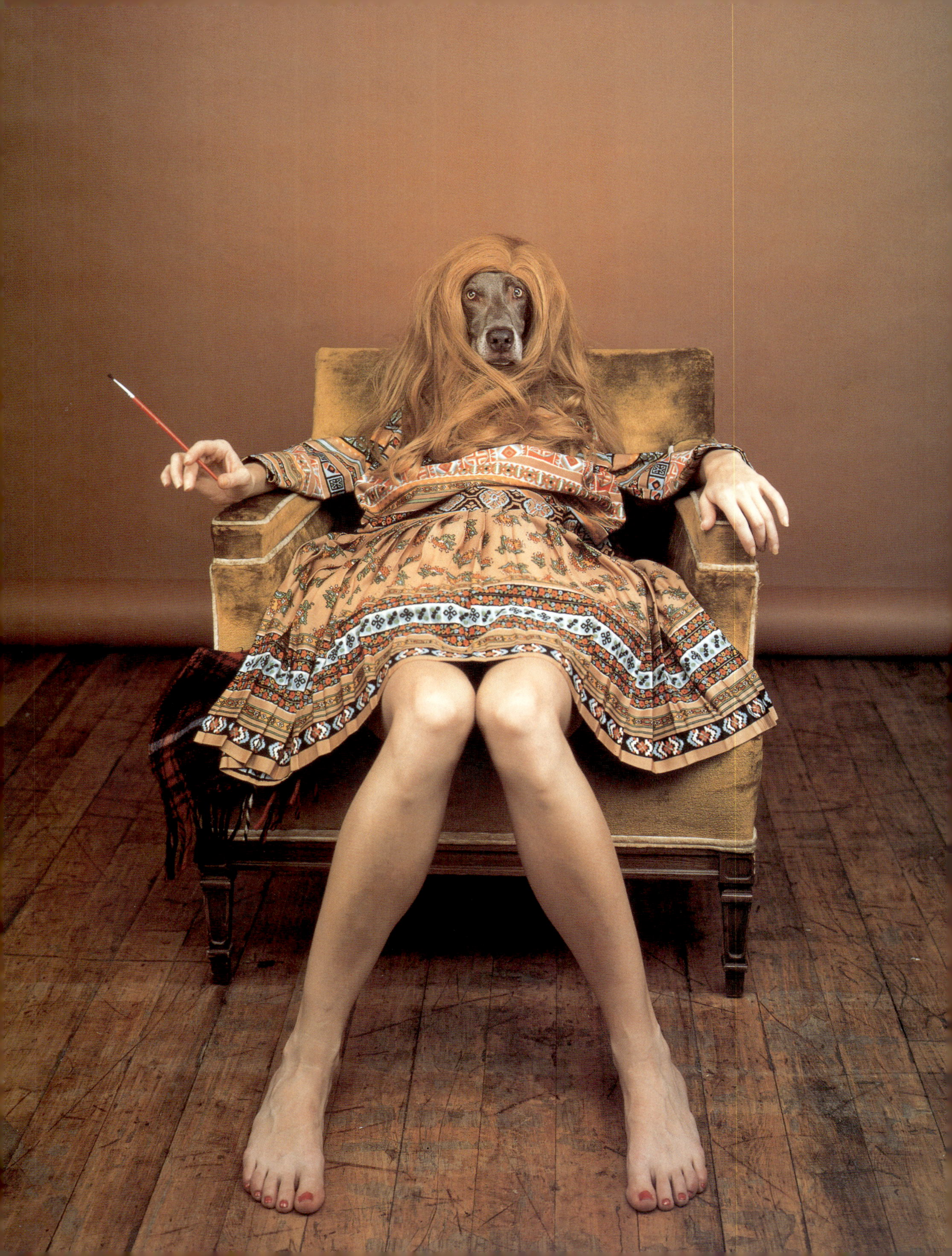

WILLIAM WEGMAN

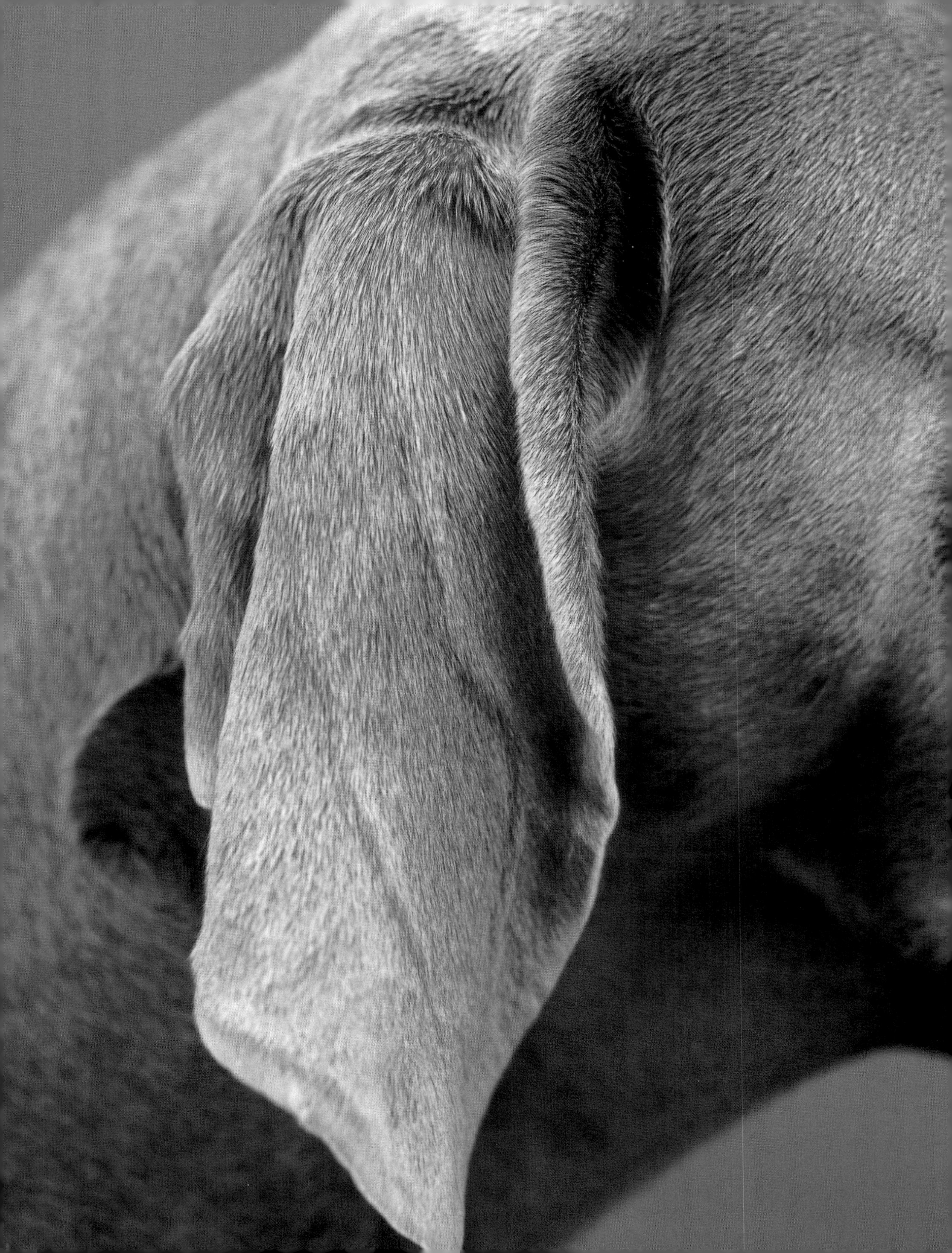

POLAROIDS

HARRY N. ABRAMS, INC.,
PUBLISHERS

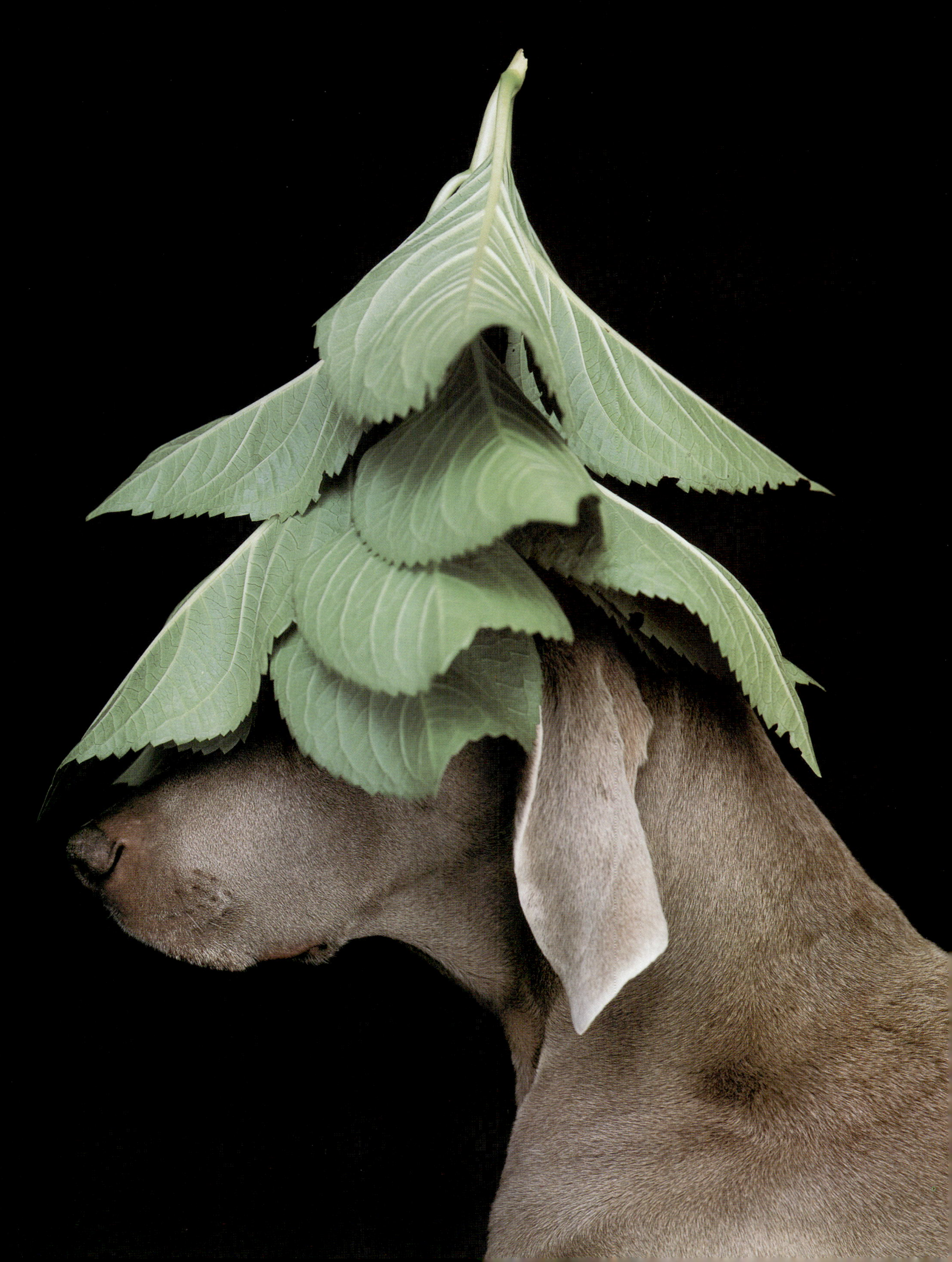

In 1978 I received a call from photographer JoAnn Verburg in Boston inviting me to experiment with an unusual camera that Polaroid research engineers had recently invented, the 20x24, designed to take twenty-by-twenty-four-inch life-sized portraits of amazing clarity and detail "in an instant." Time with the big studio camera was now being offered to artists and photographers.

I was on the list.

"Come to Boston. Bring your dog."*

I declined. I had rules: I only used black and white. My photos were never larger than 11x14. Big pictures in color were not on the list.

JoAnn persisted. "Bill, you will love this camera."

With little enthusiasm and low expectations, I accepted. In early 1979, we left New York for Boston.

Man Ray loved road trips. It's about a five-hour drive, not including a stop on the way at my parents' house in East Longmeadow, a good place for Man Ray to run and for me to rummage for props. I knew Boston fairly well, having lived there for four years while attending art school. More recently I had made several trips to Boston to participate in an experimental video work shop at WGBH during which I developed a close friendship while working with multimedia artist Betsy Connors, and it was with Betsy that we stayed during our first visits to the Polaroid studio. Her house, like my parents', was a treasure trove for props, and I raided it openly. (A great number of Betsy's belongings made their way into my pictures, including house plants, a long gray sock, a guitar, and Styrofoam mountains that she had planned on using

*Man Ray, so named after one of my artist heroes of the Dada and Surrealist movements, entered my world in September 1970, a pudgy, six-week-old puppy. In no time he grew into adulthood, a weimaraner of classic proportions, to become a central figure in my photo and video works, overshadowing all other elements. By the mid-Seventies, I had become the guy with the dog.

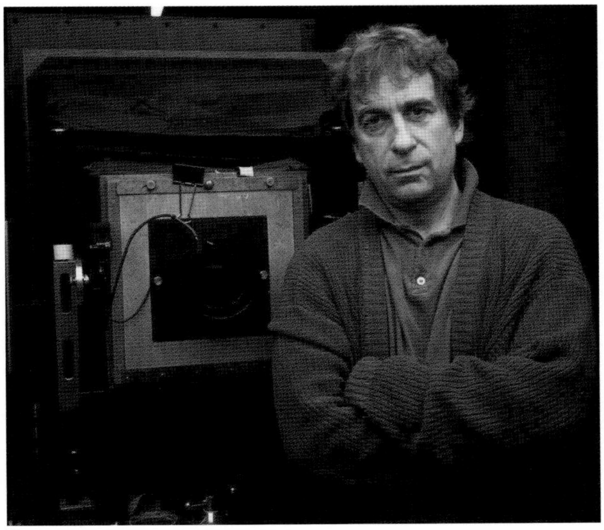

in her own photo piece. Betsy was very generous.) Armed with a carload of miscellaneous material and my trusty dog, I felt prepared for the first day.

When I arrived at the studio at Ames Street in Cambridge, Ray padded along beside me in his familiar way. Everyone wanted to meet him. He was a bit of a celebrity and I didn't mind the way he deflected attention away from me. I focused my gaze on his dark-gray almost black, coat, unusual for a weimaraner. I hadn't photographed him for a long time. At nine years Ray had grown thick and old. It hurt to see him like this. In his prime he was chiseled.

As an act of discipline I had abstained from photographing him for all of 1978. A miserable year. He was anxious to get back to work.

Seeing the camera for the first time I noticed how big it was. Big! It looked like a refrigerator—a refrigerator and a cello, both rickety and solid. Considering the high-tech corporate surroundings, its appearance was surprisingly old-fashioned, I thought. With its gigantic bellows, handmade wooden construction, and brass fittings, it looked not unlike the camera Carleton Watkins toted through Yosemite over a hundred years ago.

JoAnn and technician Peter Bass explained how it worked as I pretended to listen. There was something called a pod, fifteen of which were loaded into a rickety black tray and placed in back of the camera, where

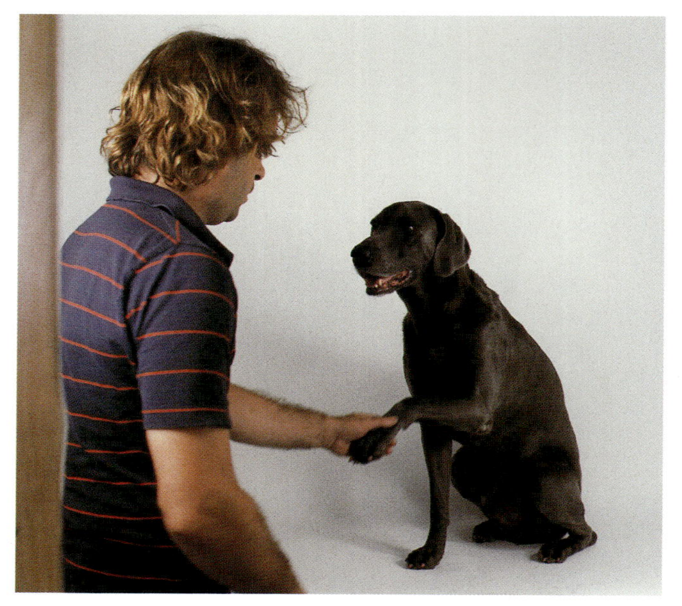

it swings open on hinges. Looking inside, an experienced photographer might see and understand how the film-and-paper roll interfaced with the pods. All I saw was a cavernous black chamber leading to a bright opening, the lens. A demonstration ensued. After each exposure a section of film and paper would descend from the back of the camera. It was sliced off the roll with a sharp Olfa knife and carried to a table. After about seventy-five seconds (the exact time is dependent on room temperature), the dark, shiny mylarish negative layer was peeled away and discarded, revealing a gigantic, fully developed Polaroid print. And a lingering chemical odor.

During the studio tour I was shown examples of work made with the 20x24. Colorful flowers, lots of red. Subject matter notwithstanding, I took issue with their glossy finish. They looked slick. My photo pieces had a low-tech straightforwardness consistent with Sixties minimalism.

Determined to preserve my aesthetic, I placed Man Ray in three basic dog command positions—Sit, Stand, Down—and covered him in a shroud of black linen. I worked to create a group of three images that together would form a triptych.

As JoAnn peeled the film from the first exposure, my attention was drawn to the goopy residue and graphically intriguing comblike pattern along the upper and lower borders of the print. This striking pattern was more compelling than my image, a barely discernable shrouded shape in a gloomy greenish field. Push-pinning it to the linen-covered wall for viewing, I noticed that after a few minutes the green gradually turned black. Greenish black. Since I had planned a triptych I needed two more.

The tedious work took all day and most of the next to complete. It was not all happy work. The room became dark, heavy, depressing, as more and more exposures wallpapered the room. It was remarkable how many pictures it took to make this group hold together—forty exposures in all! It was a struggle getting the camera to work, and things invariably went wrong. I learned new terms such as "cocked pod," "tight gap," and "light leak," for things that caused the technicians great concern. (Over time I came to see these tech breakdowns as blessings, using the delays to stop and think about my next idea.)

It was no less a struggle to learn to work at the pace the camera set—to slow down and closely examine the images as they appeared right before my eyes. The process itself propelled me in directions I wasn't ready for. With Polaroid I got ahead of myself.

More than twenty years later not much has changed.

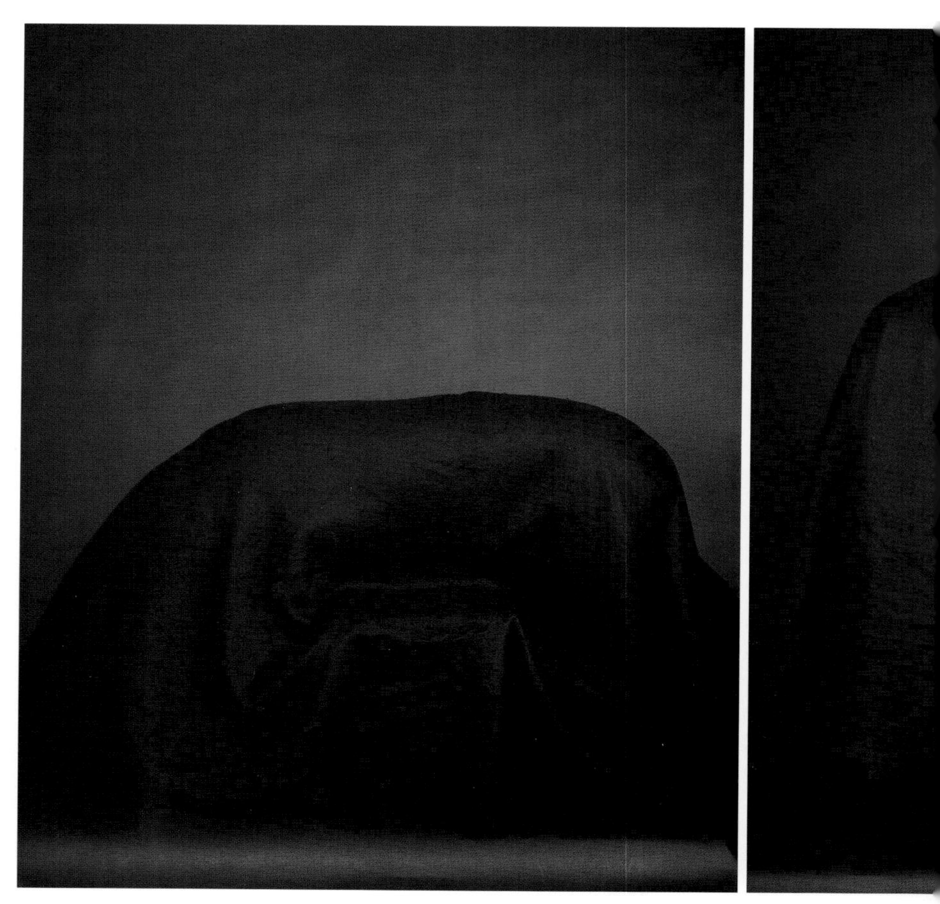

Black Triptych, 1979

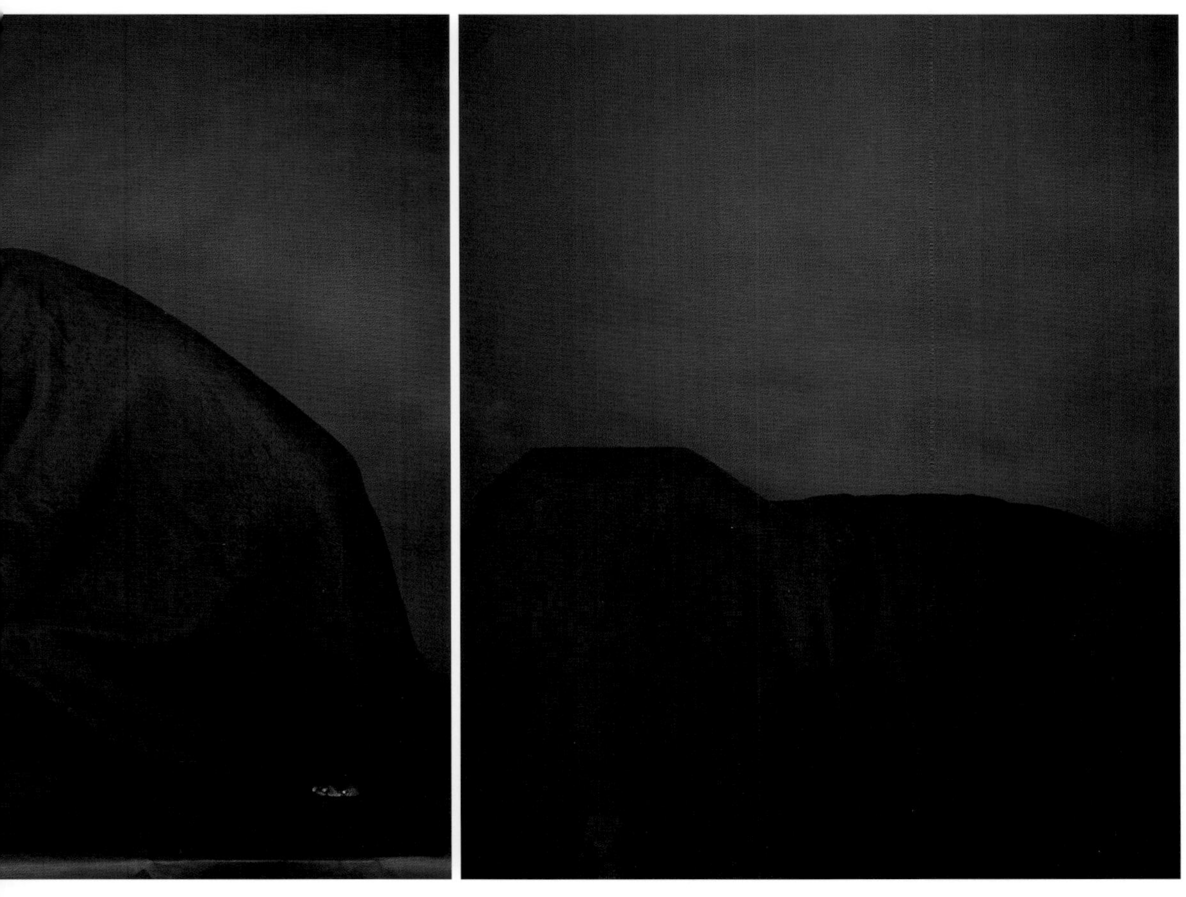

Fey Ray, 1979

I distrusted color.
Sensuous, romantic, elusive color.
Color was. . . well. . . colorful.

I began by ignoring color, using the film as though it was black and white. On my third day with the camera, a bottle of Revlon red nail polish made its way onto the set with Man Ray. The little bottle was acceptable. It wasn't simply red. It was red nail polish. As I applied it to Man Ray's toenails I convinced myself that it was OK. No one could accuse me of using color subjectively. After positioning Ray on the black set paper and composing the frame, I said "shake." As he raised his paw with the painted toenails, I snapped the shutter, and seventy-five seconds later—color! There was no denying it.

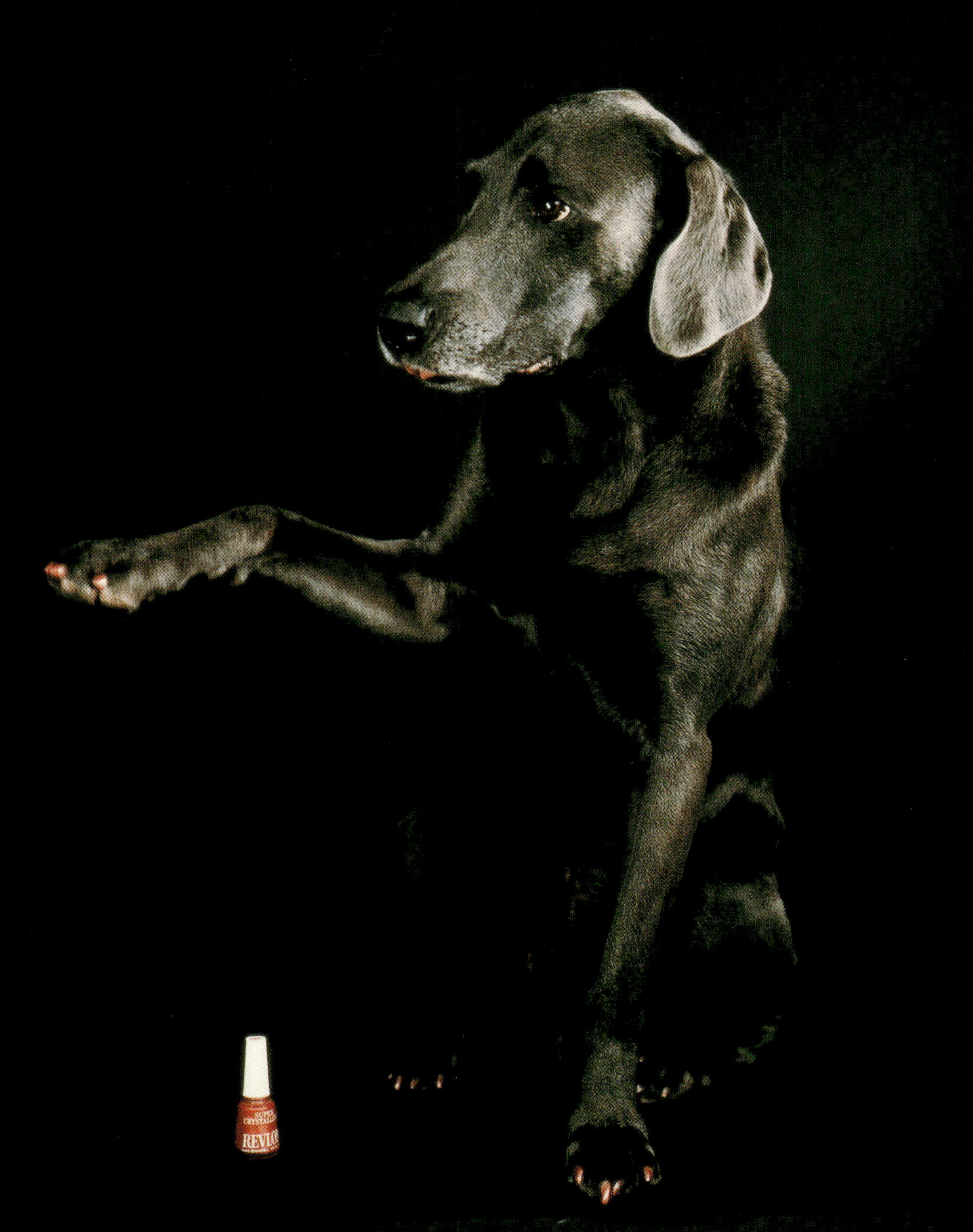

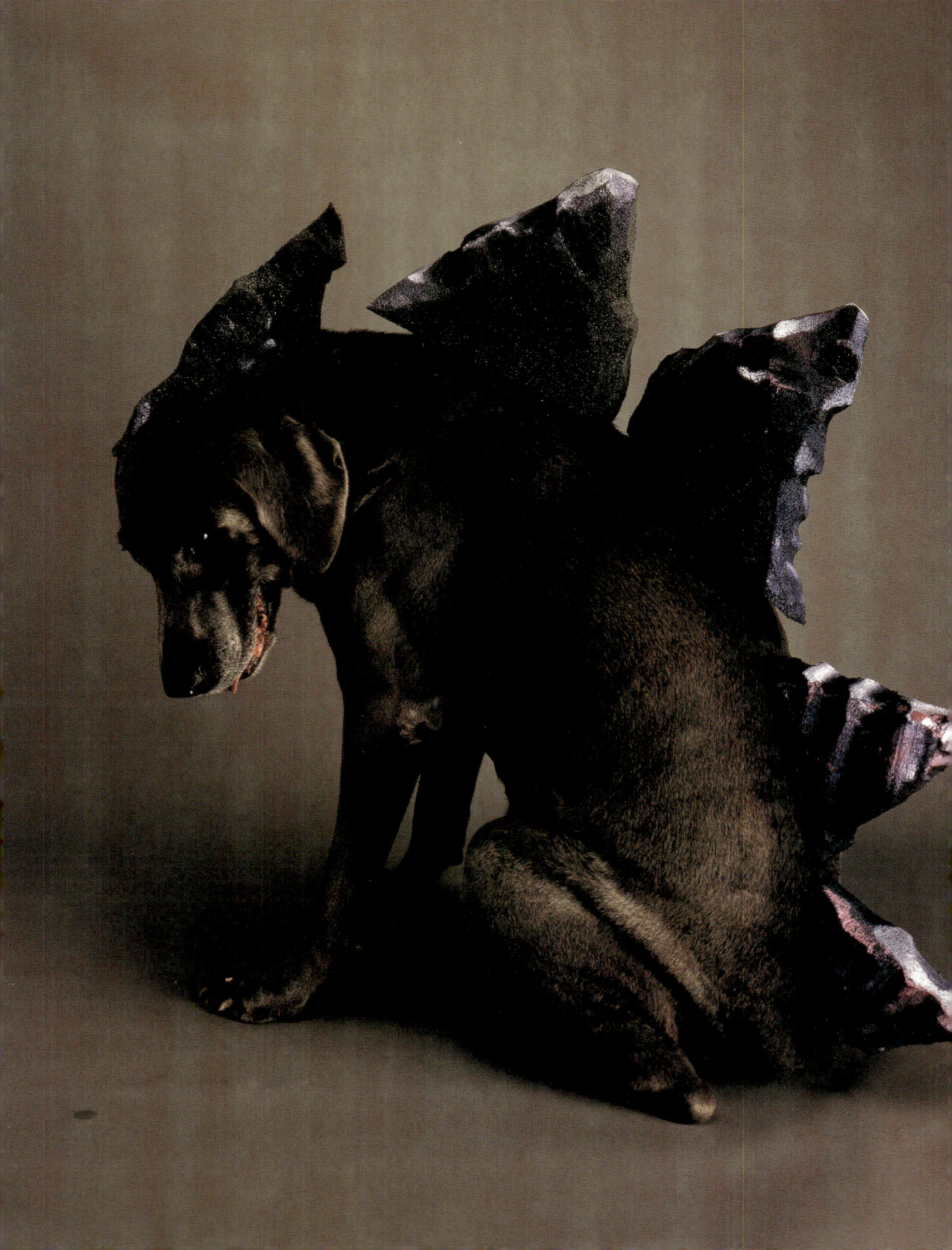

Dino Ray—Back, 1981

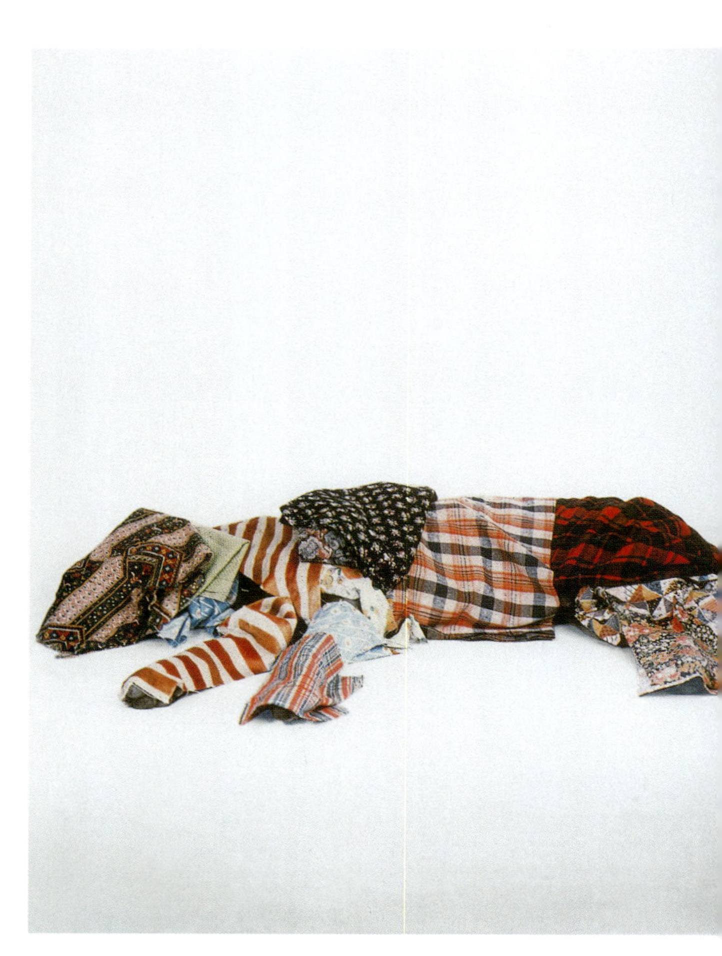

Remnants, 1979

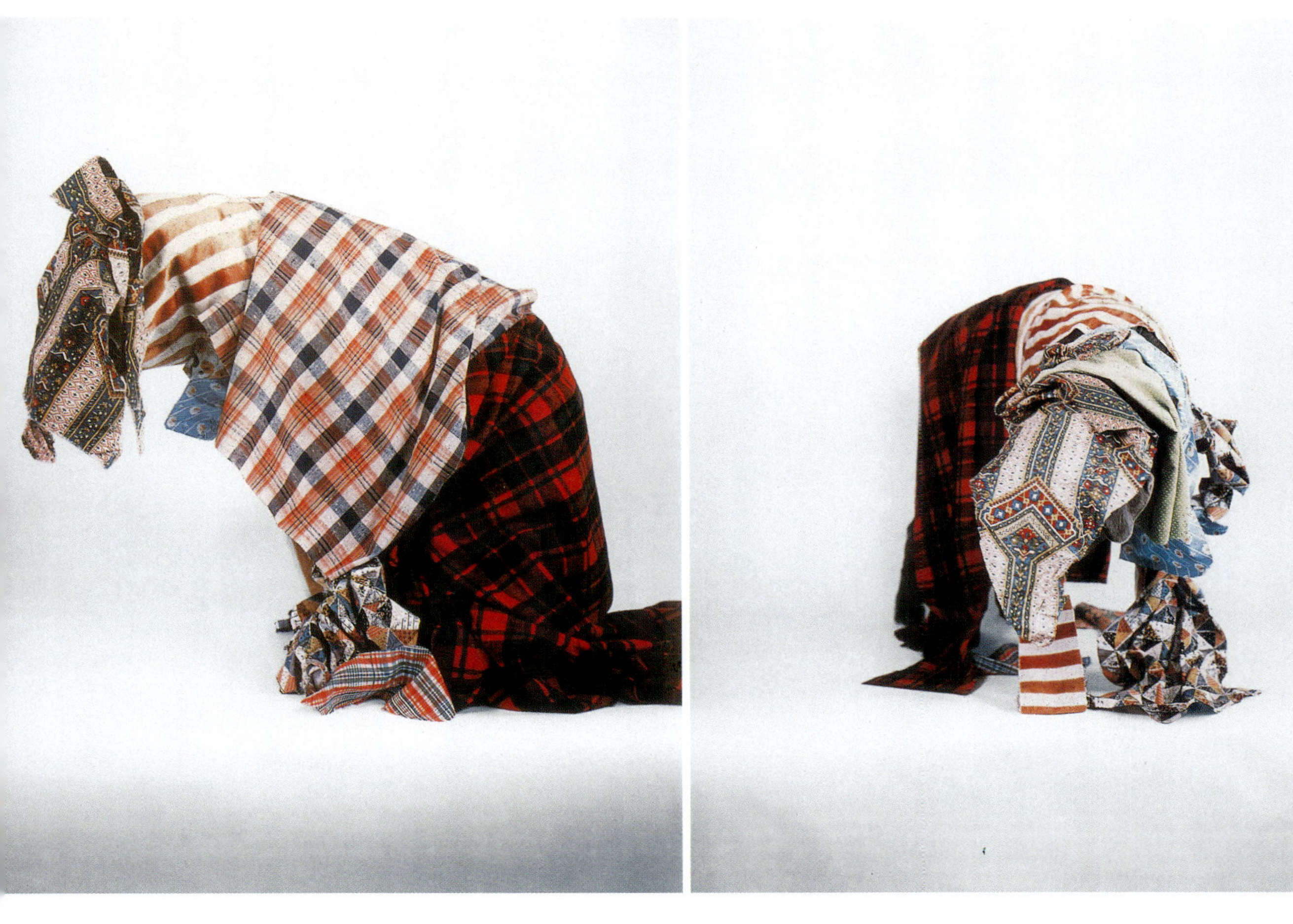

Opposite: ***Airedale #1 Standing,*** 1981
Below: ***William's Woolsworth,*** 1981

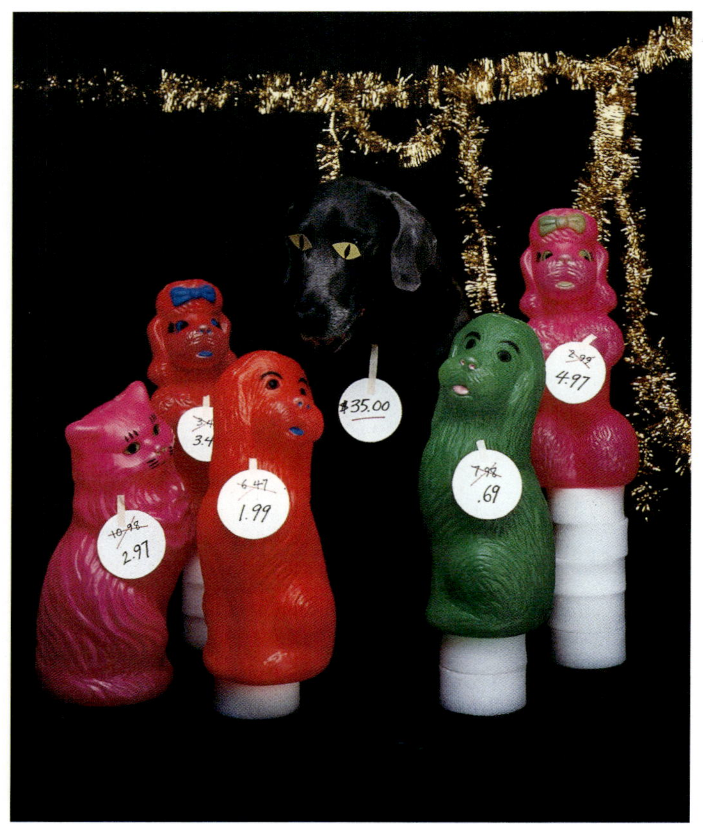

One morning at the studio I was coiling strands of tinsel garland around Man Ray, my armature, completely wrapping his torso, head, tail, and four legs.

Something unexpected began to take shape. He was turning into a different kind of dog—an Airedale. It was surprising how the Polaroid film converted the shiny tinsel into something natural looking, like fur or perhaps hay. In the photo he really does look like an Airedale.

Some dogs don't like to be stared at. Man Ray required it. Surrounded by light-boxes that flanked the cyclopean eye of the big camera, he was truly at ease, never balking as I studied him for new possibilities. As the strobes pop in a blast of light, Man Ray appears in afterimage. So illuminated, he begins to glow, growing larger in my mind. In the act of being photographed he becomes magnified.

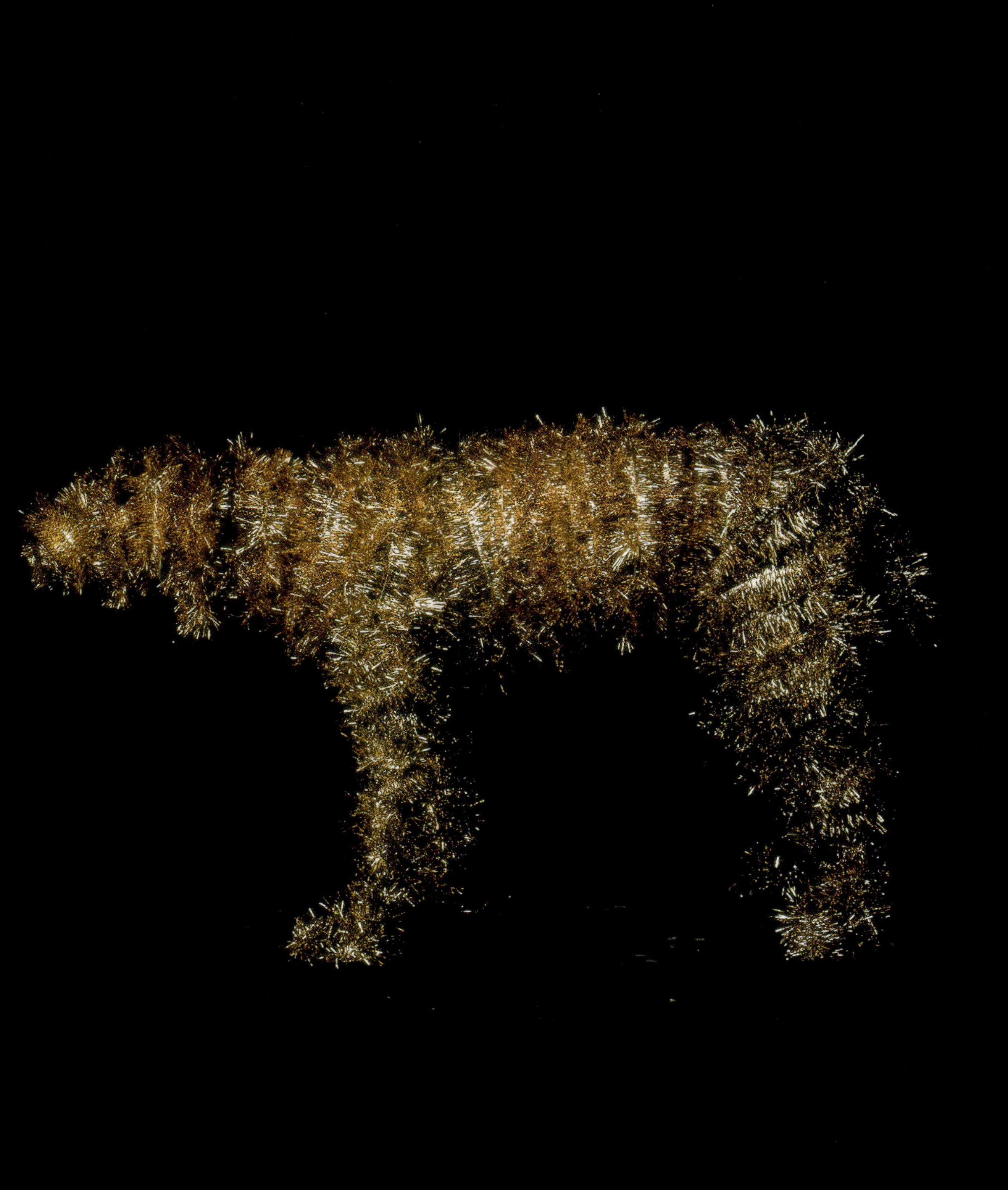

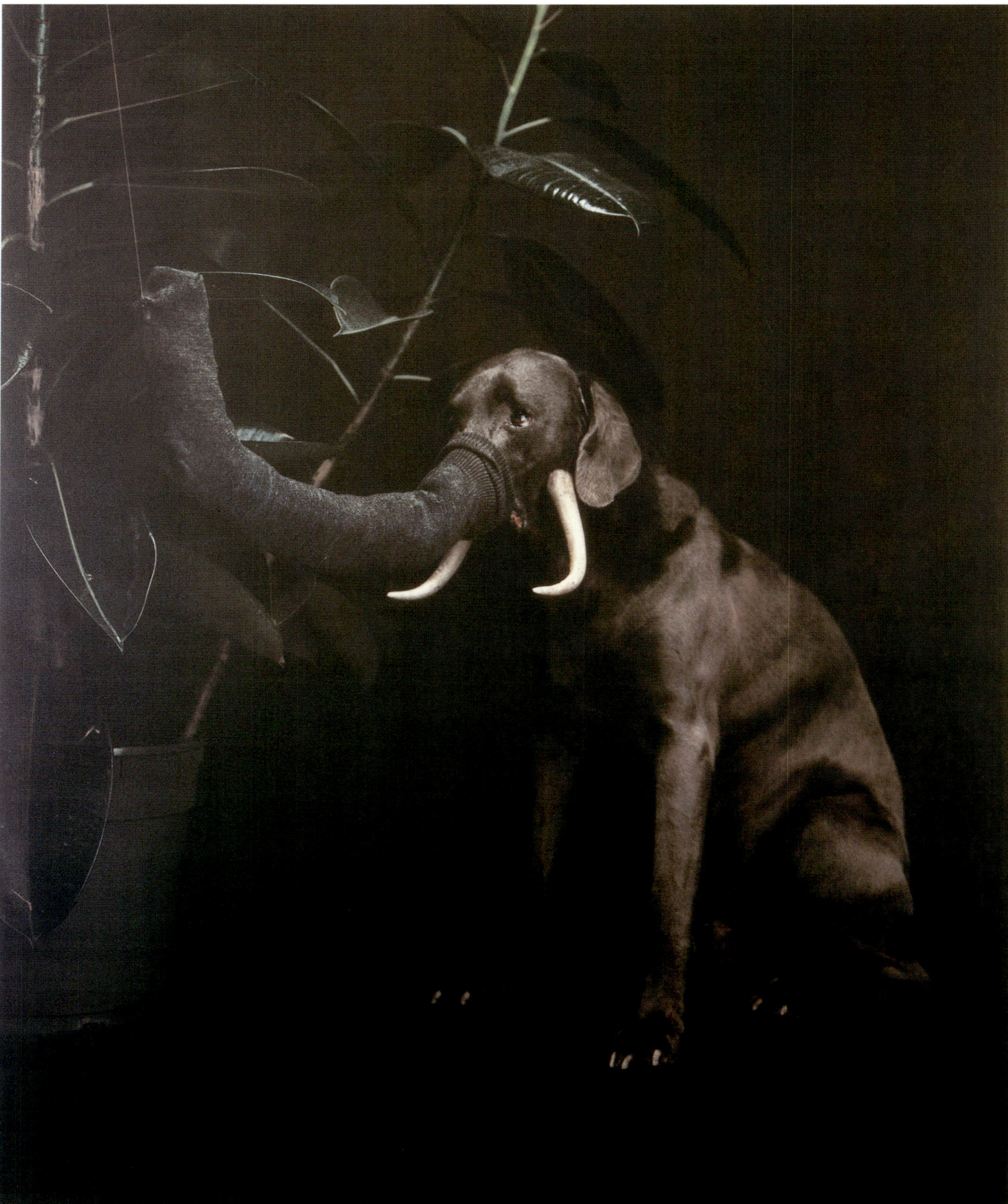

I had an aversion to anthropomorphism.

There was a distressing popular beer ad on TV at the time that featured a bull terrier dressed up in shorts, hat, and sunglasses. This I knew was a direction I would steer clear of.

I began to search for ways to transform ManRay while avoiding the anthropomorphic.

Frog/frog II came about when, after leaving the studio for a minute, I returned to find Man Ray sitting on the set waiting for me to act. He looked like a frog. The next day I returned with a pair of fins and a life-like plastic frog. A few lily pads of cut construction paper, some vinyl, and voila: he was a frog. Almost. "What about those bulging eyes?" you ask. Ans. A ping pong ball cut in half. A little twirl of masking tapes on Ray's eyebrows kept them from falling. Even in the silliest of guises Man Ray is always noble. I was unwilling and unable to make a fool out of him.

If you put a long gray sock on a gray hunting dog's nose, he begins to look like an elephant. Add Styrofoam tusks and a house plant, and he looks just like an elephant. Only Man Ray, with his gray velvety ears and calm visage could have pulled this one off. He takes up just the right amount of space in the frame. *Elephant* was the cover image of my first book, *Man's Best Friend*. It has become impossible for me to think of this picture apart from that book.

Man Ray was in the habit of lying flat on his back while resting. He resembled a dead bug. I slid him over onto green set paper and snapped an exposure. For some reason I pinned it to the wall upside down. He looked like a bat . . . or a dog Velcroed to the ceiling. I redid the shot, positioning a lamp and floral bouquet at the top of the frame to enhance the illusion.

The color green is not well-reproduced by Polacolor II film, the type used in the 20x24 camera. Rather than the wholesome green of nature, what appears is an ominous sickly dye. In fact most people who use Polaroid to "capture" a landscape are probably disappointed. The film was designed with birthday parties rather than vacation scenery in mind, I suspect. It's a "people" film. But I liked the icky green. It was creepy. And perfect for *Ray Bat*.

Frog/frog II, 1982

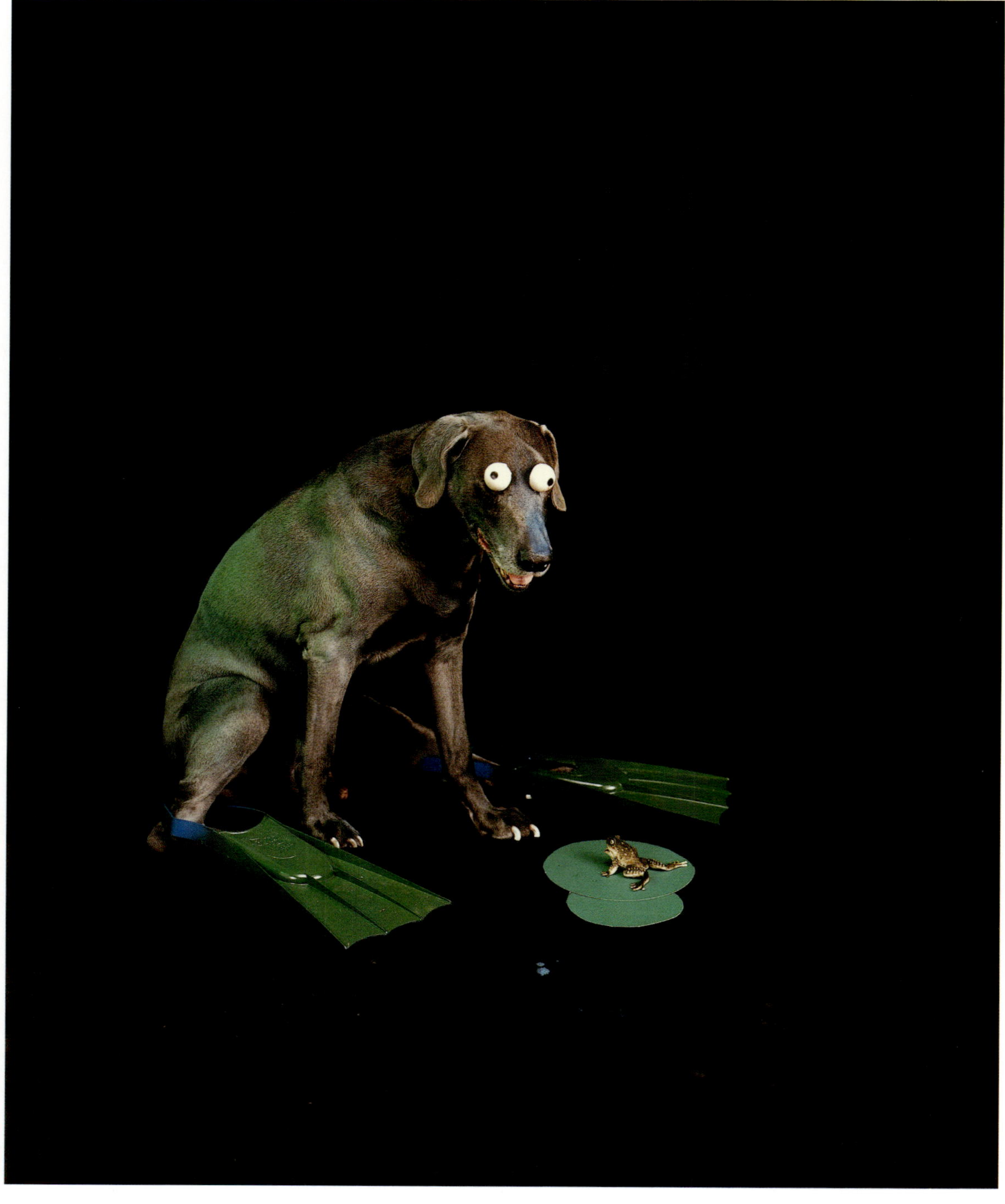

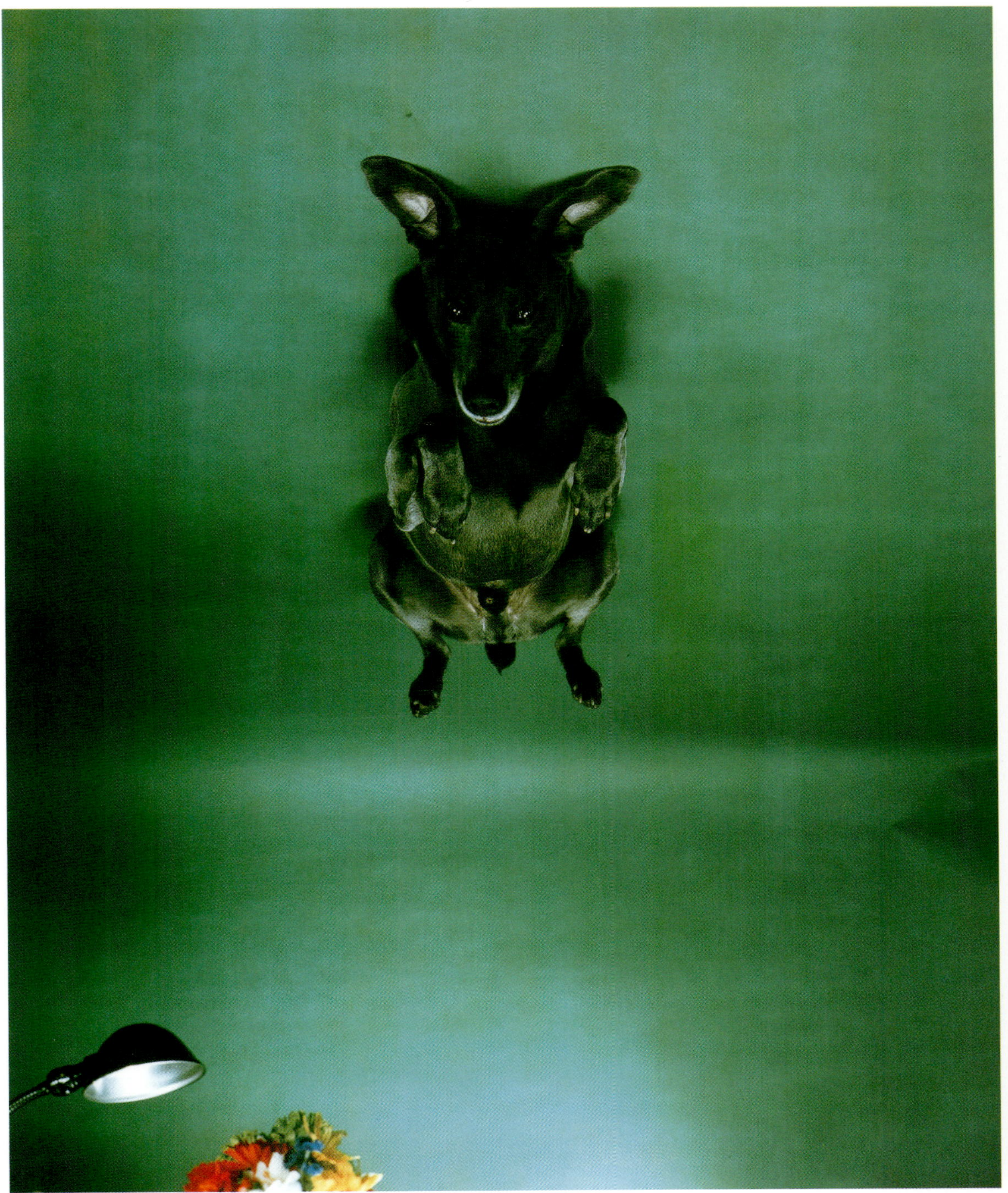

Ray Bat, 1980

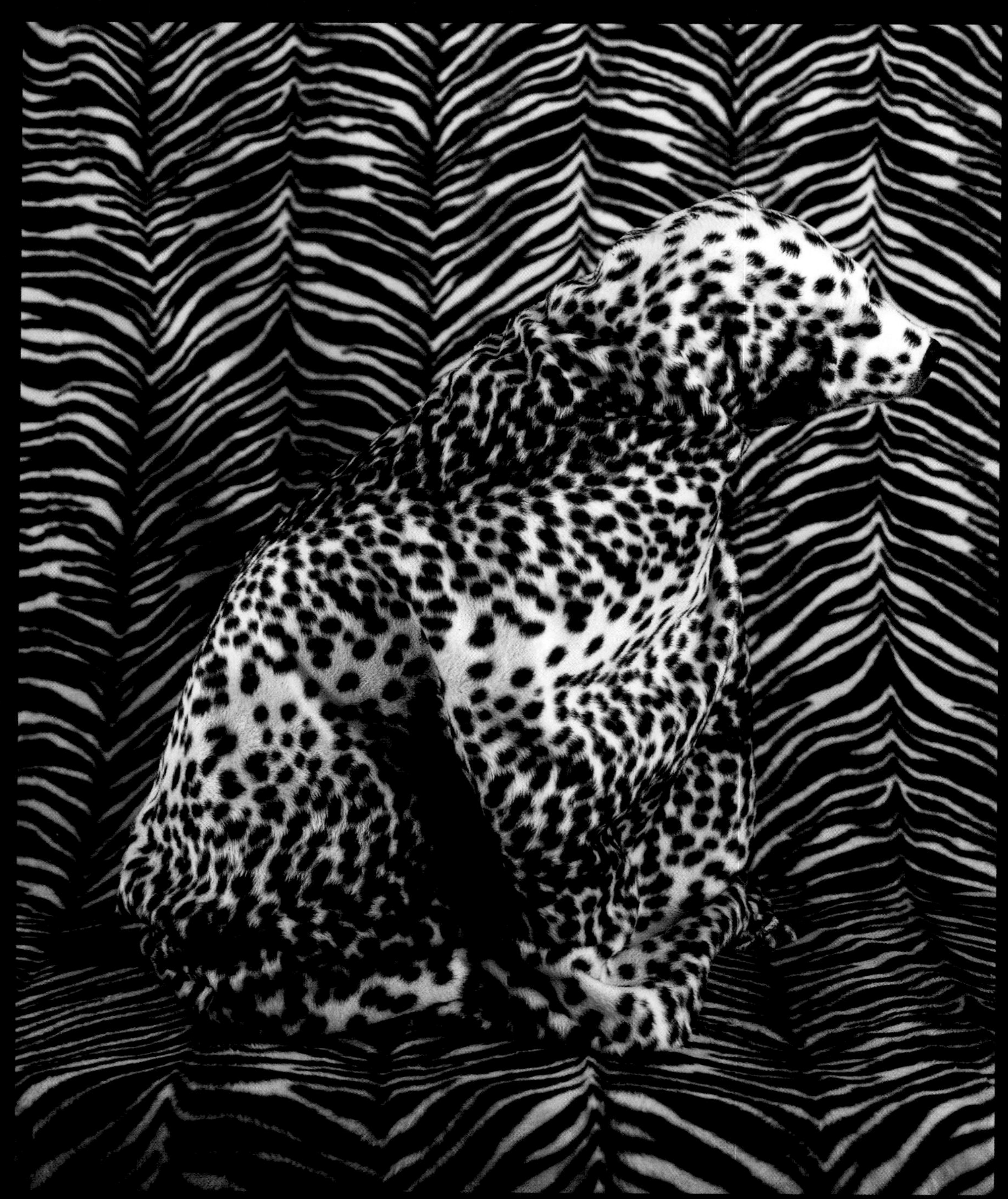

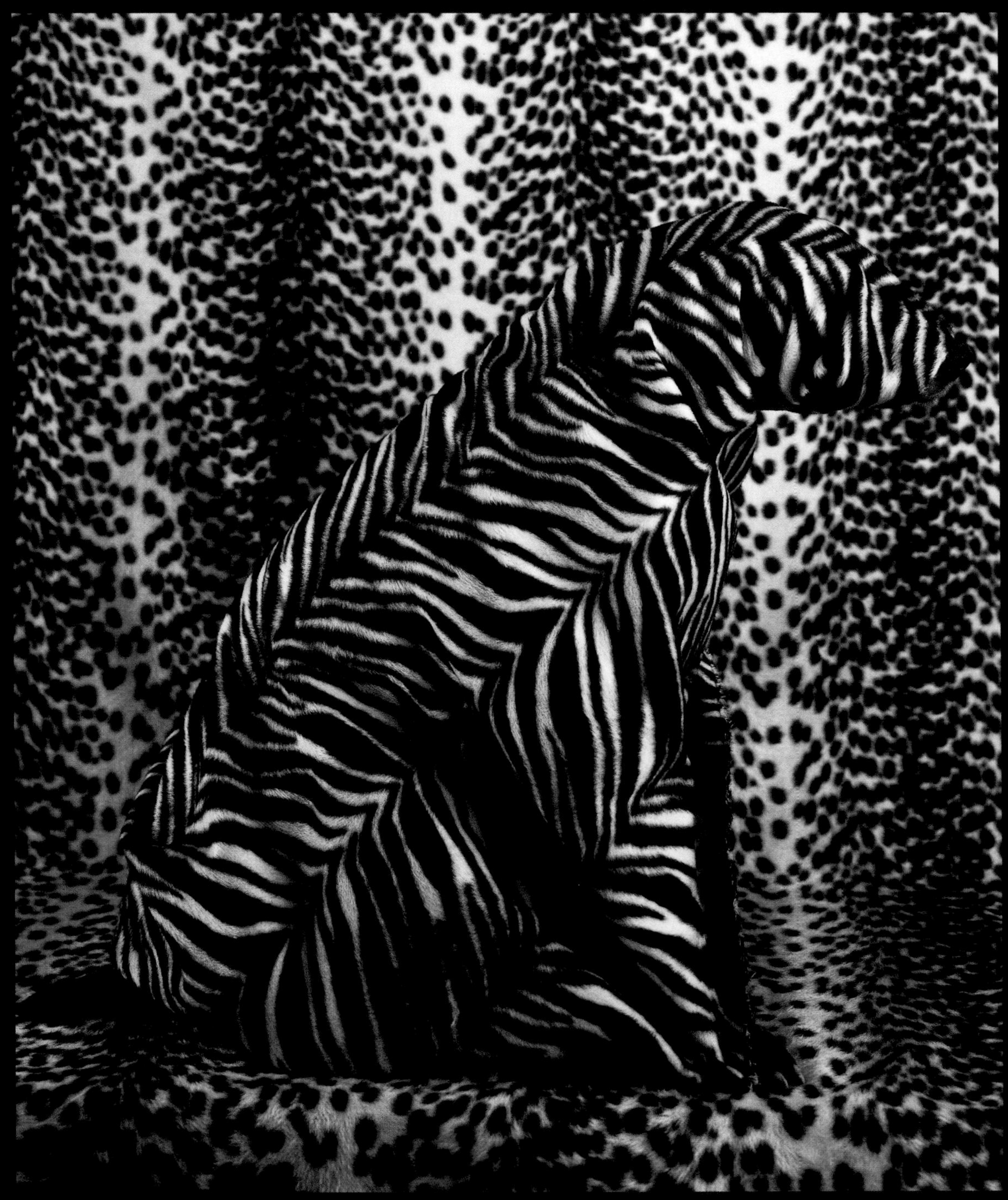

Leopard/Zebra — Zebra/Leopard, 1981

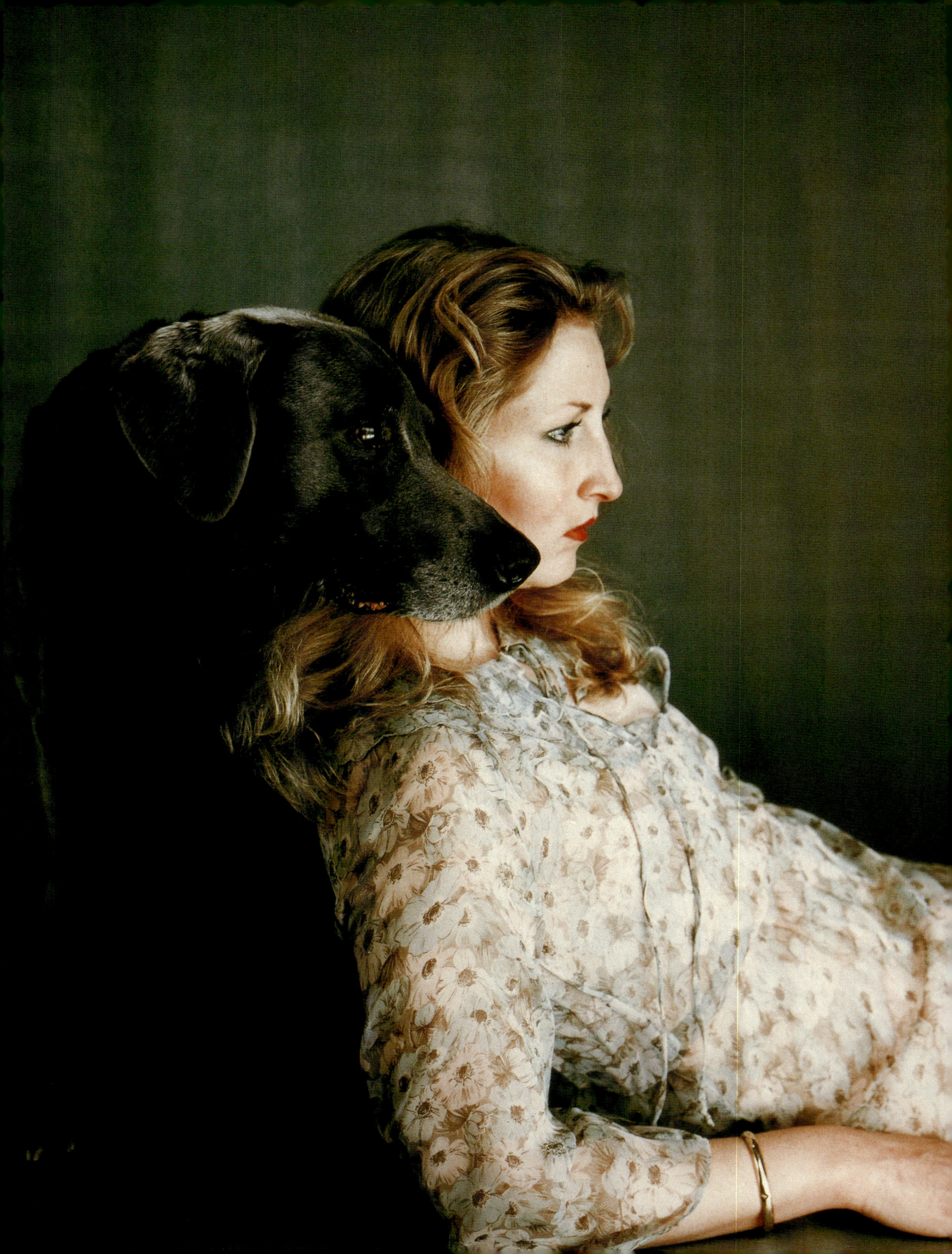

Opposite: ***Double Profile*, 1980**
Below: ***Broken Arrow*, 1980**

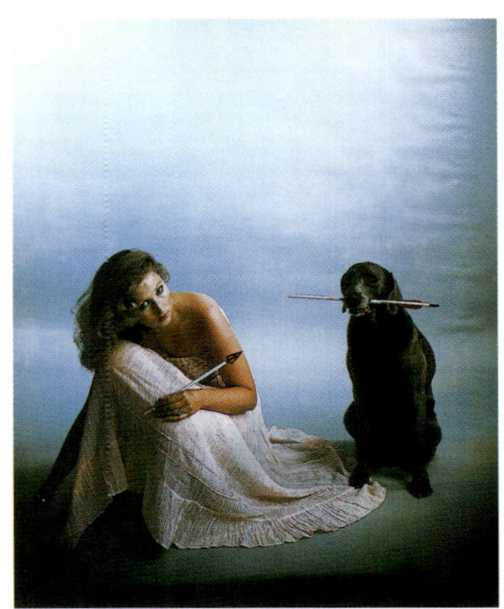

Some people are born to be in pictures.

Hester Laddey, a former student at California State University in Long Beach, where in 1978 I taught a class in performance art, was one. Big, blond, wickedly smart, and full of exhibitionist tendencies, Hester continually pestered me to photograph her. She moved to New York as soon as she could. She wanted to meet Warhol (she did), and I lost touch with her for a while. In 1980, after seeing the Polaroid 20x24s I had recently taken, she wanted to be in them. I was a little afraid of her. She always got her way. And so off to Boston we went. Hester, Man Ray, me, and Hester's wardrobe.

Rogier Gregoire was now running the studio. Like JoAnn, he was a photographer, but Rogier had a strong background in fashion photography and portraiture. Rogier and Hester were magnetically drawn to each other. He knew lighting. She knew makeup. I watched. Besides being charismatic and beautiful, Hester had a special talent for mimicry. She could do Man Ray's shifting expressions as they occurred, almost without looking. I got the funny idea of putting false eyelashes on Man Ray to make him look more like Hester. Rogier set up the camera and the lights while Hester and Man Ray got into position in profile on the set of pale gray. I snapped the picture. It didn't seem to work. Hester looked good but Man Ray was too dark. You couldn't see his fake eyelashes. It wasn't funny. We took more exposures with different lighting and pose. My eye kept returning to the first exposure, the double profile. Beauty and the beast, I thought. It wasn't what I was after. It was better.

I took several more pictures of Hester over the next two years. She brought a vivid spark to the sessions, but none equaled *Double Profile.*

I didn't study photography in art school. My background is in painting. What I learned about photography on my own was slim, and so I was always being surprised by the waywardness of it. From the beginning, color shifts and surface aberrations caused by defects in the film or faults in processing intrigued me.

Sometimes, due to incorrectly adjusted gap I was told, the backgrounds broke down into streaky moirés of light. When flat gray set paper background became a dusky sunset in *Broken Arrow* with Hester and Man Ray, it reminded me of those dramatic movie posters from the age of Technicolor.

Blue Period, 1981

In my own work I have visited many art movements,

but none more often than Cubism, the epitome of modern art. As a student of art history, my mind is filled with names and dates and art-historical facts. In *Blue Period*, I combined Picasso's Cubist and Blue Period styles. The shallow depth of field of the large-format Polaroid camera requires a cramming of subject figures into a rather shallow space. Add a guitar to the equation and you get Cubism. I came by the little framed reproduction of Picasso's *Guitar Player* in a Goodwill shop. Man Ray is blue thanks to Zauder's liquid makeup. Picasso's Blue Period is moodier than his Cubist period. My Blue Period lasted one afternoon.

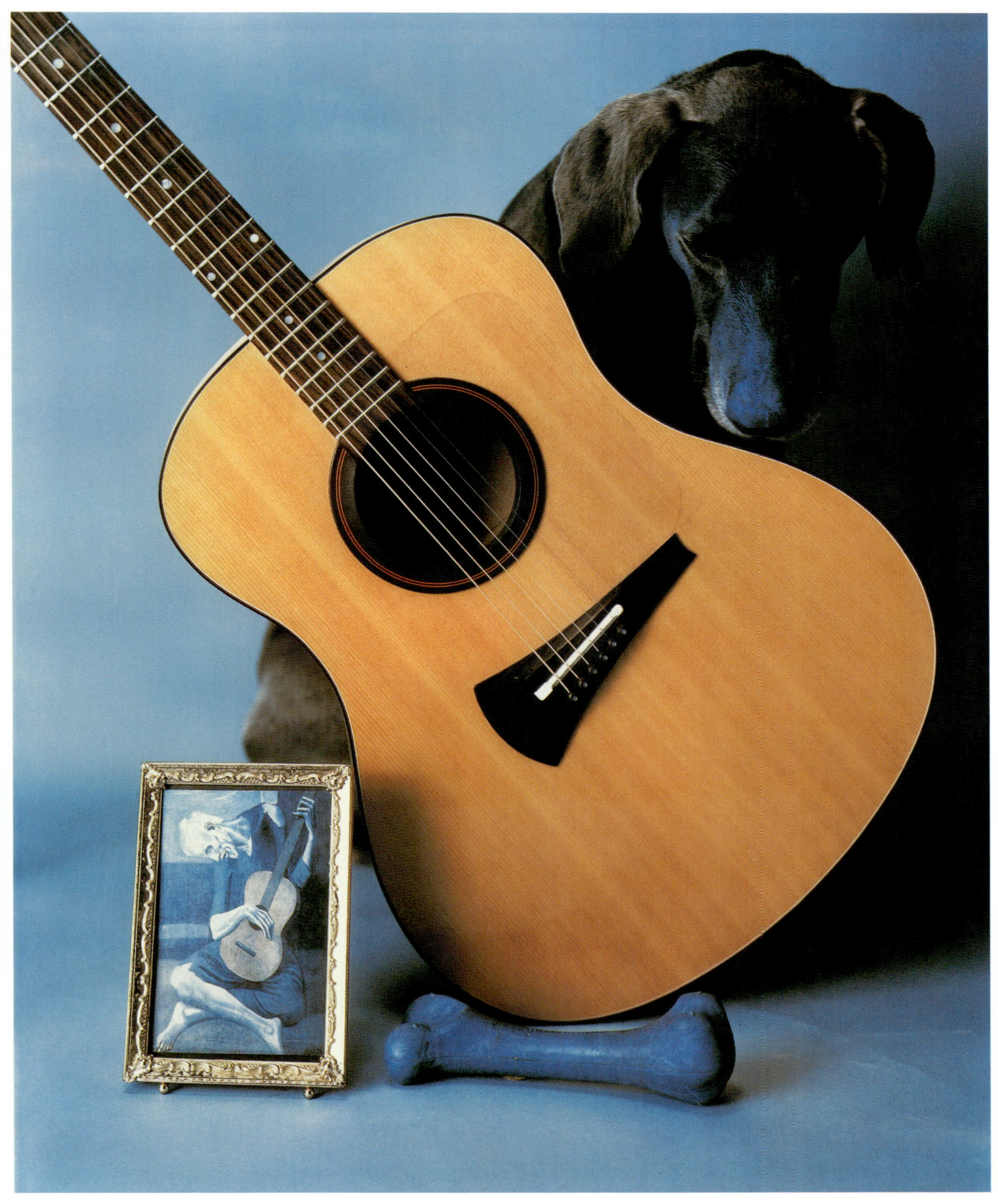

Heels, 1981

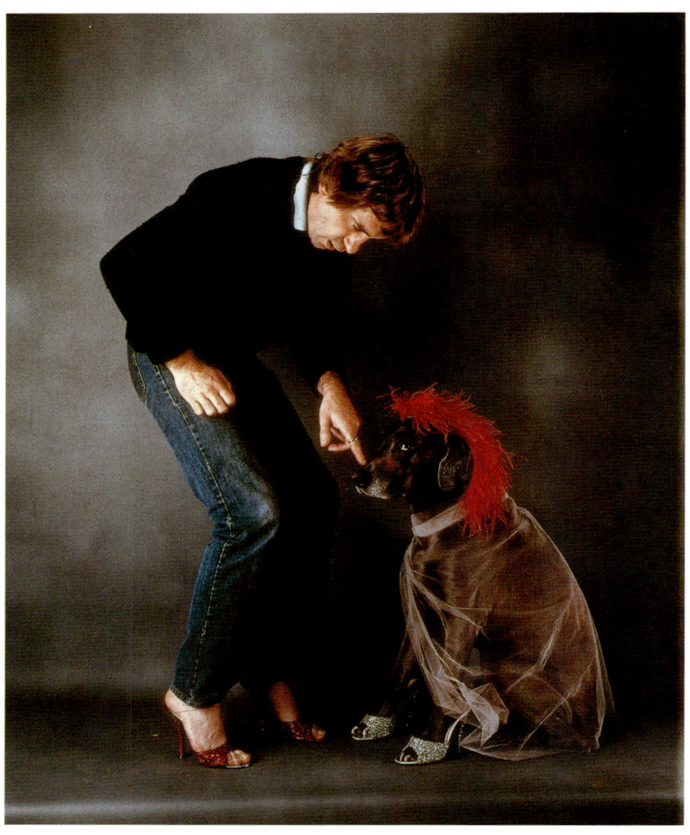

At some point in 1980, the Cambridge 20x24 studio was relocated from Ames Street to an even more corporate-looking space at Tech Square.

Barbara Hitchcock and Eelco Wolf joined Sam Yanes in the Polaroid Corporate Communications Department, with John Reuter now operating the camera. I was getting used to working with assistants. At the studio there was always at least one helping John. Sometimes photographer Stanley Rowin, sometimes engineer Peter Bass. Betsy Connors was still helping me with the set and models. Then there were the visitors. The camera was becoming a tourist attraction. It's a fact of life at the studio. People gather around the big camera. It's a conversation piece. This hardly bothered me. I was beginning to accept the audience.

John Reuter and I made a good team. He had a great technical command of the camera, and as an artist himself he could follow my thinking and anticipate my sudden changes in direction. Best of all, he had a sense of humor. This was good. Running the studio and the camera is physically and mentally demanding. It's the catcher's position in baseball. Everything about the camera is hard. It's hard to load, hard to move, hard to raise and lower, hard to focus, hard to process, hard to keep hearing "What's taking so long?," "What's this goop?," "Can we make it horizontal?," "Why aren't you getting this?"

Bad Dog, 1981

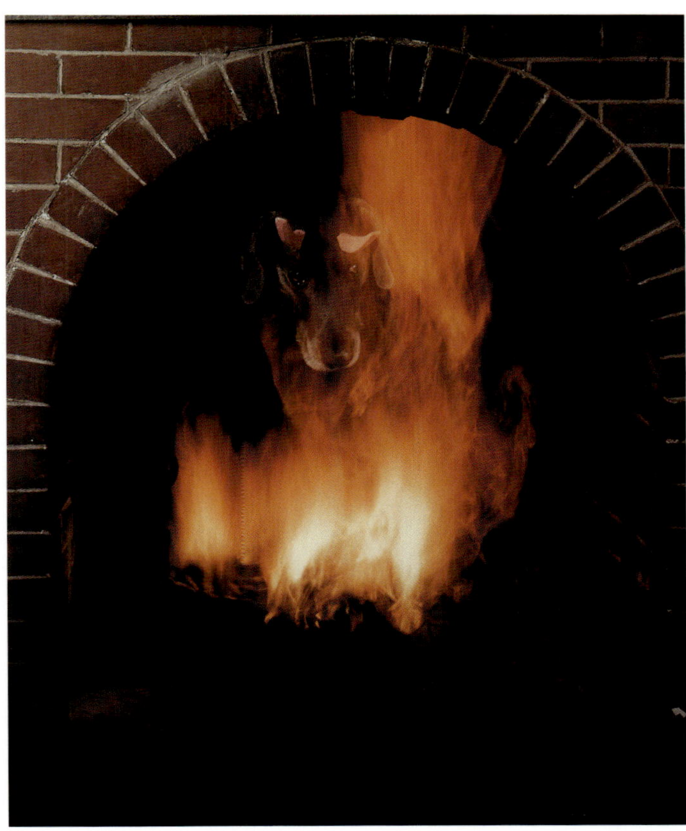

John and I had discussed bringing the camera to Rangeley, Maine, where I had a summer camp. In September the leaves change color and there would be less green. Polaroid green belongs indoors.

It takes a lot of stuff to put the camera on the road. Besides the camera itself, film, negative pods, strobe lights with power packs, and drying racks for the prints. Include grip equipment, light stands, clamps, a generator or two, extension cords, sandbags, apple boxes, wedges, two 4x8 sheets of 3/4-inch plywood, a roll of black Polyethylene, a hair dryer, black gaffers' tape. Did I forget anything? Insect repellent? Maybe not in September. Some of this stuff we had on our first trip.

Shooting outside presents certain logistical difficulties. Polaroid film likes to be 68 degrees. Colder and it looks cloudy, milky, purple. Light streaks in through the bellows. Dust blows on the wet print. Wind kicks up suddenly and the picture becomes a sail. The camera likes to be in a nice clean room, warm and level. Its little wheels are useless on the sandy, rocky, swampy shore of a Maine lake. We came to the conclusion the camera has no business being outside.

During bad weather, we set the camera up inside my log cabin. After the lights were set up and the drying racks brought in, the space became ludicrously cramped. My sister, Pam, who recently moved into the house next door to mine at the lake, had a dog named Liebe. Liebe was a weimaraner, and naturally I wanted to photograph her. Liebe was not a good dog. Even my sister Pam will tell you that. Liebe would not sit still for a second. For 1/60th of a second? Just. By sheer persistence, I managed to pull off one work: *Man Ray & Mrs. Lubner* (that was Liebe) *in Bed Watching TV.* After each strobe blast she bolted, taking lights and set with her. Finally after several takes, I got the shot.

Bad Dog was another rainy day picture. By utilizing the old double-exposure trick, Man Ray appears as a devil dog burning within the cozy chamber of my brick fireplace. To make him look evil, I had to get him to keep his eyes up and his head down. No mean trick. It took of lot of patience. In using his expression to drive the work, I may not have been aware at the time that I was onto something. Many people are fooled by this picture, believing when I tell them it was his last work.

Below: *The Kennebago*, 1981
Opposite: *Man Ray & Mrs. Lubner in Bed Watching TV*, 1981

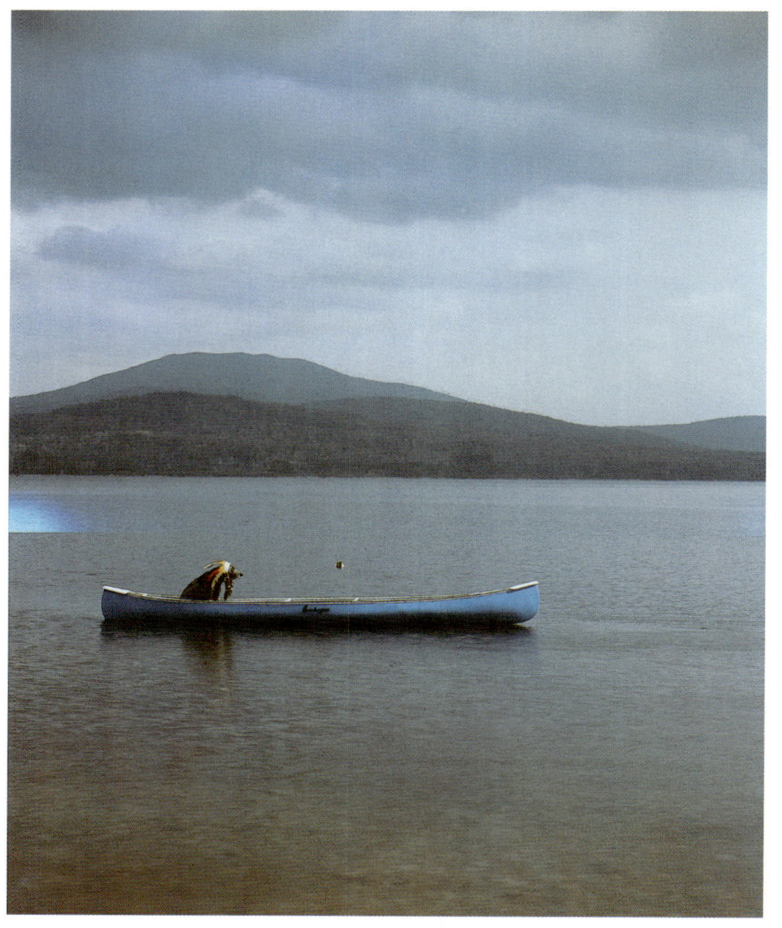

Man Ray was eleven-years old during the Maine trip and I began imagining a kind of last picture:

Man Ray, vanquished Viking warrior adrift on a funeral pyre or revered Indian chief floating off into happy hunting waters . . . or something. With that in mind, we packed our rented Ryder truck with equipment and headed for Kennebago Lake, fifteen miles from the Canadian border: moose, loon, trout, salmon, pristine waters, foliage in the mountains just beginning to turn.

As luck would have it, we were able to borrow a canoe from a fisherman at nearby Grants Camps. John and Stanley unpacked the truck and set up the camera, while I waded into the lake, guiding Ray in the canoe to a point about eighty feet from shore. After placing a touristy Indian headdress on his head, I backed out of the frame. John snapped the shutter. I stayed with Ray and the canoe between shots while Stanley processed the film. He held each exposure up for my approval. From a hundred feet away they looked like postcards. We needed the sun, or the canoe would not be properly illuminated. It came and went. I stumbled around desperately to get the canoe into position in time and then get out of frame. When the water settled, John would take an exposure. One was good, except for a small light leak that caused a blue flare to appear in the photograph's upper left hand corner, which everyone who has ever seen it asks about.

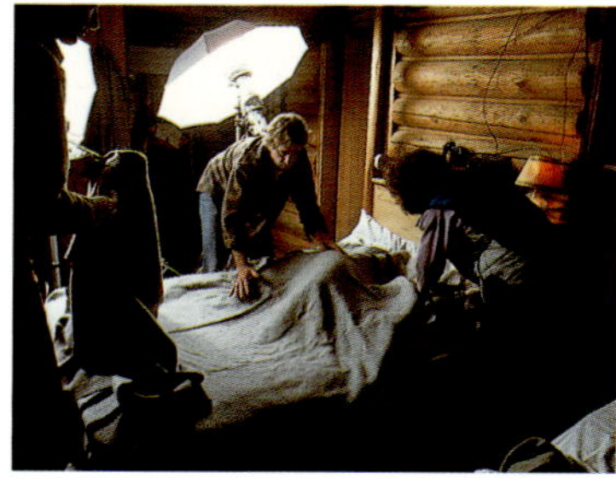

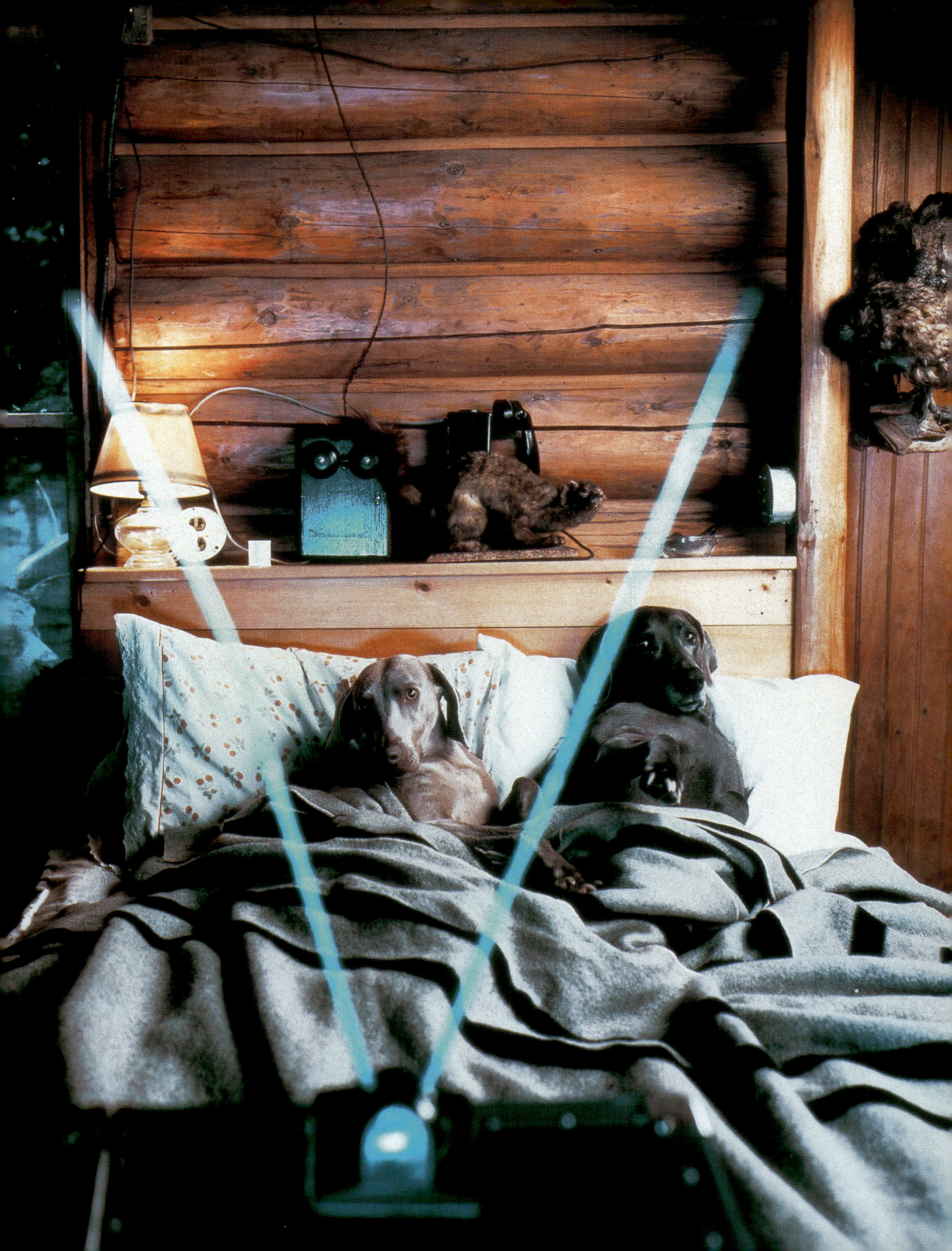

Dusted, 1982

Polaroid photography, with its instant feedback feature, was closer to the way I worked in video,

where I could review the "take" before moving ahead, than it was to traditional photography.

It became possible to stay with an idea and spin off into directions I never thought I would go. In working with the 20x24, images occasionally popped out of the camera belly that I had difficulty owning up to. Some have taken time for me to accept as mine, but the immediacy of the physical presence of the image has a way of exerting a powerful persuasiveness over my prejudices. Then again, certain photographs seemed to be predestined. As if it was only a matter of time before I got around to creating them.

I was heading in a very different direction in the Polaroid studio on the day *Dusted* came to be. I was transforming Man Ray into a raccoon when I noticed that the white flour I was sprinkling on the top of his nose as a highlight shimmered in a beautiful way. I climbed high up on a stepladder and began pouring the flour over Ray on the black set paper. John made three exposures. One stood out: Ray is caught in a beam of white glowing particles. To me the photograph is full of allusions, but their meaning escapes me. Jimmy Durante meets Philip Guston.

Two years later, someone from the B-52's commissioned me to photograph members of the group for the cover of their record album *Whammy*. I dumped flour on them like I had Man Ray in 1981. Some viewers thought it represented cocaine.

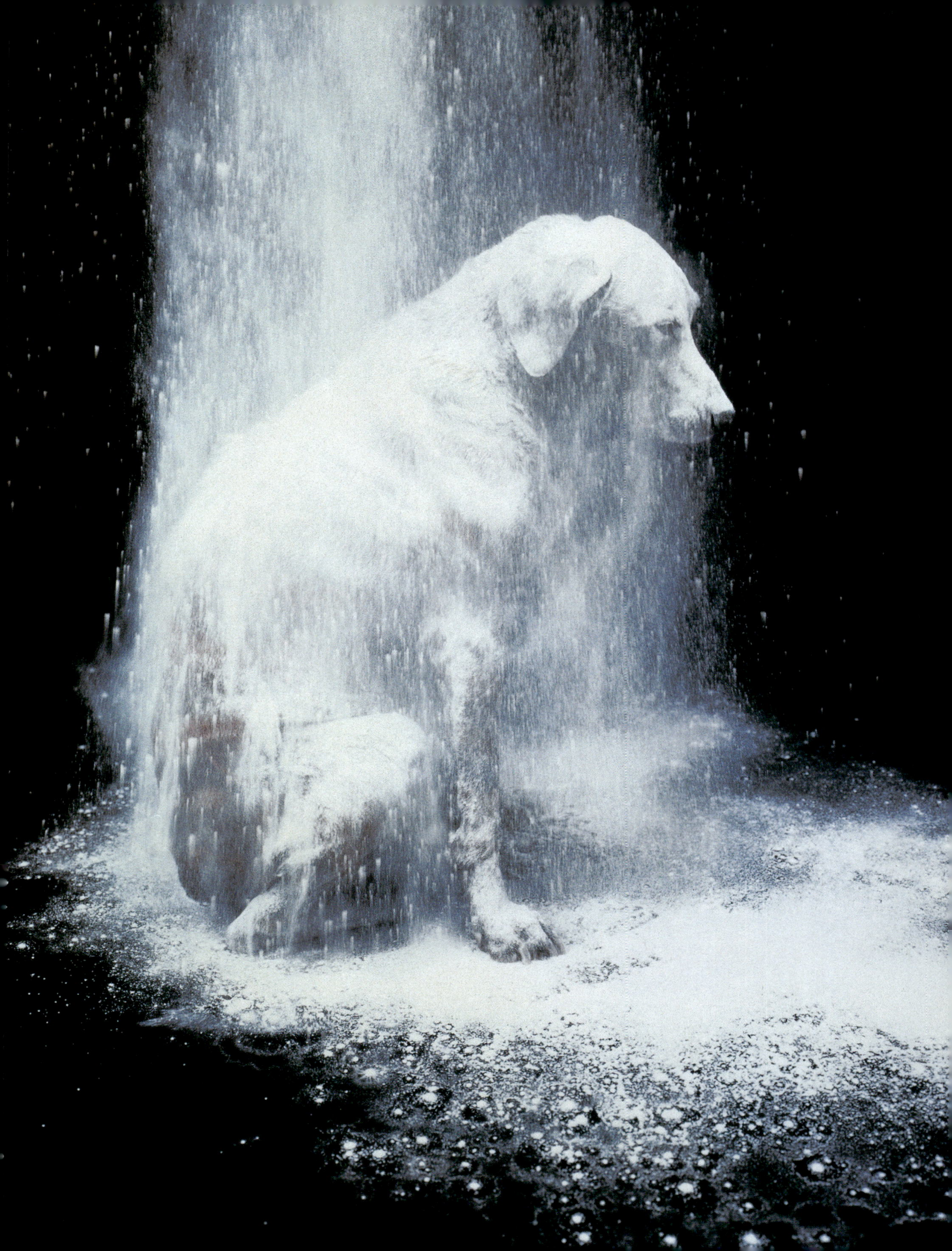

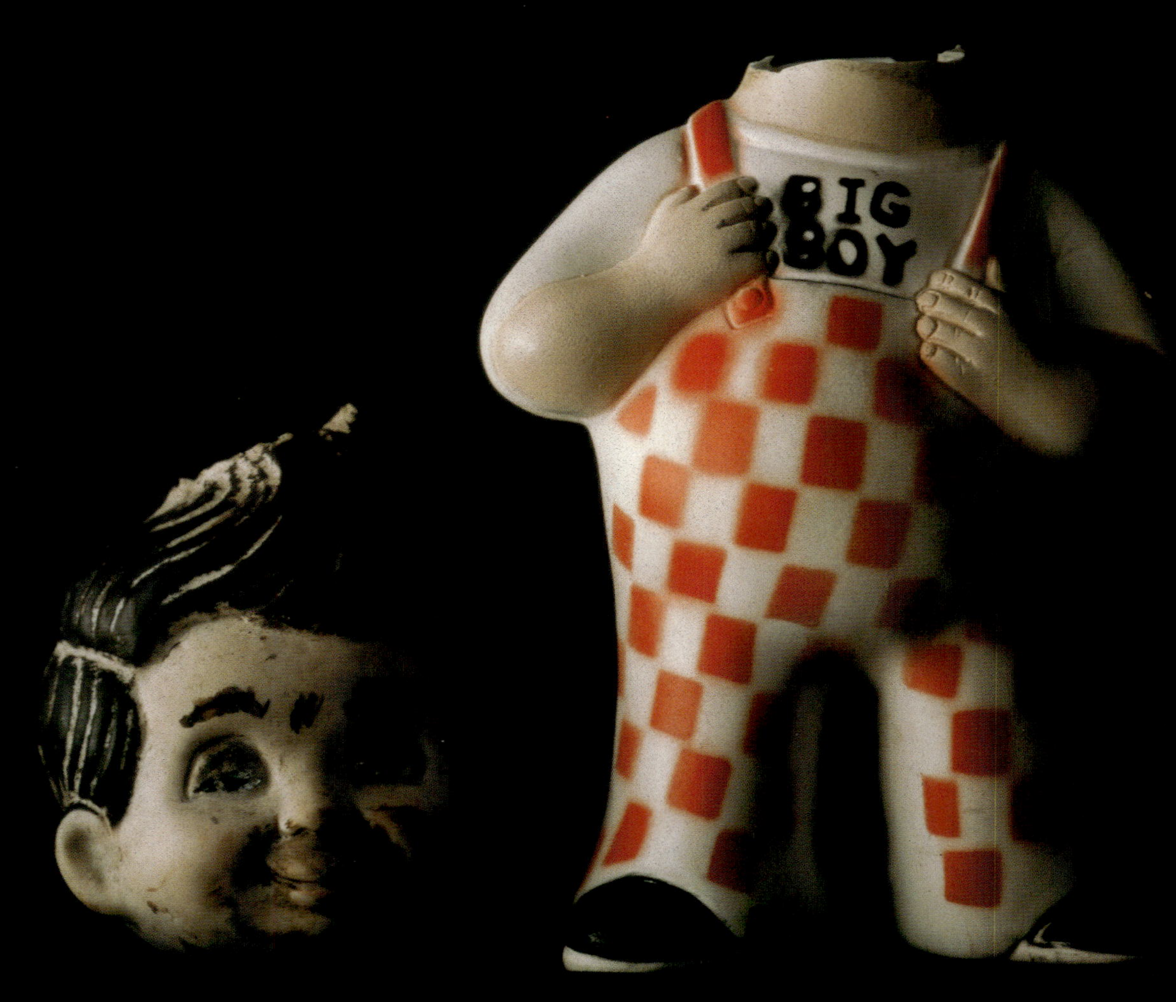
BIG
BOY

Not every picture featured Man Ray.

He didn't like being sidelined, but I wanted to explore other possibilities. Sometimes a prop would inspire such an occasion. He watched from the couch as I prowled the studio for colorful subject matter. Soon, I began to import enormous quantities of props and materials and the studio became a teeming mess.

To enhance the macabre effect of *The Head of Big Boy,* I painted the head to look dirty and roughed up. Not many still-life objects inspired continued attention, however. Man Ray's job was safe, much to his relief.

Opposite: ***Rouge*, 1982**
Overleaf: ***Silver and Gold*, 1982**

Man Ray had been ill for a few months, but at the time I did not know how serious it was.

Only anemia had been diagnosed, through a blood test. Still, I must have sensed the end. That would explain my urgent desire to memorialize him. I had strong ideas of how he should look.

We needed to bring the camera in very close, almost touching him. With the bellows fully extended the camera required rigging to keep it from tipping forward. Working this close meant any movement would cause key elements of the composition to shift out of frame. Man Ray had to hold his pose and remain extremely still during the time-consuming process of closing the camera, rolling down the film, and setting the lens. I felt a sense of urgency about these sessions and for the first time worked uncompromisingly to get what I was after. There was no straying from the idea.

Like portraits featured on commemorative coins, the gold and silver heads have the effect of having been issued posthumously. The gold and silver hair spray (Disco Dazzle brand) had the effect of stiffening Man Ray into a stately Neoclassical relief, calling to mind Julius Caesar, George Washington, John F. Kennedy. At least to me.

In *Rouge*, Man Ray looks soft and fragile, physically and psychologically. This picture makes me remember him more intimately than in any other. His feet smelled like movie popcorn.

For *Red Head*, I envisioned a portrait of Man Ray in red against black with his eyes open, but it never happened. His eyes remained shut. After a few attempts I gave up. One of the exposures was hauntingly beautiful and reverent, reminding me of Rothko. This proved to be the very last 20x24 of Man Ray.

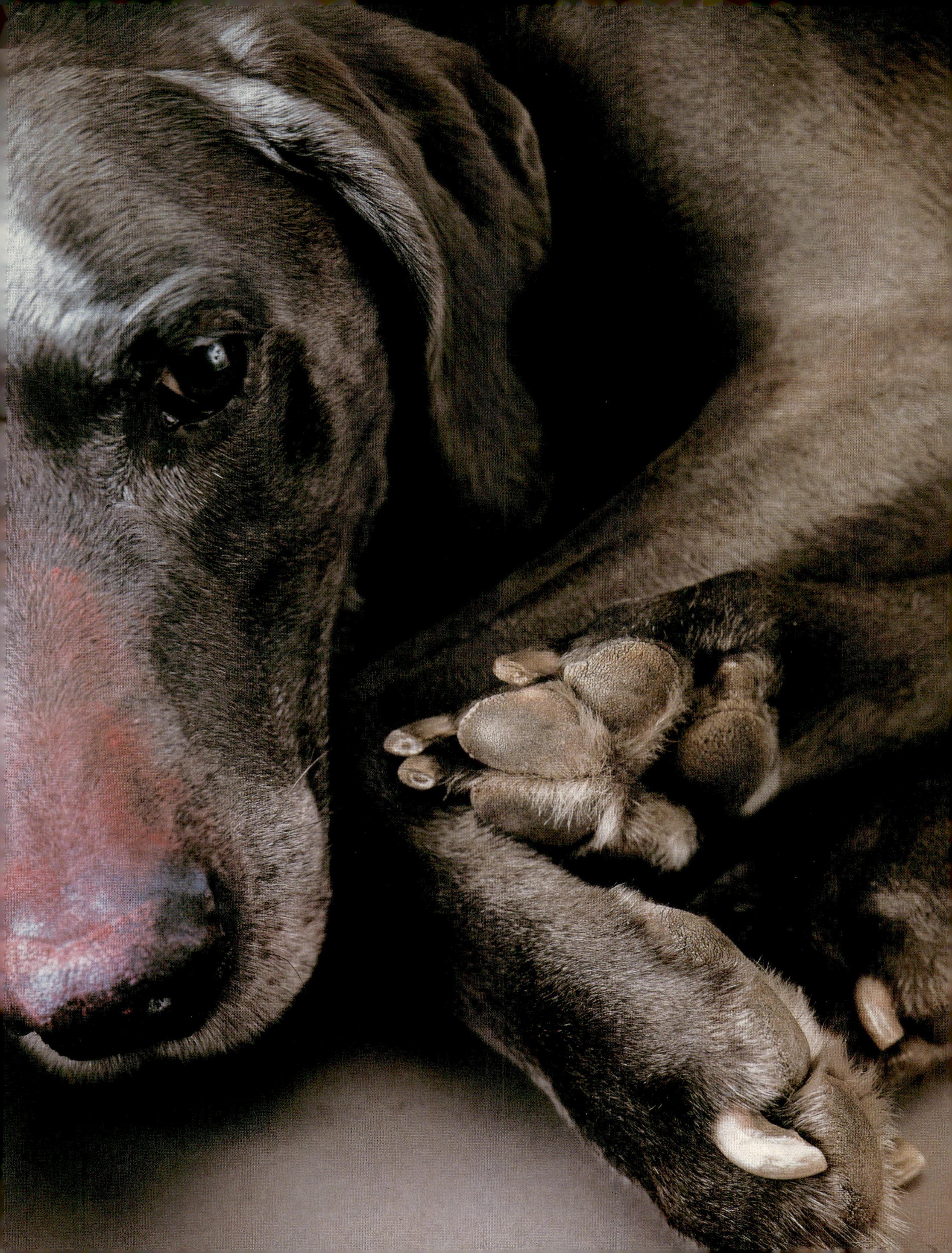

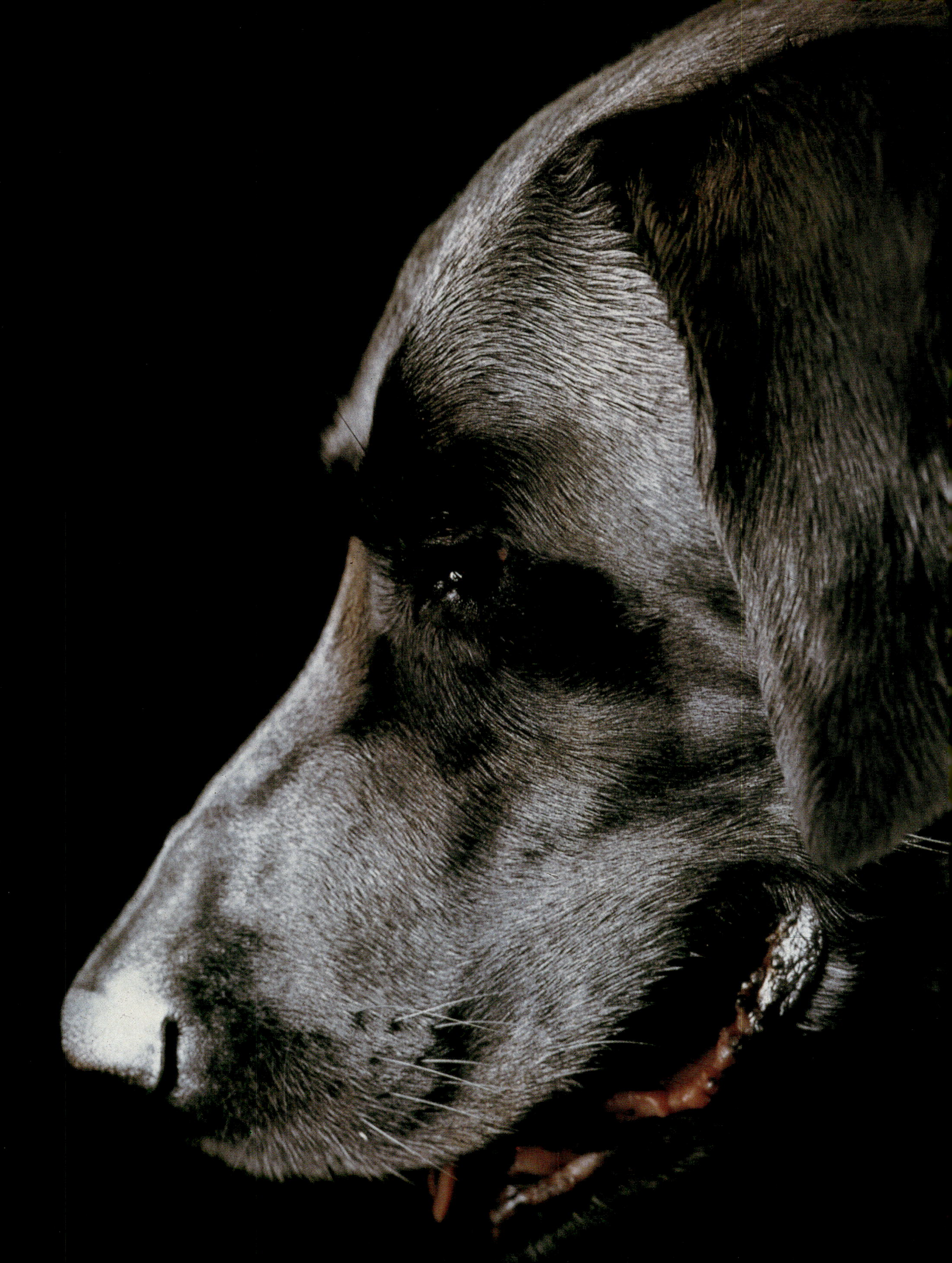

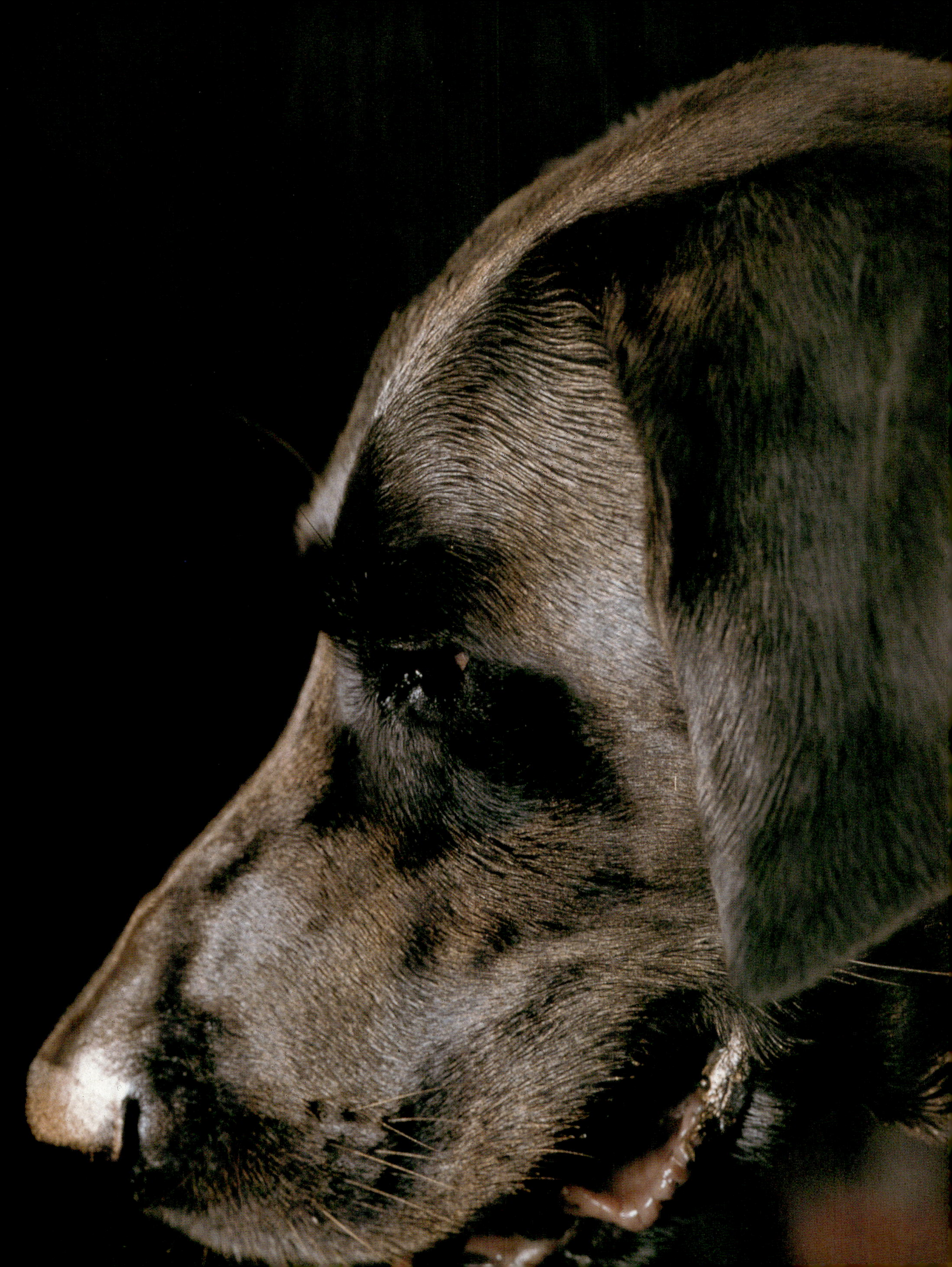

Red Head, 1982

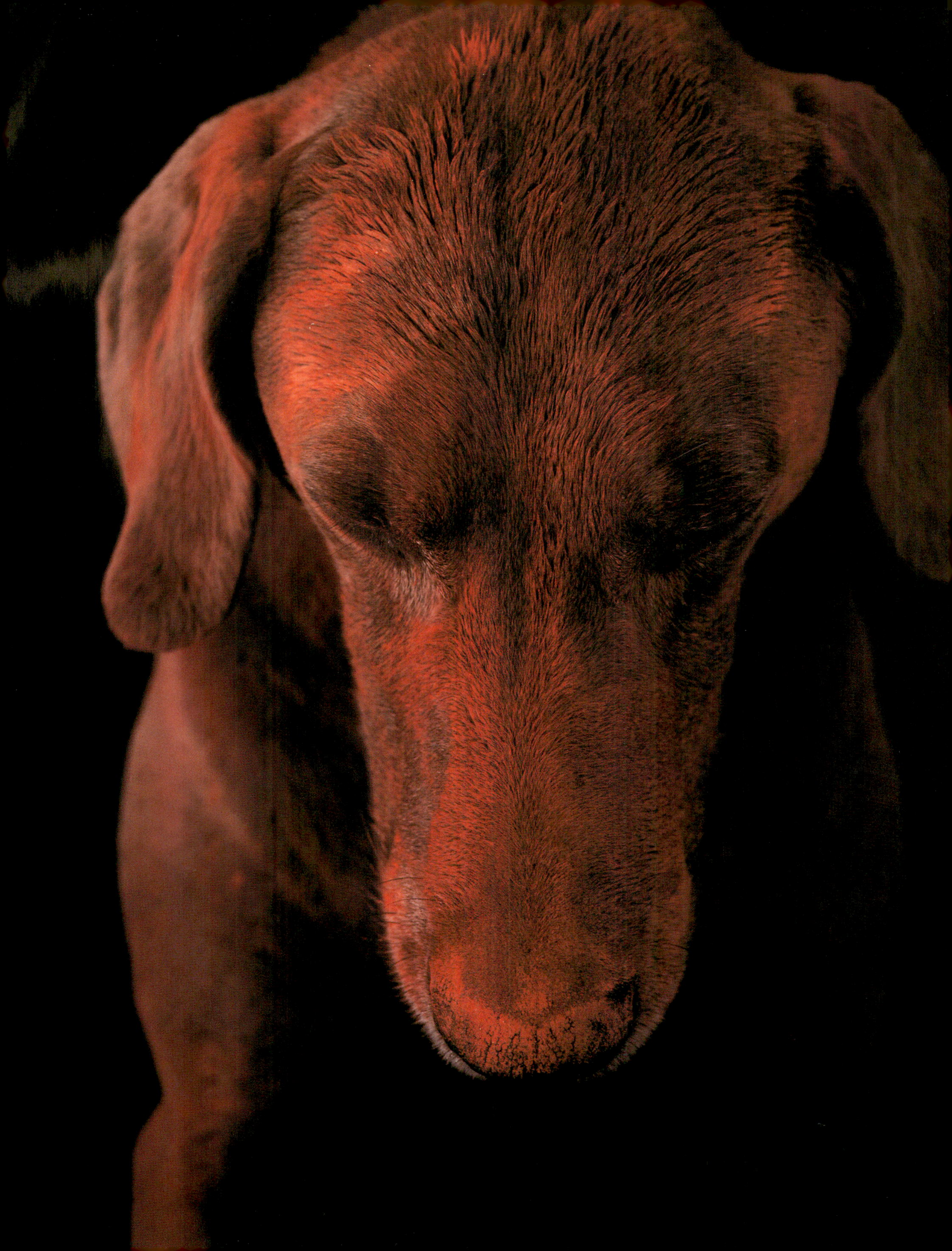

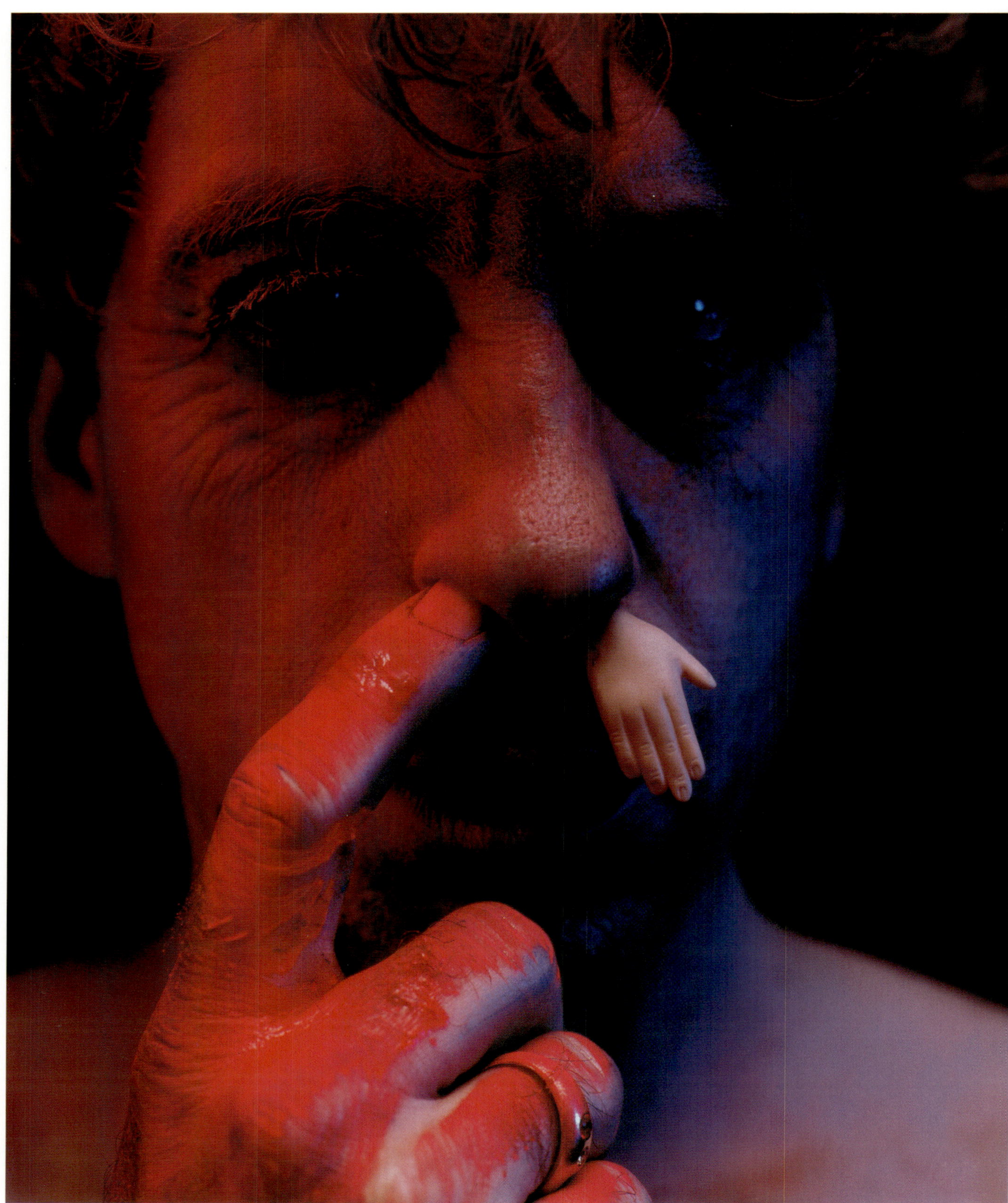

Opposite: ***Handy*, 1984**
Below: ***Foamy Aftershave*, 1982**

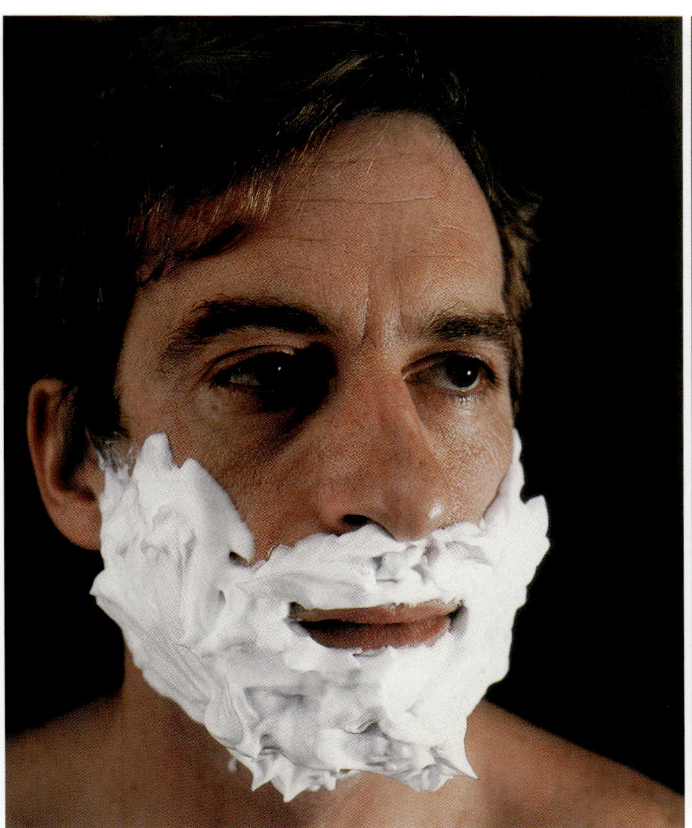

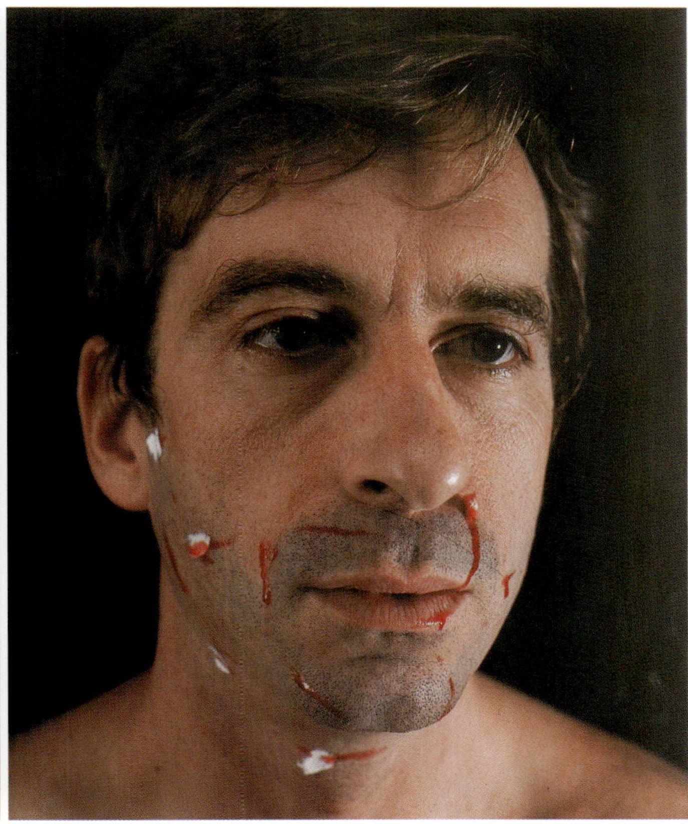

When Man Ray died I lost a best friend and a muse.

I missed him in the deepest way. Yet somehow, it was a relief not to have to photograph a dog. I returned to some of the ideas I had left behind when I lost myself in our collaboration.

I had frequently used myself as performer in my videos, less so in the photographic works. In video, where the monitor is separate from camera, it is possible to see oneself obliquely, and that, I found, generated ideas. I could convince myself that I was having a dialogue with another person. While using myself in photographic works like *Handy* and *Foamy Aftershave*, I had a sense of freedom to slobber myself with goopy substances that I might not have had the nerve to apply to another human. Had Man Ray been available, I might have spared myself the trouble. I don't know, though. Some of the things I put on myself you would not want to see on a dog.

Greek Restaurant, 1982

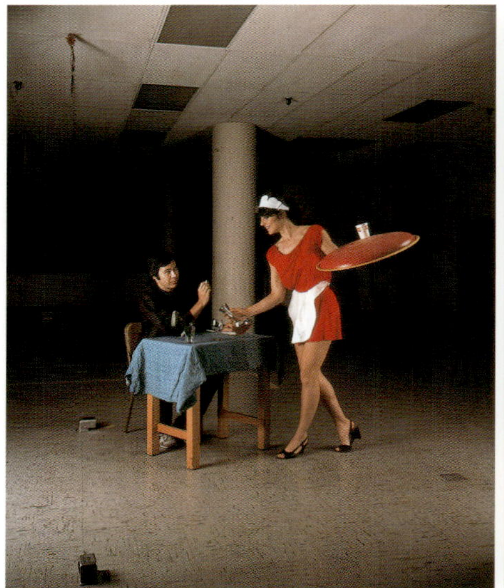

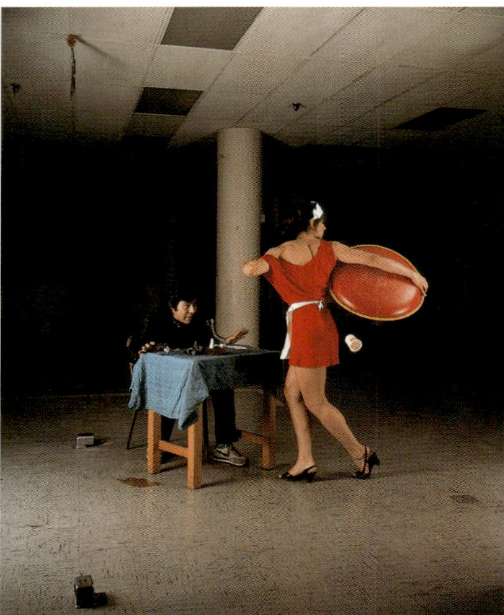

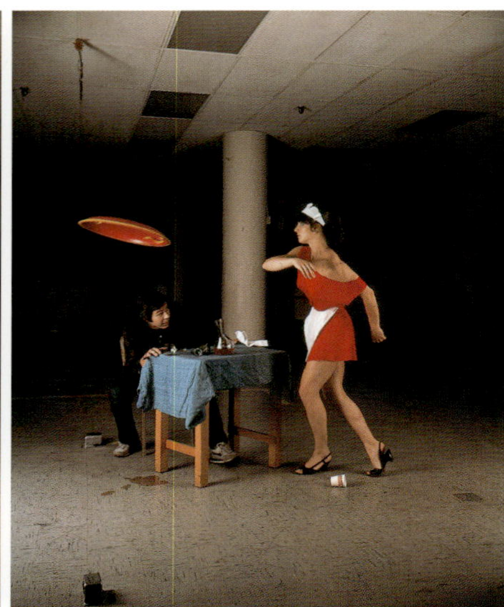

In 1982 the Polaroid studio closed.

The camera and all the stuff were locked up a warehouse in Cambridge. I missed it, but not terribly. One day John Reuter called. He had a key.

The space was cavernous. With me came Eve Darcy.

Eve was beautiful and strong. She had muscles. Like Hester, Eve was a born performer. She projected cool detachment and a half-hidden silly streak. Hester's beauty was in her radiance. Eve's was classical, sculptural. With Eve I found myself staging works that showed off her physical prowess, usually in absurd or contrary settings. *Greek Restaurant* combines the athlete with the waitress. John Reuter sat in as the customer. In this triptych, I was able to take advantage of the huge space of the warehouse, which allowed lots of room for the subjects to move about.

With the help of a lot of green body paint Eve became a green giant in one picture. In another work, *Eau II*, she became Catherine Deneuve. By juxtaposing conflicting but plausible factors in *Eau II*, my intention was to confound the sense of an ad.

And that was it for the warehouse. Too bad. It was a great studio.

Eau II, 1982

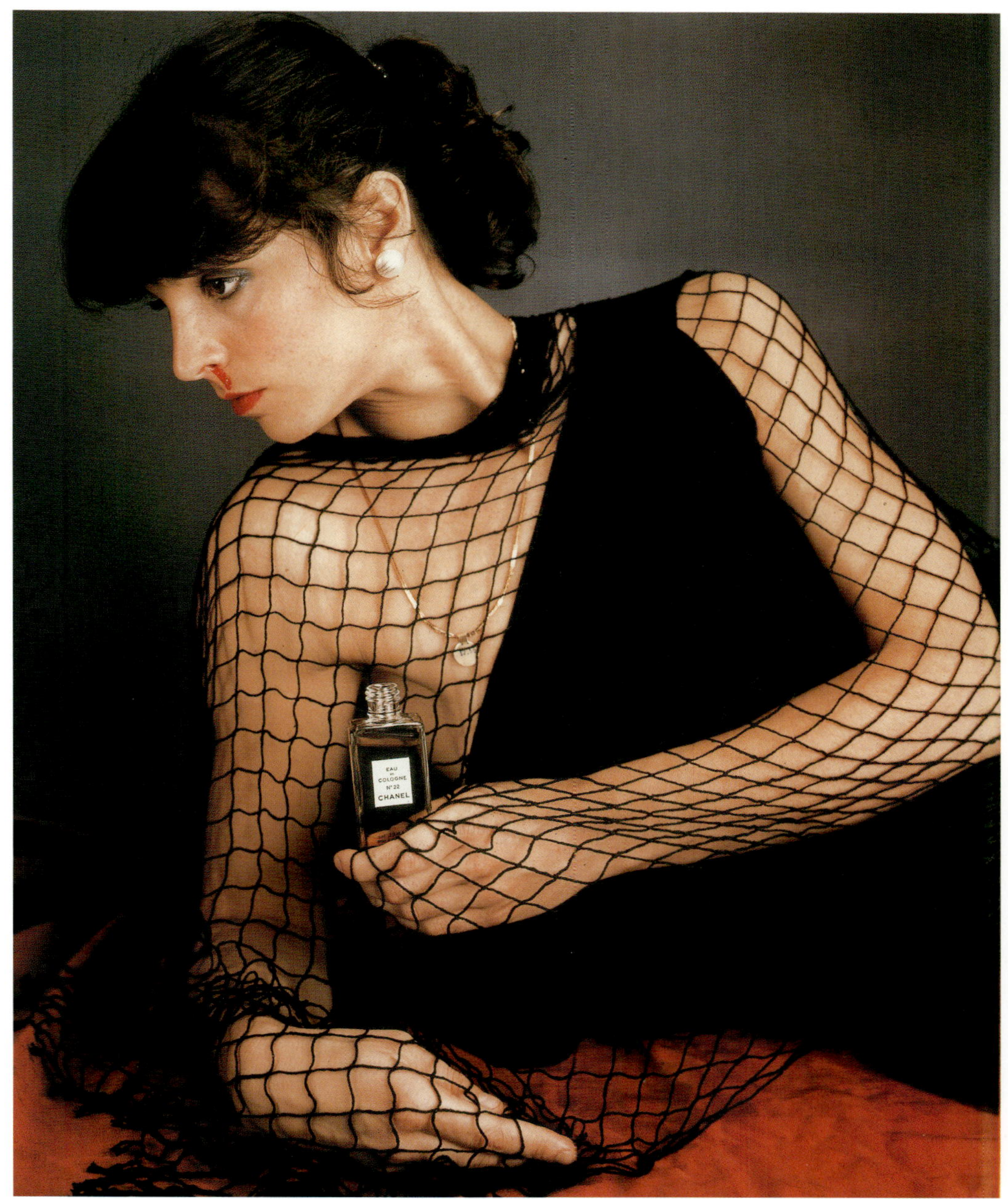

Left: *Charlie*, 1987
Right: *War and Peace*, 1979
Opposite: *Foster Parents*, 1984

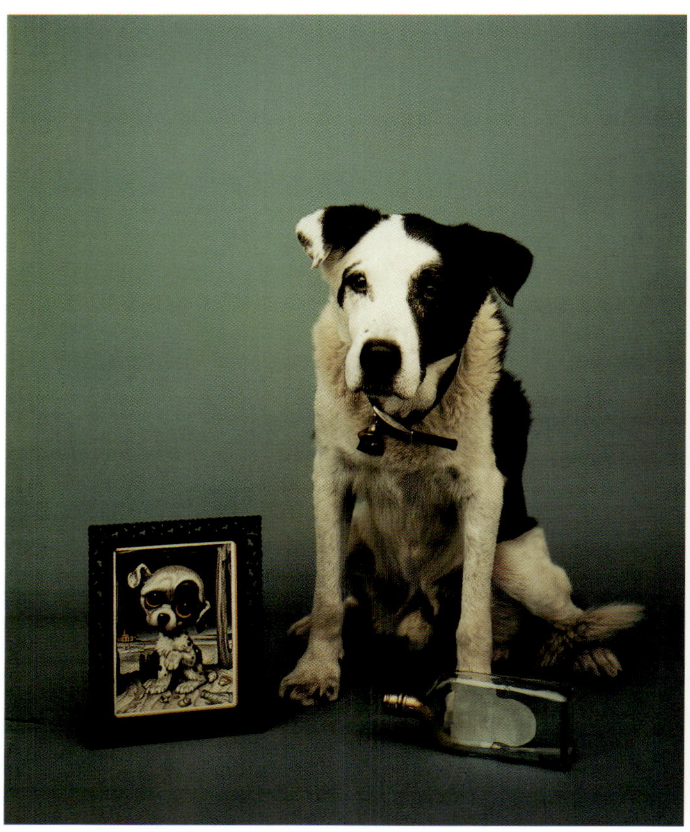

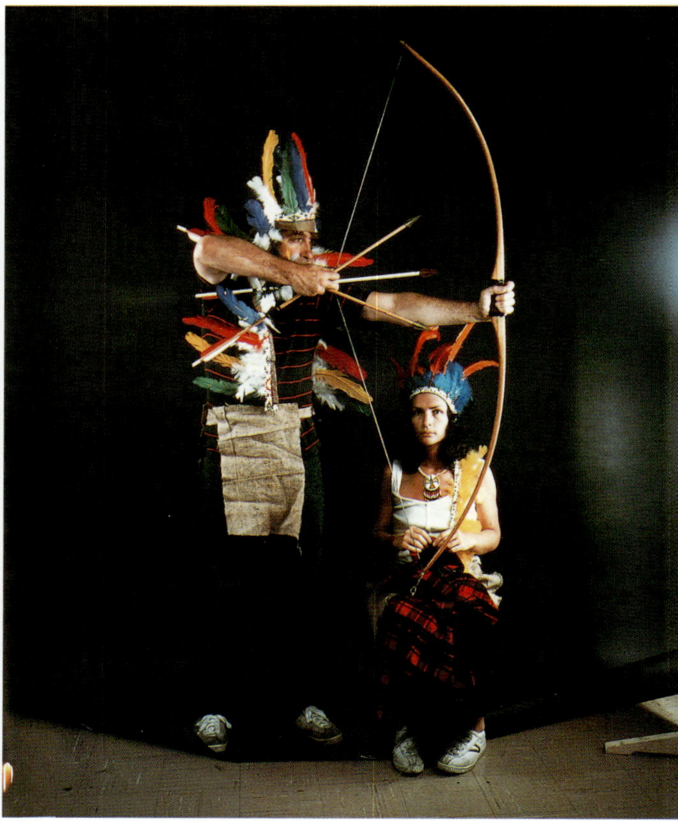

By the fall of 1982 the big camera found a new home at the Boston Museum School,

in a special arrangement where both students and outsiders could use it. The school atmosphere was familiar to me in contrast to the corporate settings of the earlier studios. The smell of oil paint in the halls, the physical space of the studio, who walked through, and the type of props found in it, all had a way of playing out in the pictures.

One day museum director David Ross and his daughter, seven-year-old Lindsay, visited the studio. I took several pictures with Lindsay and a few with David, Eve, and others who happened to be there. Lindsay was an interesting subject. She had an aura of unfathomable wistfulness about her. At the time children to me were something like dogs, except more abstruse. In *Foster Parents,* Eve and David were covered in animal-print fabric and holding hands. Lindsay is outside the shroud. Like some of my other pictures, this one seems to mean something. I am never after meaning per se, but sometimes it flickers by.

Fussing with material keeps me occupied on the set while I think of what to do. Sometimes the fabric takes over and becomes the subject of the work. I began to use fabric in the way that painters sometimes use paint. My attraction to fabrics, which began with the aged Man Ray, really took over after he died. I would show up at the studio with chintz, duck, felt, net, satin, velvet, wool. What was I doing? Could I have been trying to cover up that I no longer had Man Ray? During this period John called me the Fabric King. A label I proudly wore.

Before leaving Boston for good, I should mention one more dog. Charlie was the constant companion of Randy Johnsen, my former student and assistant, builder and world-traveling surfer. Man Ray didn't want Charlie in any of the pictures, so Charlie had to wait. I thought of Charlie as a kind of everydog to Man Ray's everyman. In *Charlie,* I was thinking about the derelict and the leftover. My next dog, Fay, was more accepting of Charlie.

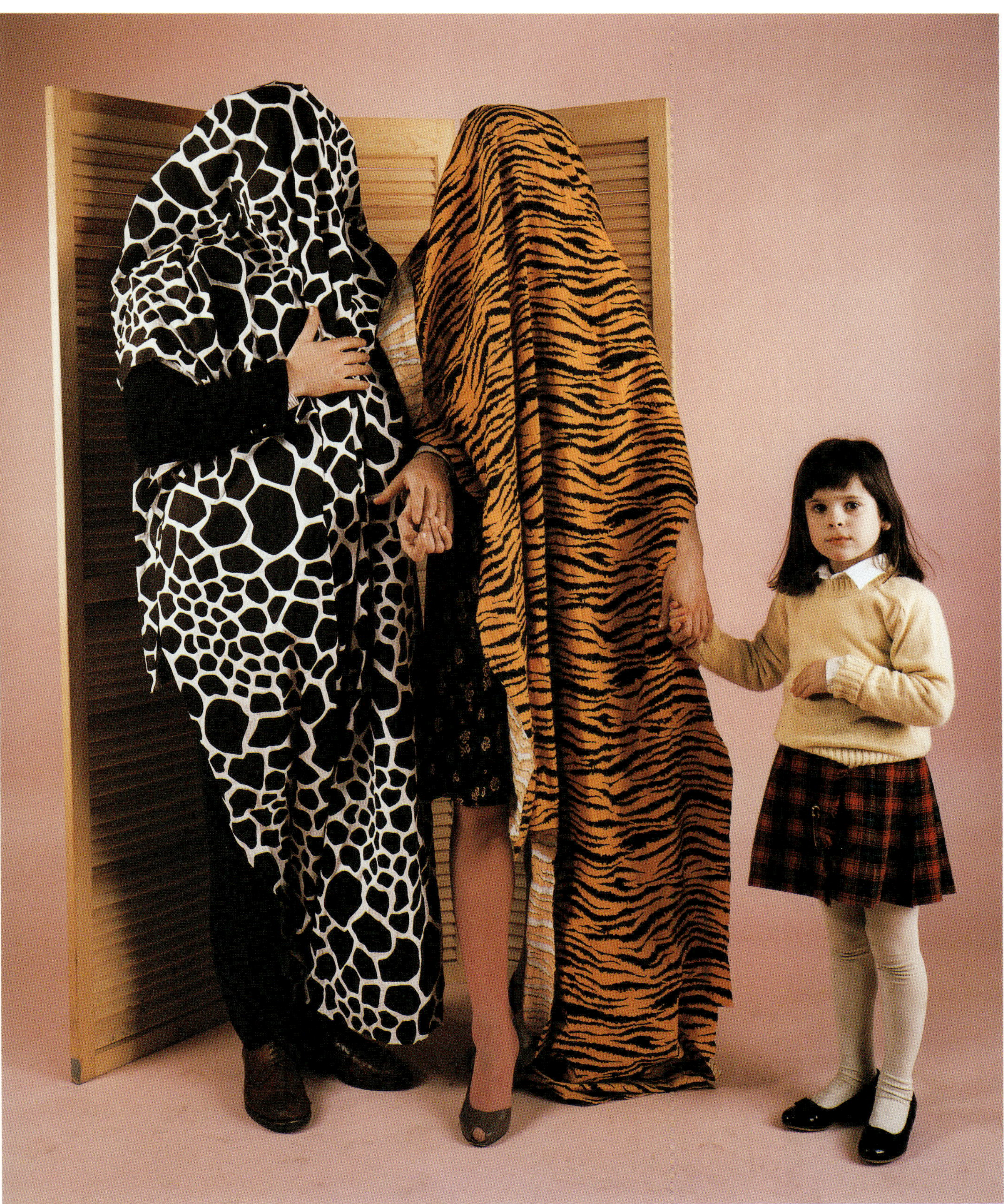

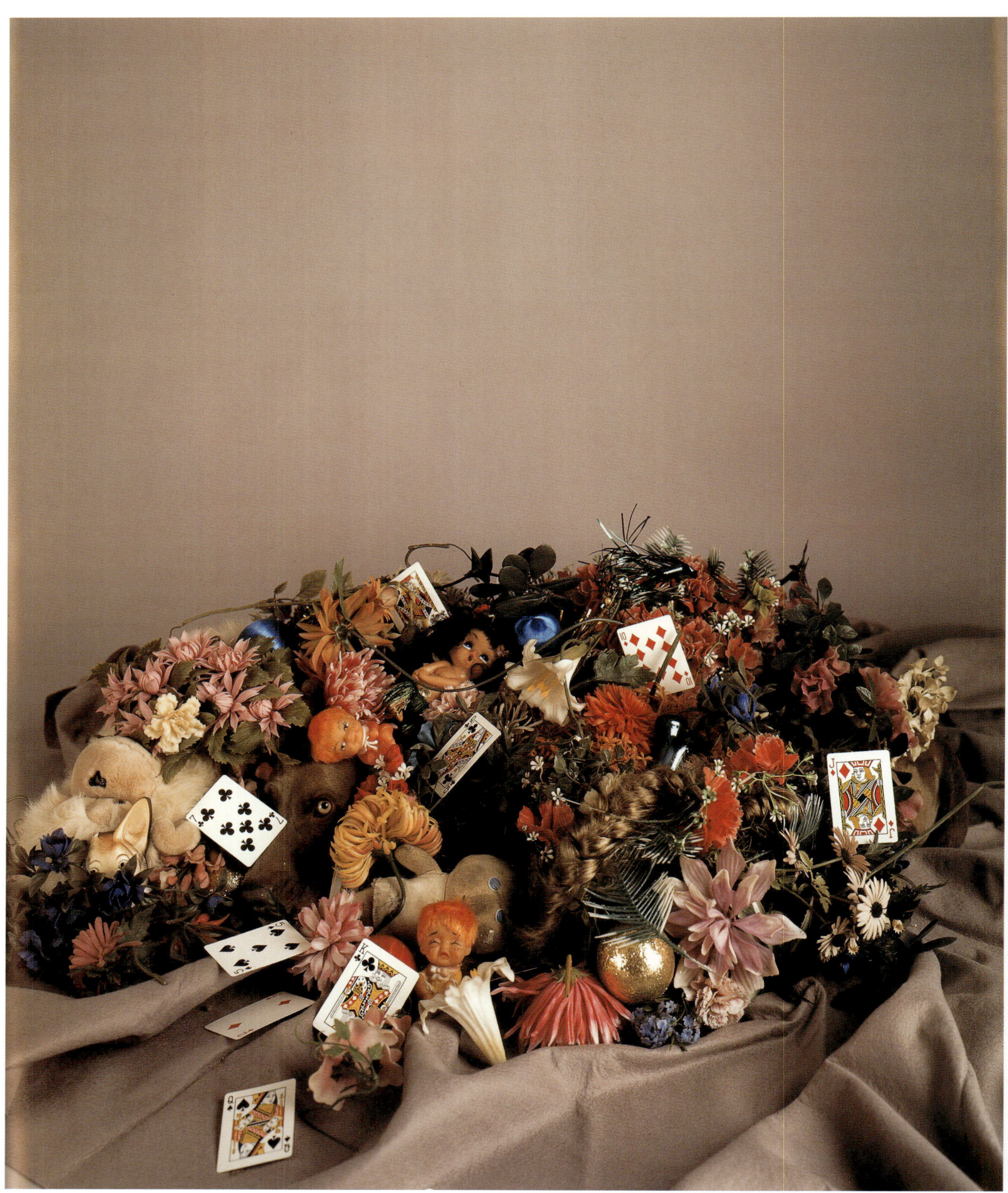

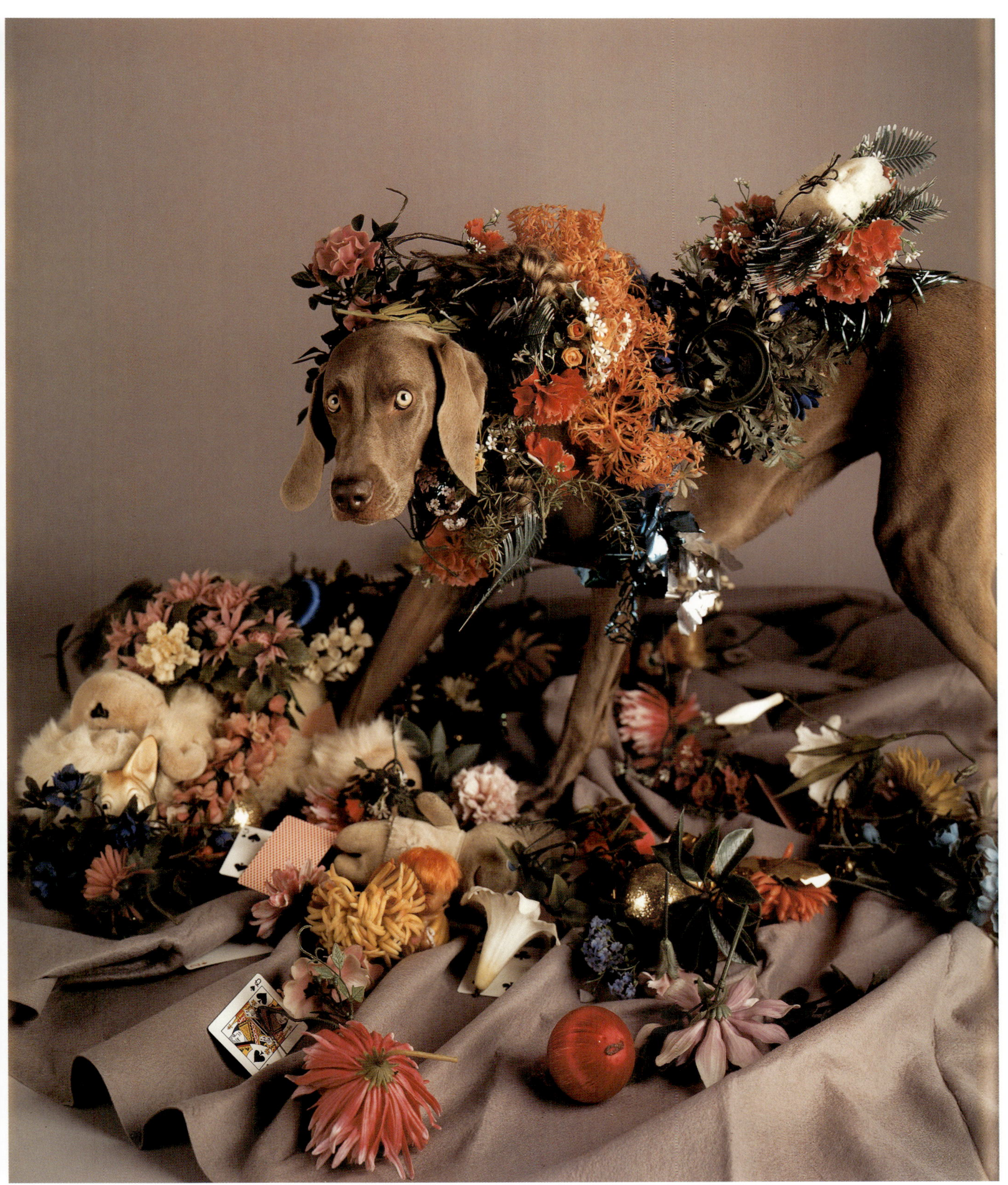

Previous: ***Rising,*** **1987**
Opposite: ***Sphinx,*** **1987**

In 1986 Polaroid moved the 20x24 studio to New York City.
It made sense. That's where the photographers were.
Going my separate way, I had returned to painting.
I gave the camera no thought. Until . . .

When we first met in Memphis, Tennessee, she was six months old and her name was Cinnamon Girl. I named her Fay after Fay Wray, of course, but also after my first color Polaroid with Man Ray and the nail polish, which I had titled *Fey Ray*. Her fur was taupe, lighter and warmer-toned than Man Ray's, and she had yellow eyes like in a Rousseau painting.

I had no intention of photographing Fay. Man Ray was irreplaceable. I didn't want to mar my memory of him.

Inside the house she was lovely. She looked especially good on furniture. Outside was hell. Our walks became a gauntlet of terror. A New York City special, the excruciating noise of metal roll-down gates, especially, tormented her. And so we spent a great deal of time in the farm fields and apple orchards of Upstate New York, where I had recently built a painting studio.

One day John Reuter called to remind me that I was a photographer. I hadn't booked the camera in a long long time. It was 1987. Fay was just over a year old.

When we arrived at the studio at 568 Broadway, Fay made a beeline for the storage closet to hide. I dragged her out onto the gray set paper and, recalling where I had left off with Ray, began blanketing her in props, a studio mix of plastic flowers, playing cards, wigs, and stuff. She relaxed and settled nicely into the poses, responding favorably to the warm lights and cocoon-like studio atmosphere. I snapped the shutter. The strobes fired. In afterimage her pupils dilated smoke rings of blue light. Good news. The big flash did not bother her.

In reviewing the first exposures, I noticed how strikingly Fay differed from her predecessor. Fay reflected light, Ray absorbed it. Fay, the shy thoroughbred, invited the viewer in with her powerful grace and beauty and hypnotic "village of the damned" eyes. Man Ray, less animal, more human as a subject, held the page as a steady masculine stoic form. I need different adjectives to describe Fay. Lying on the ironing board, Fay is a feline sphinx full of effulgence and grace, the yellow dot of her eye a beacon of light, leading me to her. Fay was not Ray. This made it all OK.

We kept returning to the studio, as Fay seemingly demanded. With each session she grew stronger and more confident. As I photographed her I came to know her better, My work was changing, becoming less cynical. I became a warmer, gentler, fuzzier, more open, caring person. The art world seemed far away. Sparta, meet Athens. Athens, meet Rome. Rome, meet Paris . . .

In a short time Fay matured from a coltish youth into a Garboesque beauty. My pictures grew with her. Now she was the muse, the adored one. Skin-deep beauty became the soul of my work.

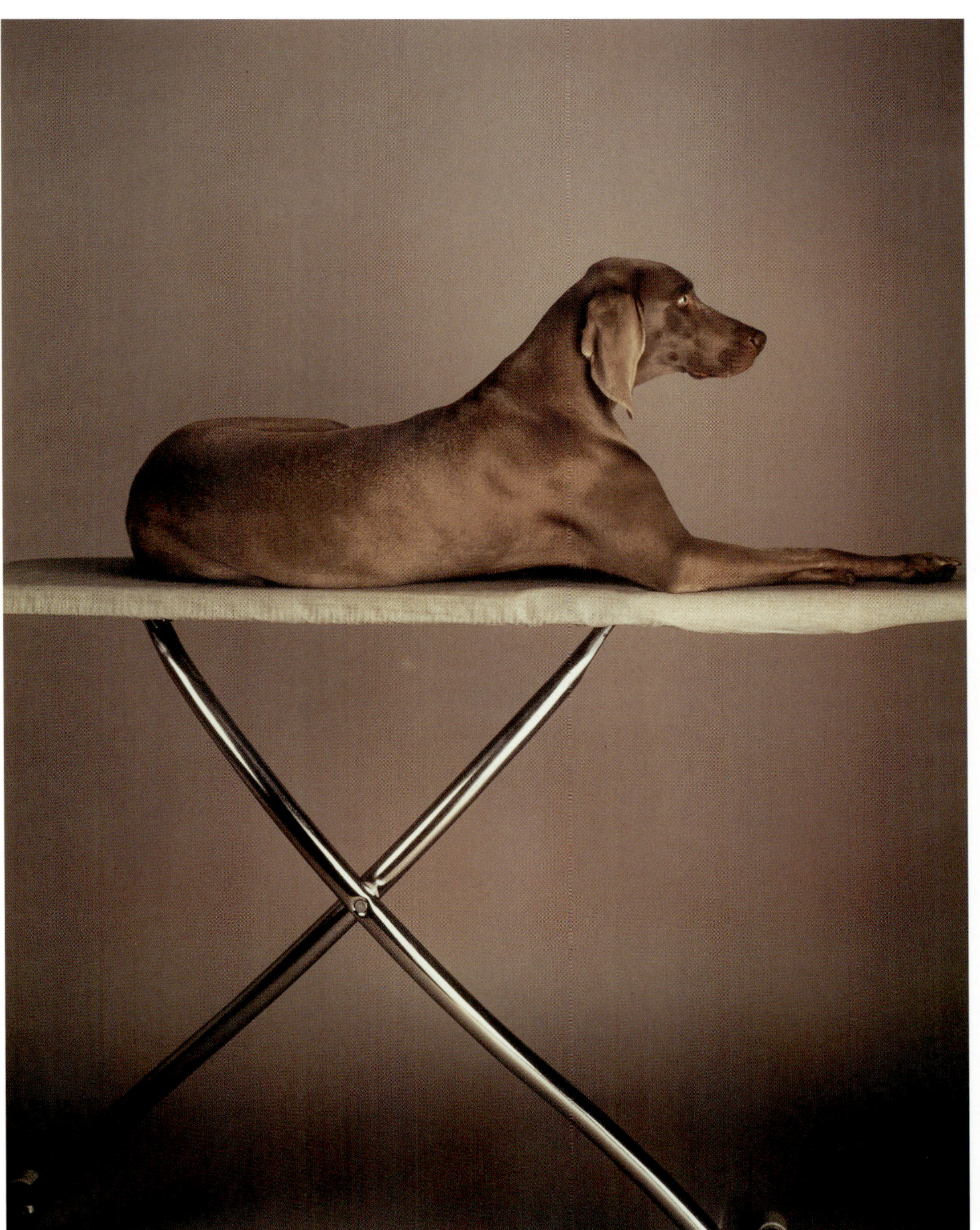

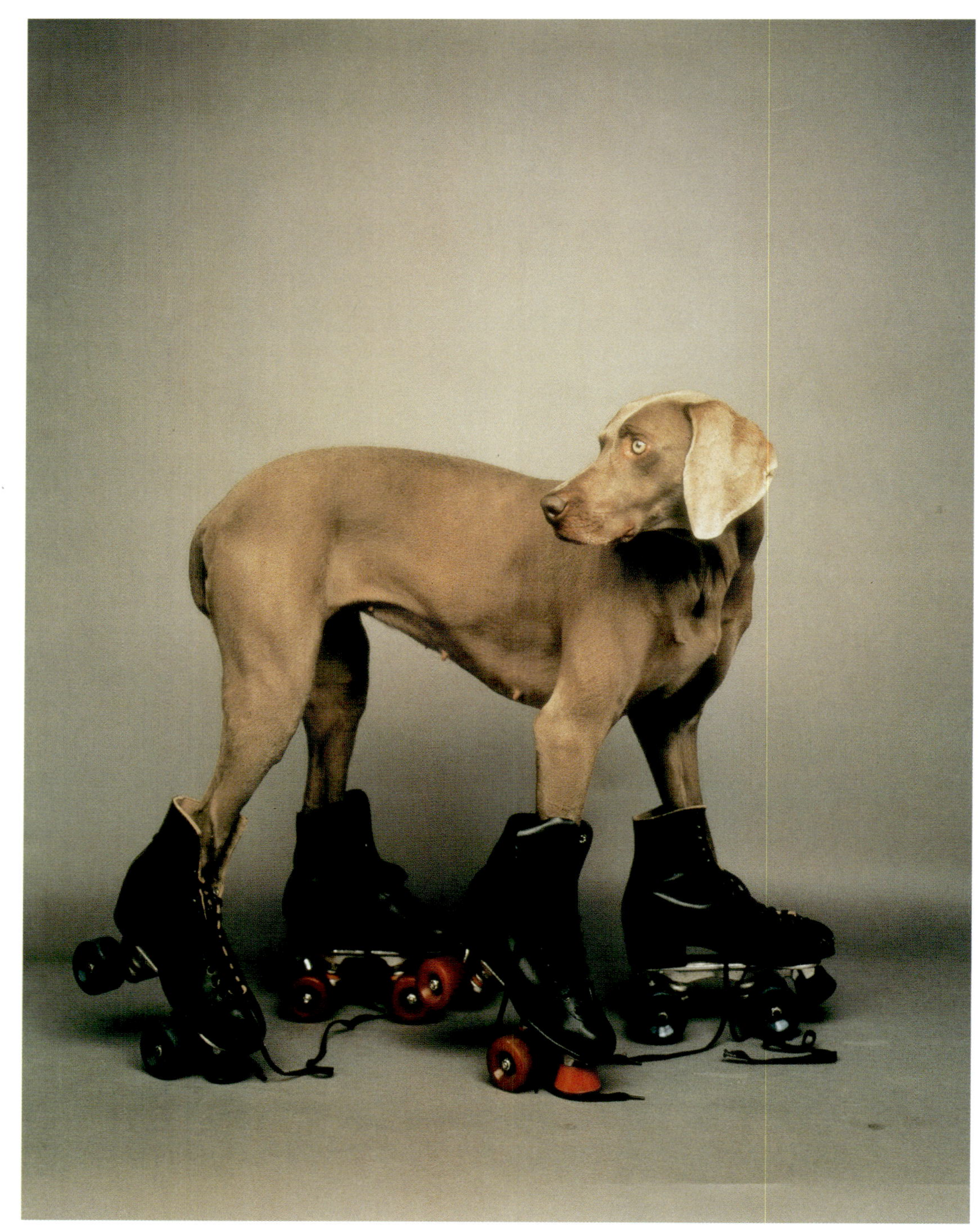

Opposite: ***Roller Rover*****, 1987**
Below: ***Afghan*****, 1987**

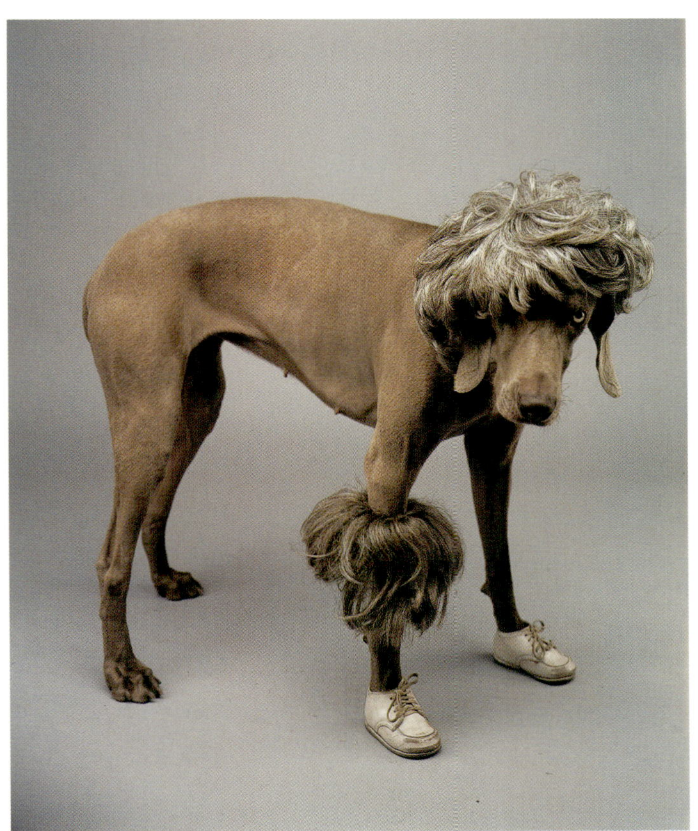

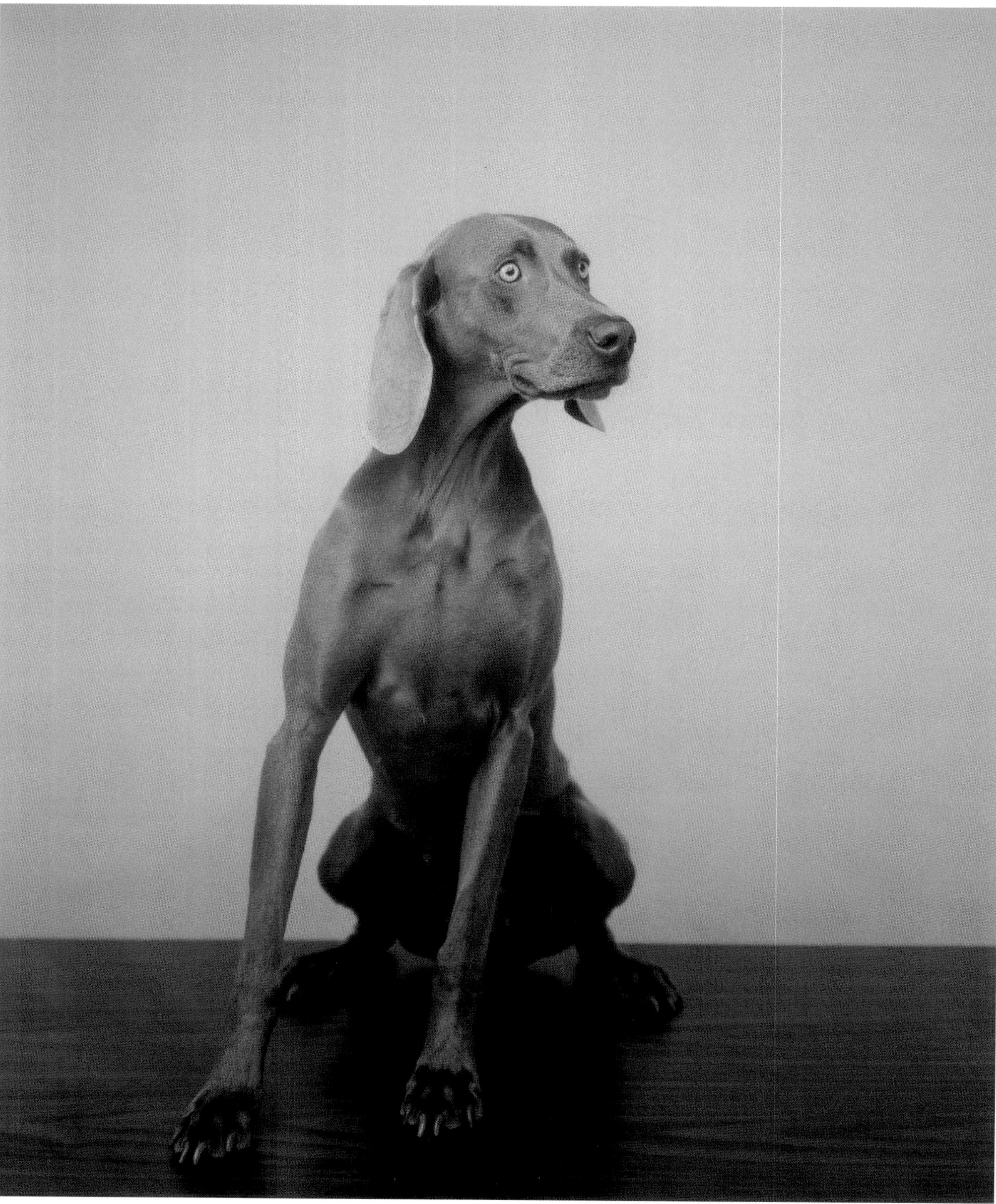

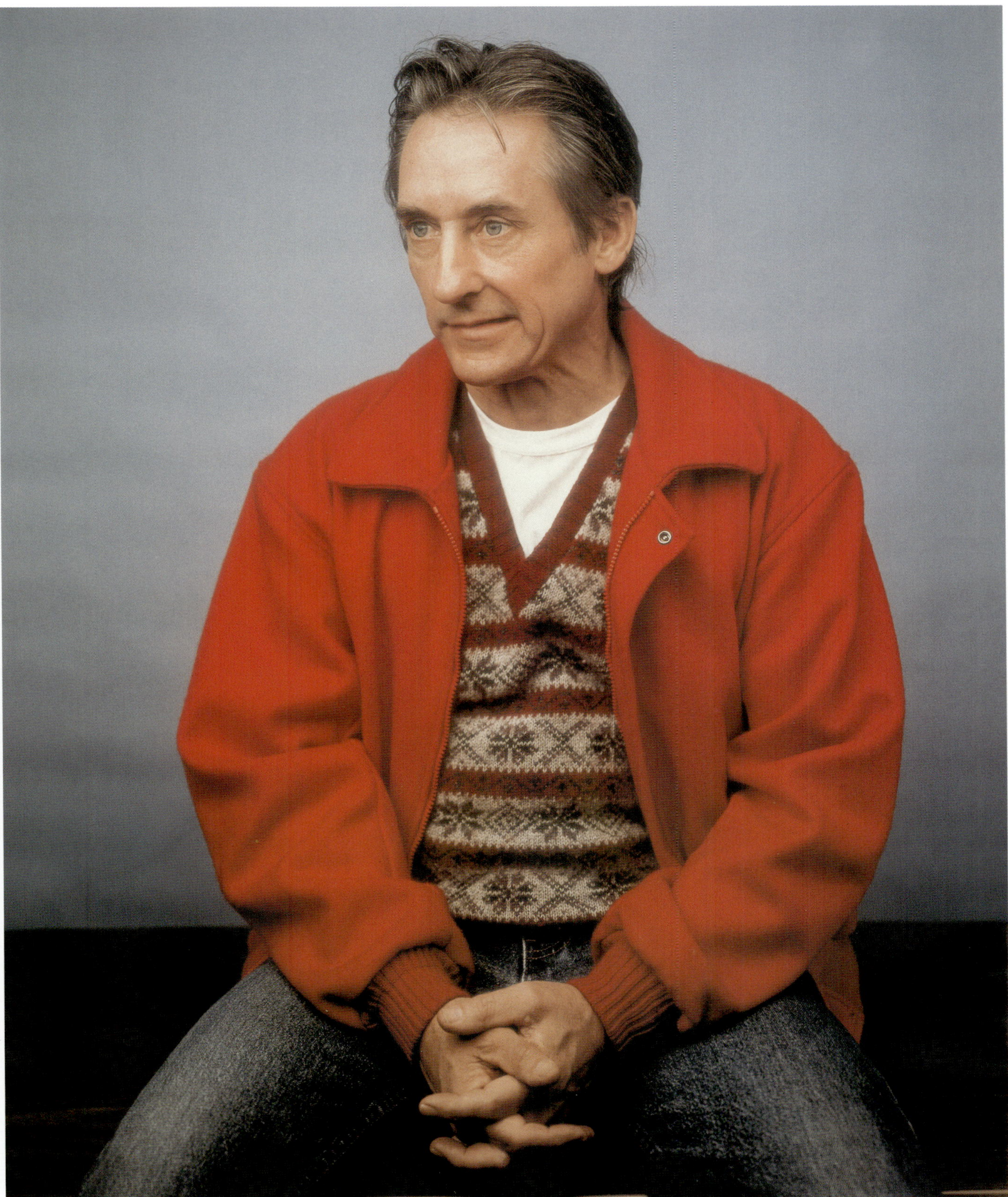

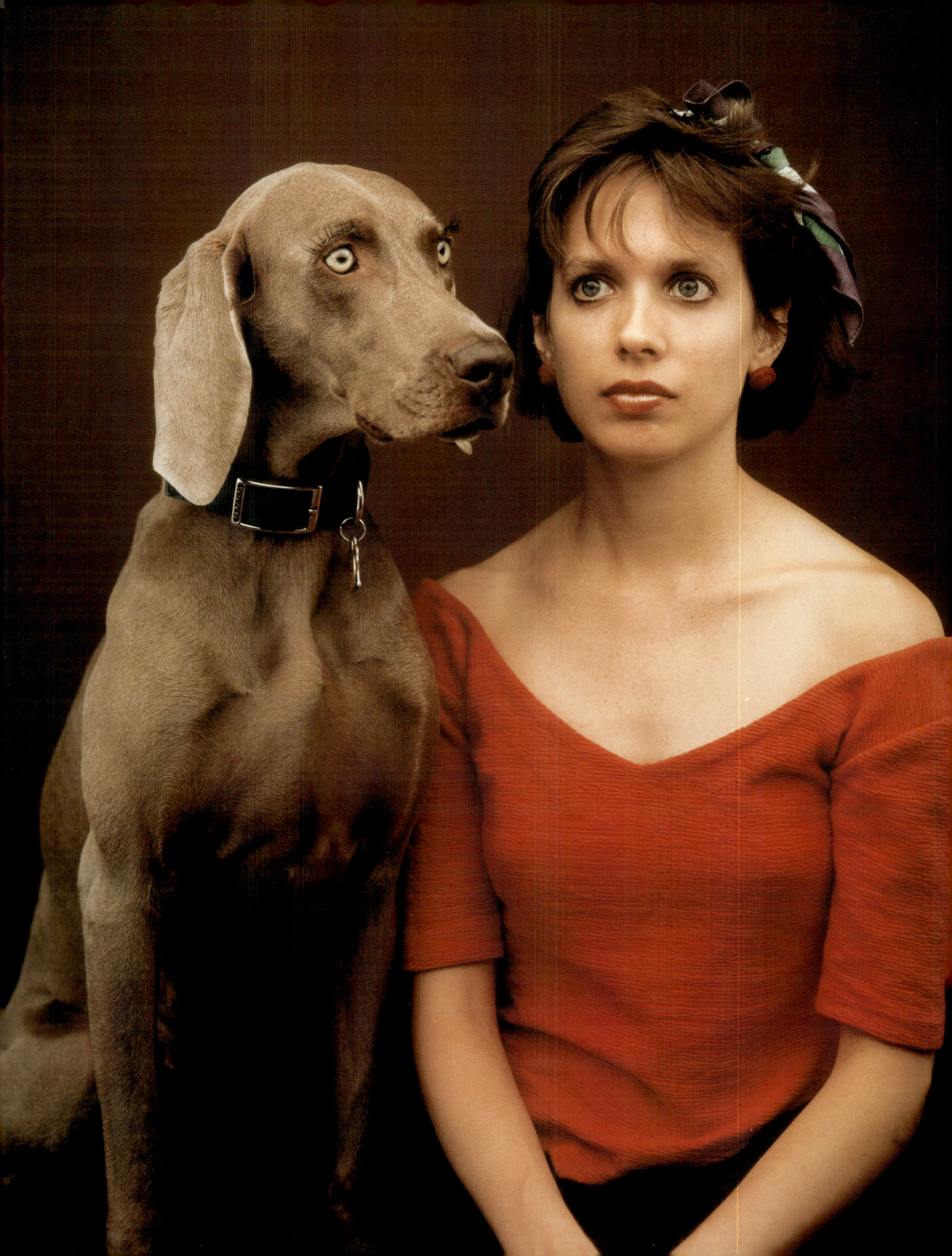

Previous pages: ***Fay/Ruscha*, 1987**
Opposite: ***Fay and Andrea*, 1987**

I never just photographed dogs.
Humans occasionally pop up
in my photographs,

although I rarely brought subjects in just for that purpose (Hester was the exception). Andrea Beeman accompanied me to the Polaroid studio not as a model but as my photo assistant. She and Fay had a similar look—they were two young and pretty girls. Looking at the pictures of Fay and Andrea, I see an innocence and bright sweetness very different from Hester and Ray's dark romanticism. Hester could not have posed with Fay. They would have clashed. Andrea returned again and again in my pictures with Fay. One day they came together as one.

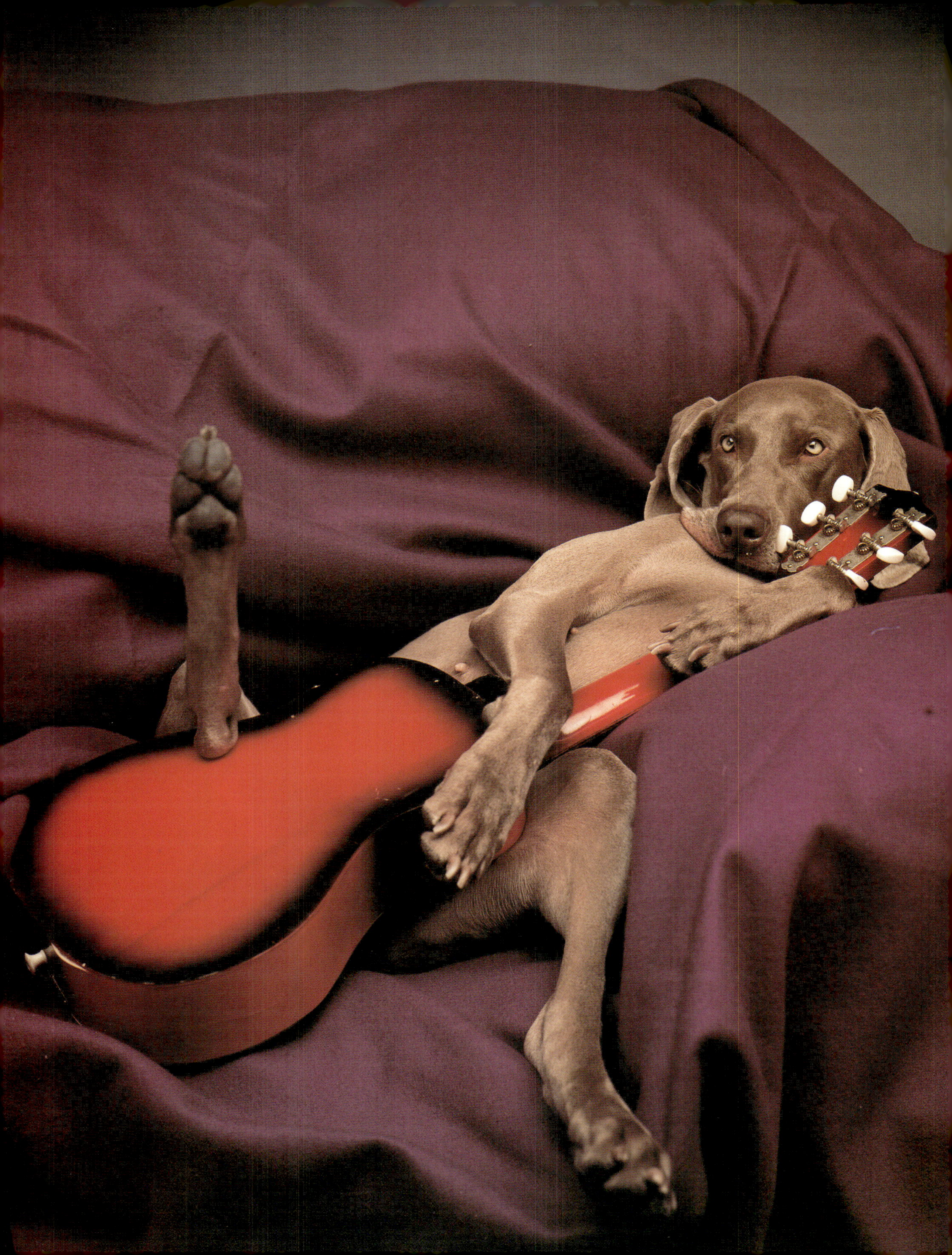

Slow Guitar, 1987

Below: ***Sculpture*, 1990**
Opposite: ***Back, Front, Top*, 1989**

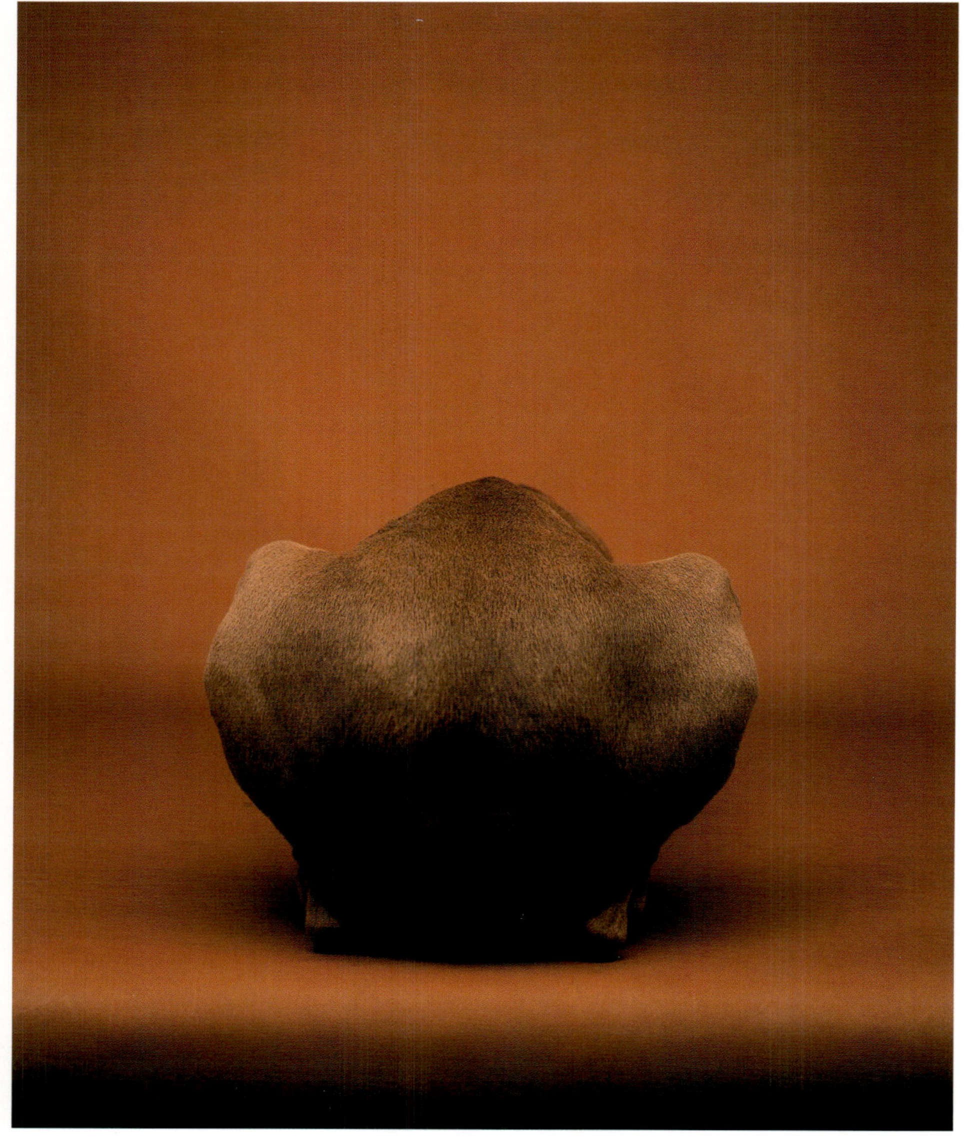

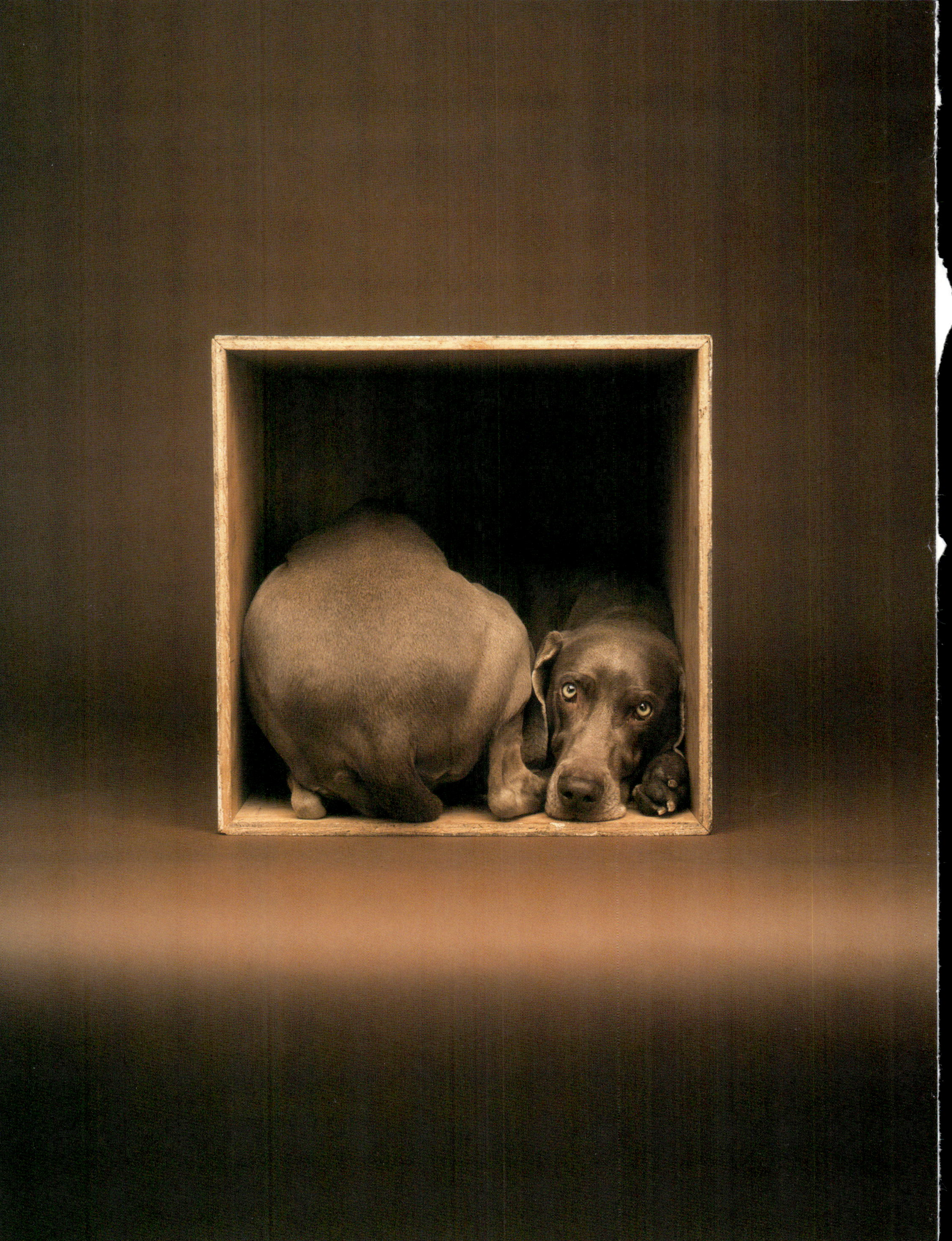

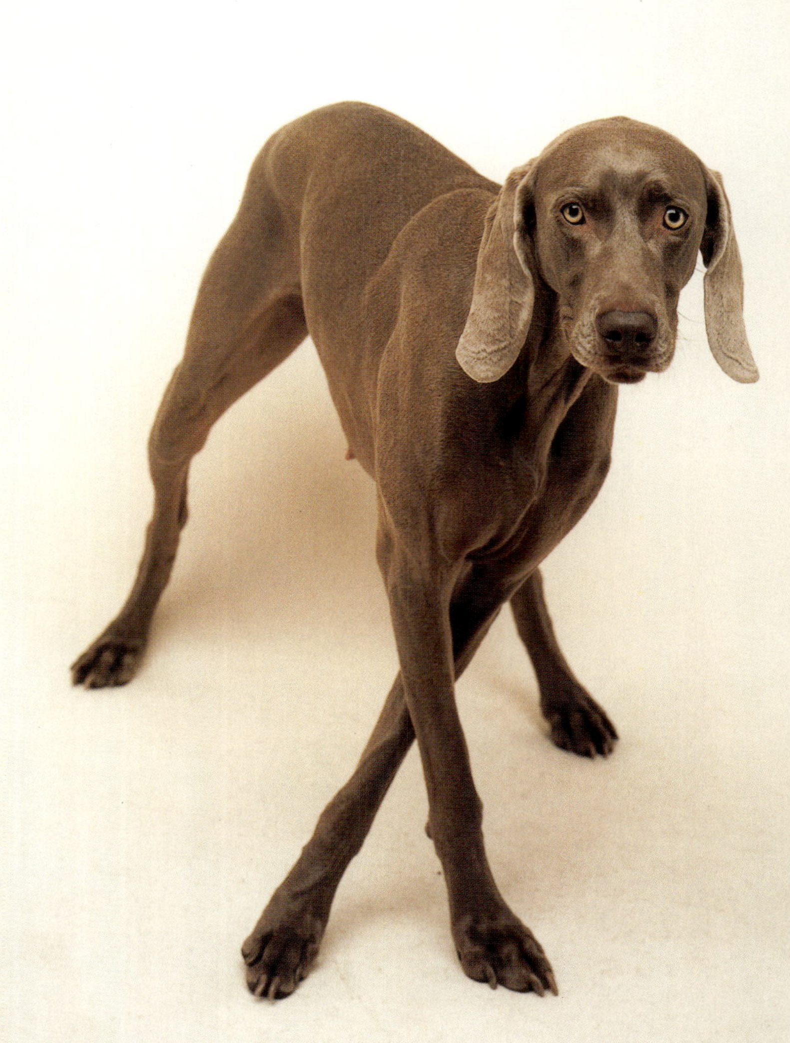

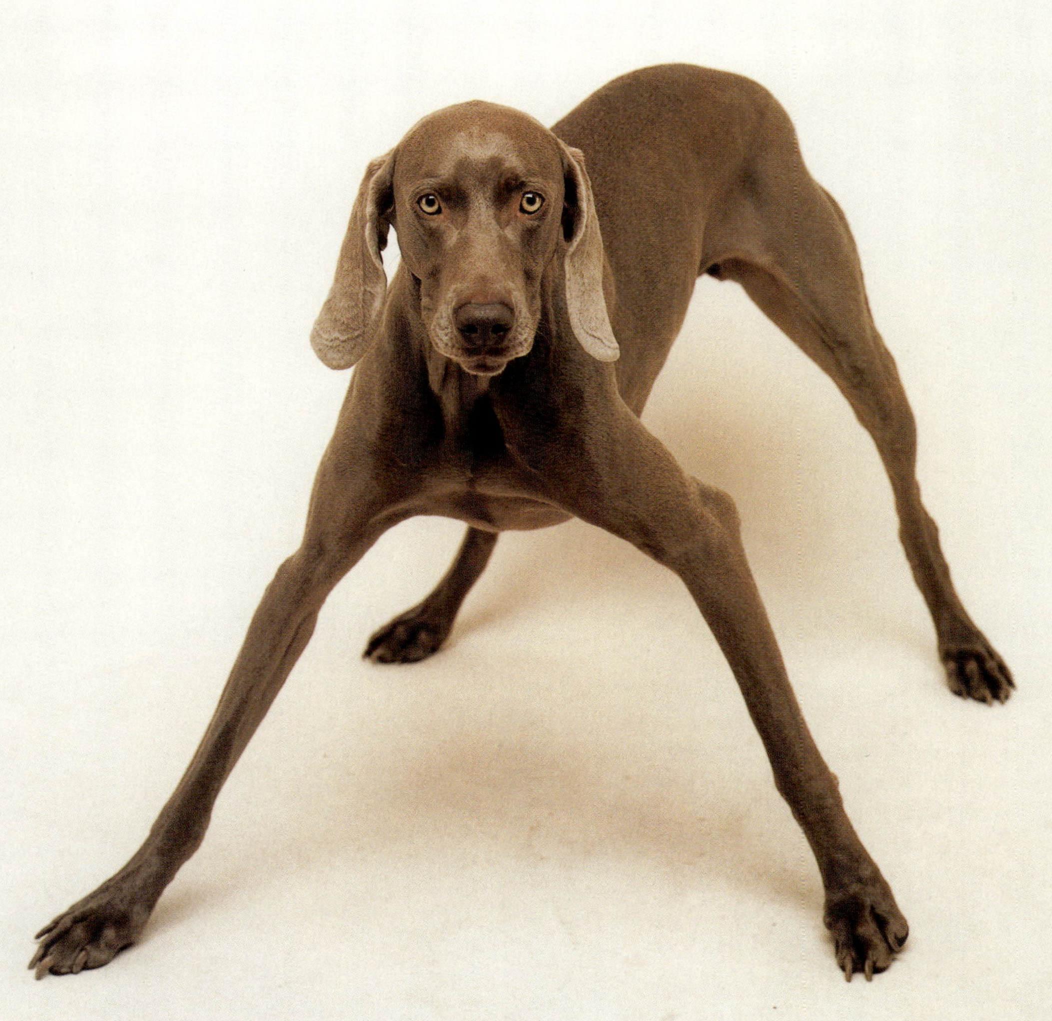

Reveling in Fay's leggy agility,

I concocted a series of anatomically challenging poses, positions I could not have thought up with Man Ray. Cross-legged, bowlegged, slant-legged, torqued, folded, flexed, flipped, flopped, flupped—you name it, we tried it. I came to understand very well her balance and points of physical tension. Fay apparently liked the challenge of a difficult pose. I think she liked to impress me.

Although I scheduled the Polaroid studio regularly, there were plenty of breaks. Given the continued presence of the dog and the unvarying format of the 20x24, you might think I had a master plan for a series of images, but I never experienced a sense of continuity in my work with the camera. I never found myself saying, "Now where were we?" Instead I looked forward to surprising myself. I developed a trust in the process. Don't make any plans. Just bring a lot of stuff. And Fay.

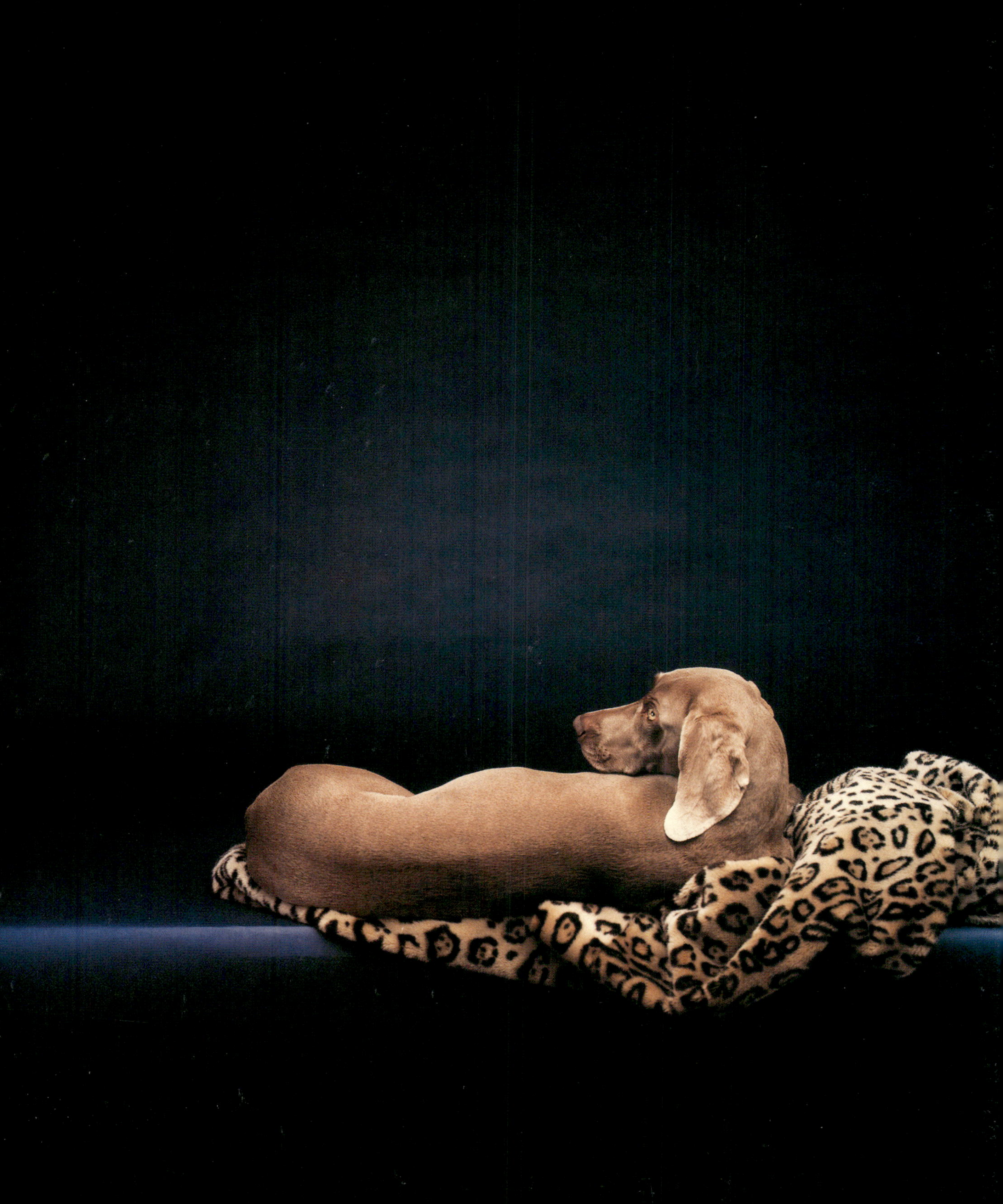

White Water, 1989

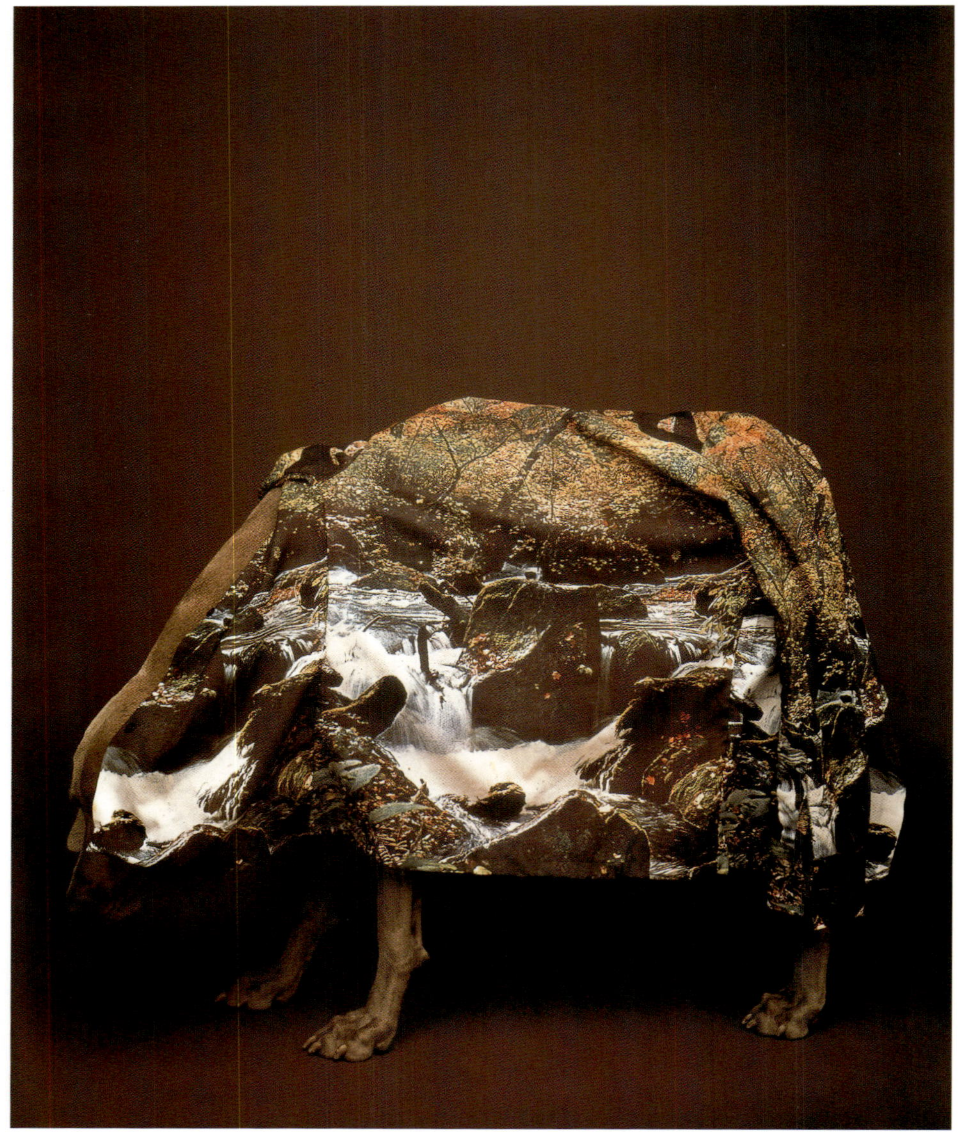

In my prop collection there are a great many articles of clothing from thrift stores and yard sales.

While avoiding anthropomorphic solutions, I found new ways to address the dog. I became particularly fond of those slippery shirts with photographic images on them, which when pulled over Fay's form became waterfalls, ships, becoming bison ships, becoming a menagerie of birds and invented fauna. Fay's rounded contours in her top line might have cost her style points in the show ring, but to my eye they were a perfect ten.

Polacolor ER film is very beautiful within a limited range. Man Ray was too dark for this film. He looked darker in the photographs than he was in real life. Fay's fur was right for this film. Through her, I began to explore color and light.

I started to collect screens, netting, and sheer fabrics that I could use with Fay to exploit shimmery light-trapping effects and spatial illusions. Fay got very used to being cocooned. She probably found it protective. I recalled using these materials for sculpture in the Sixties, long before I ever thought or heard about weimaraners. It was gratifying to bring this spirit back to my work.

Boating, 1141, 1079, Etc., 1989

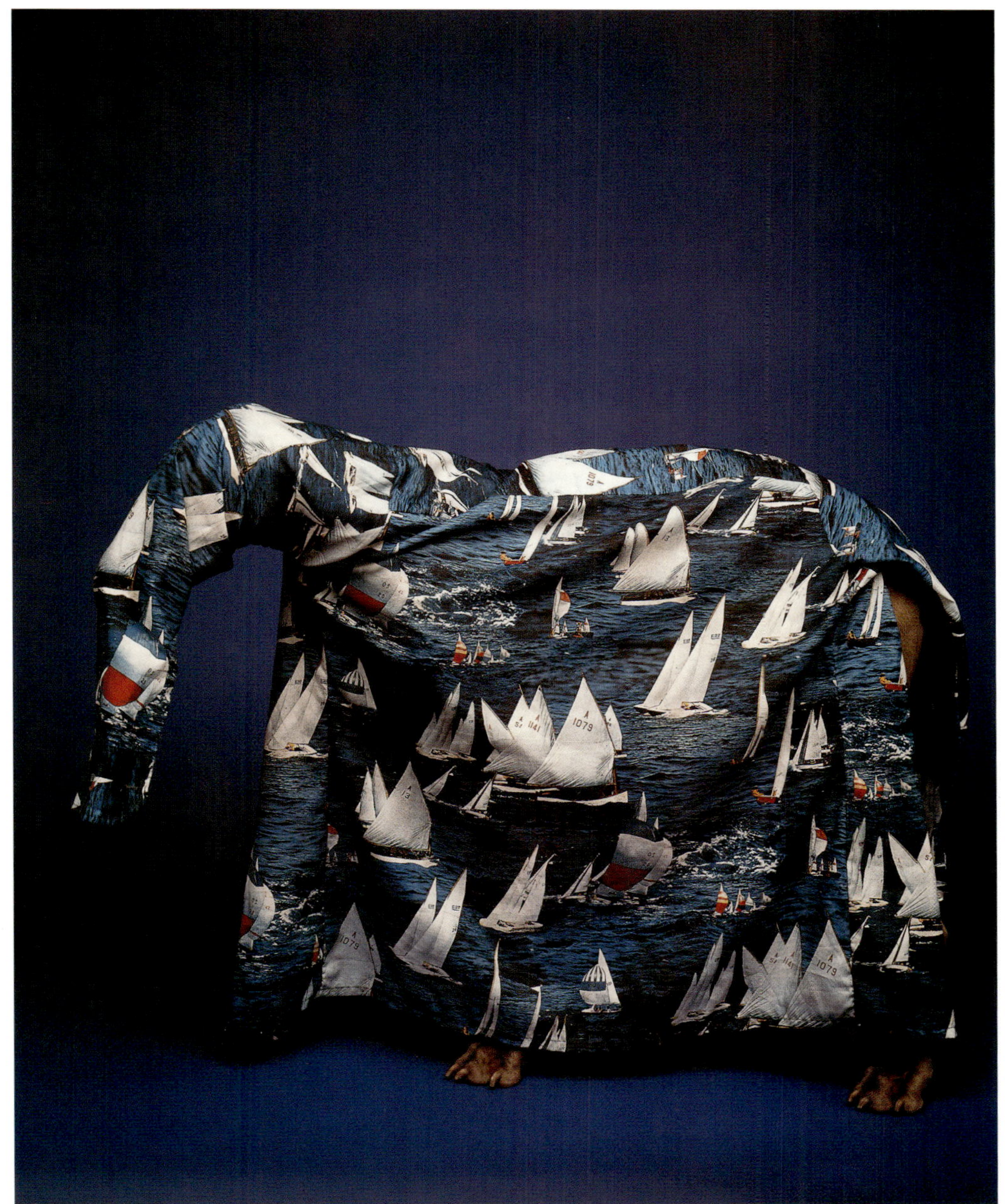

Old Crow, 1988

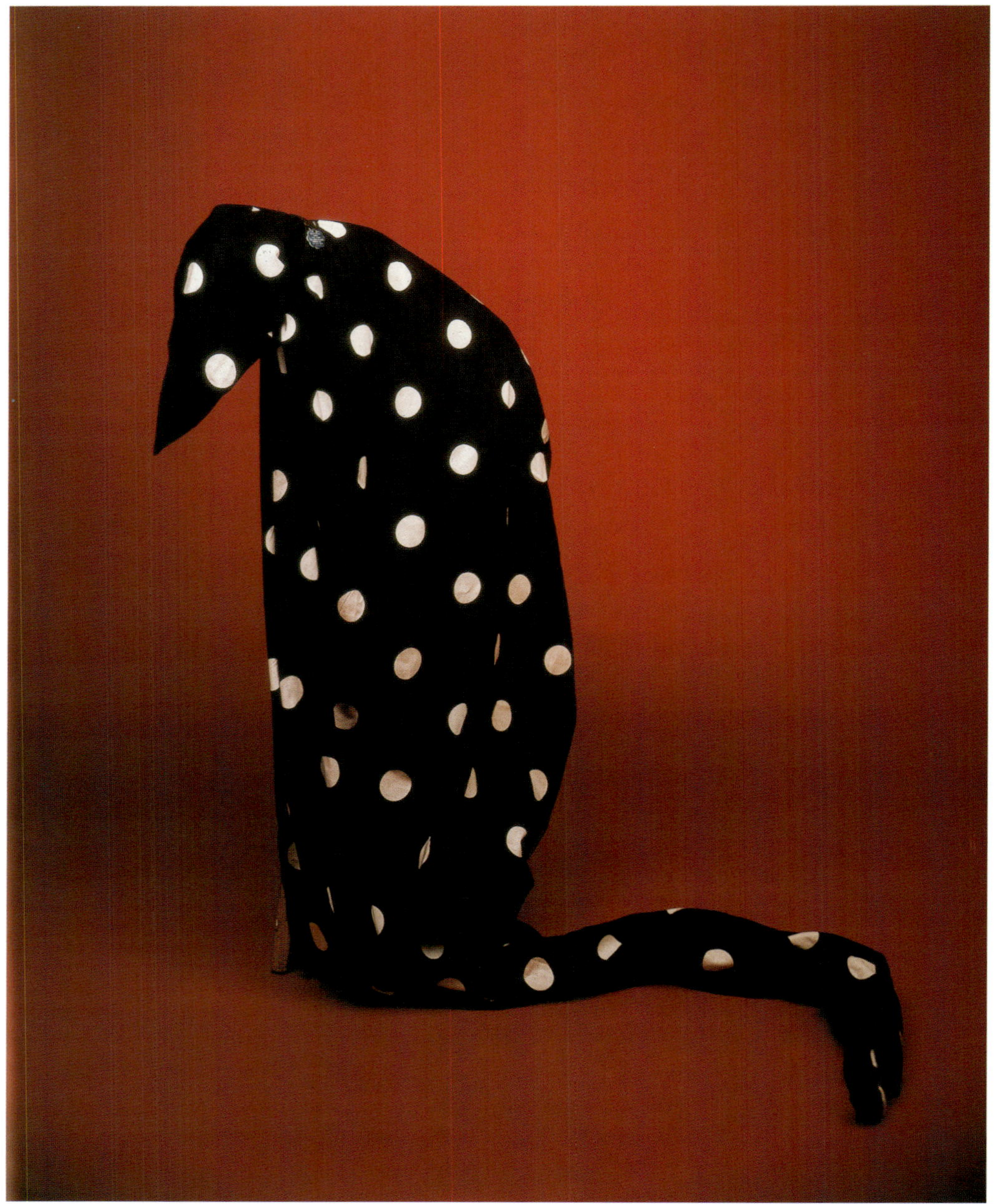

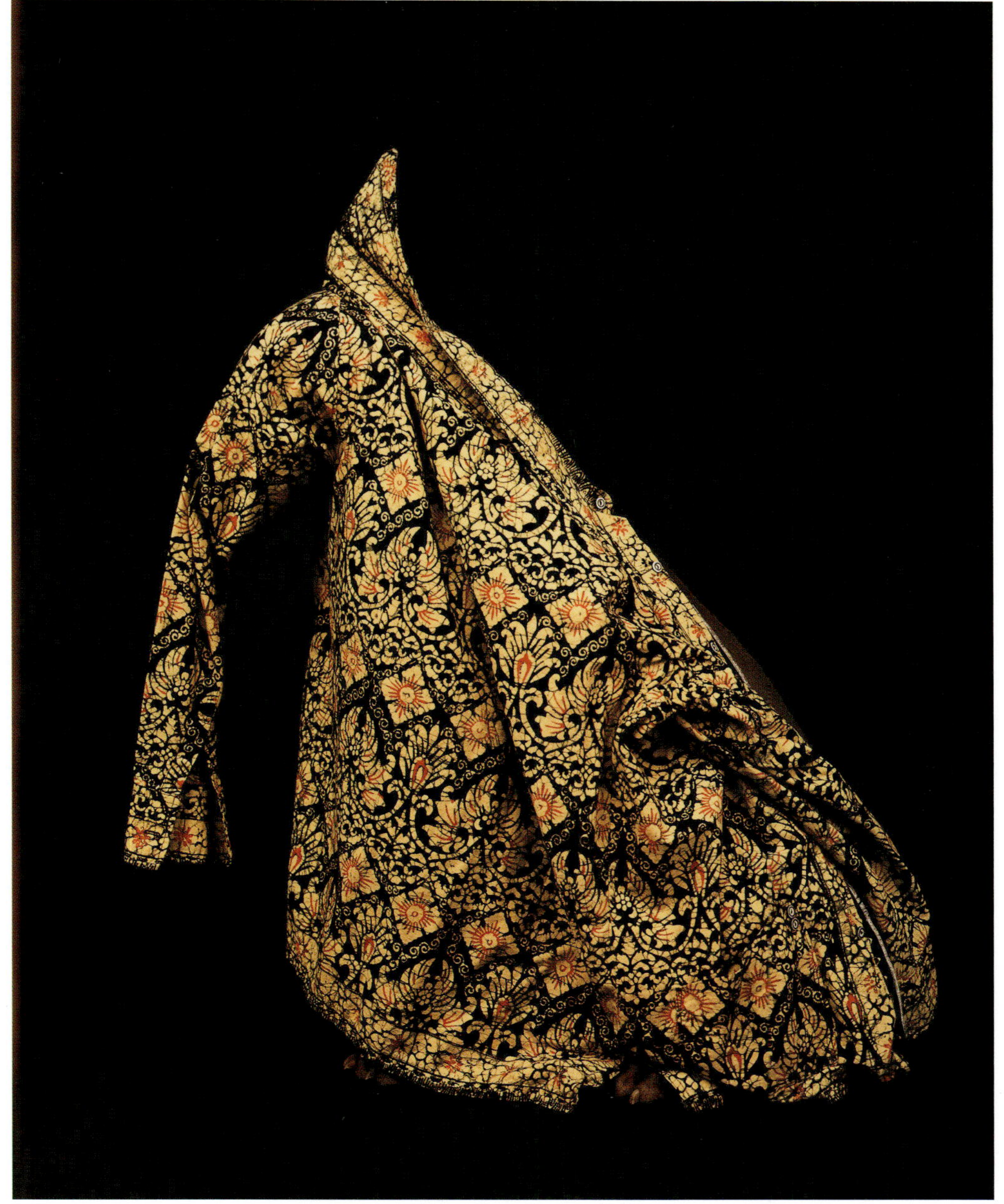

Coat Pig, 1990

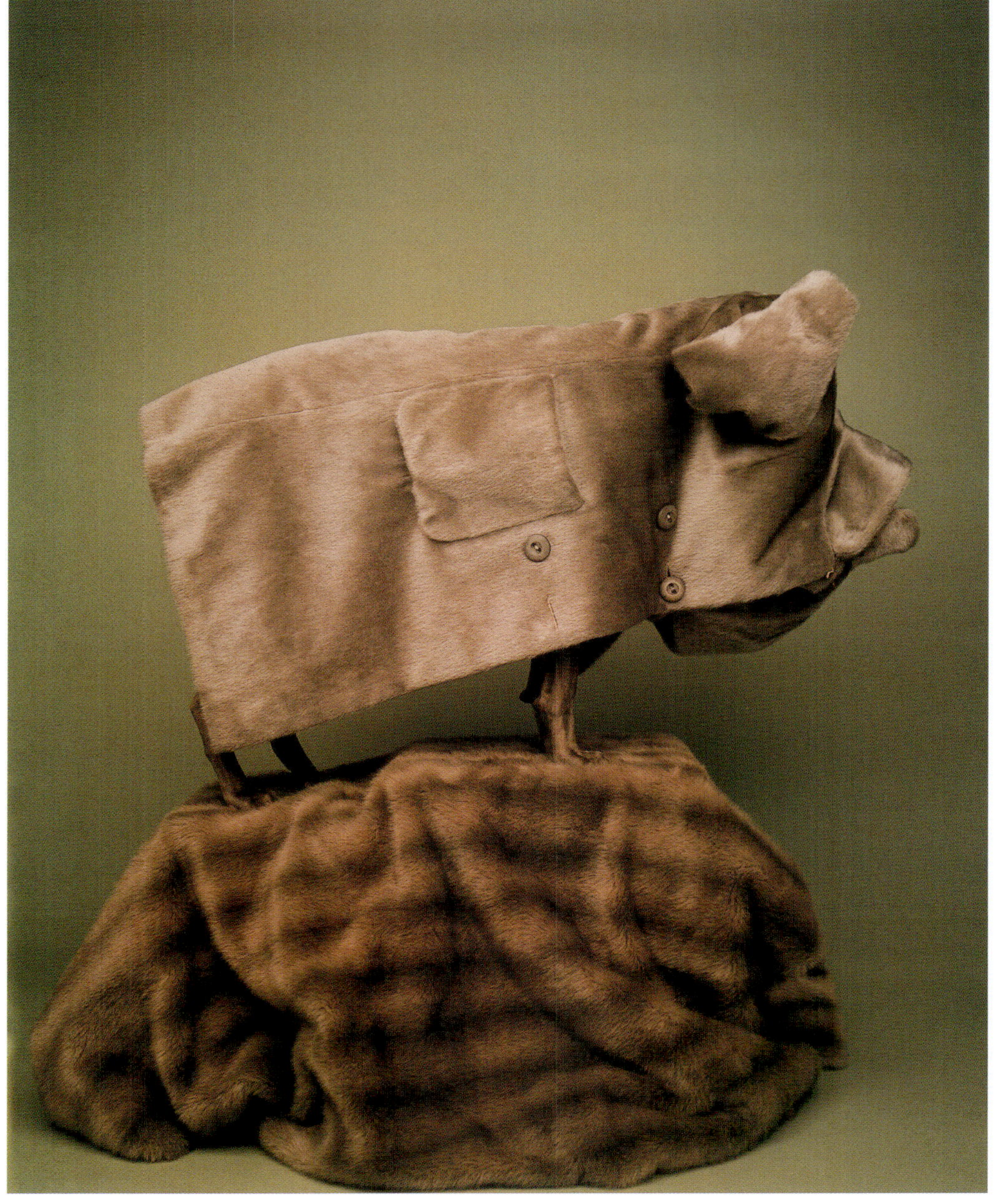

Hog Speaker B, 1989

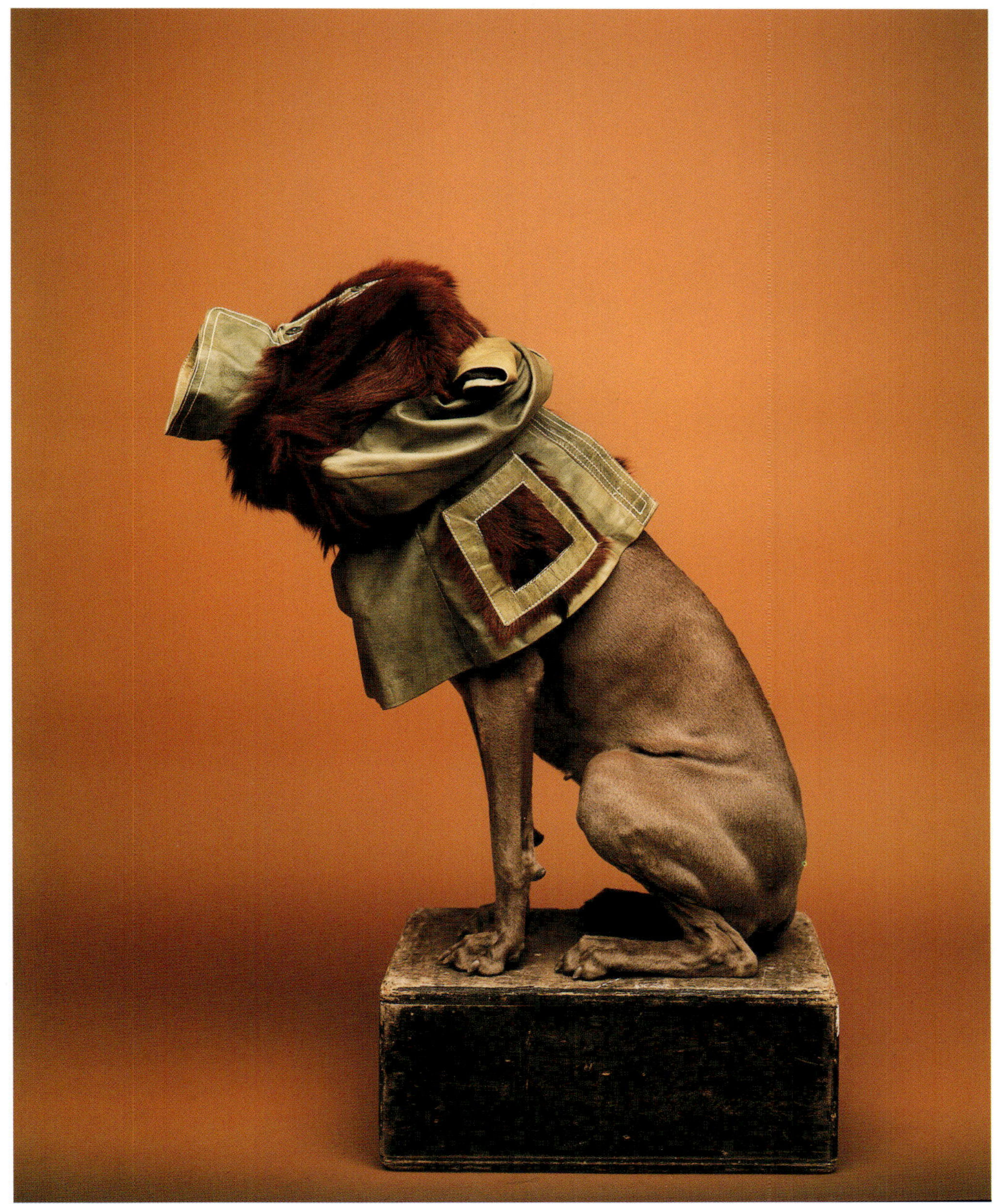

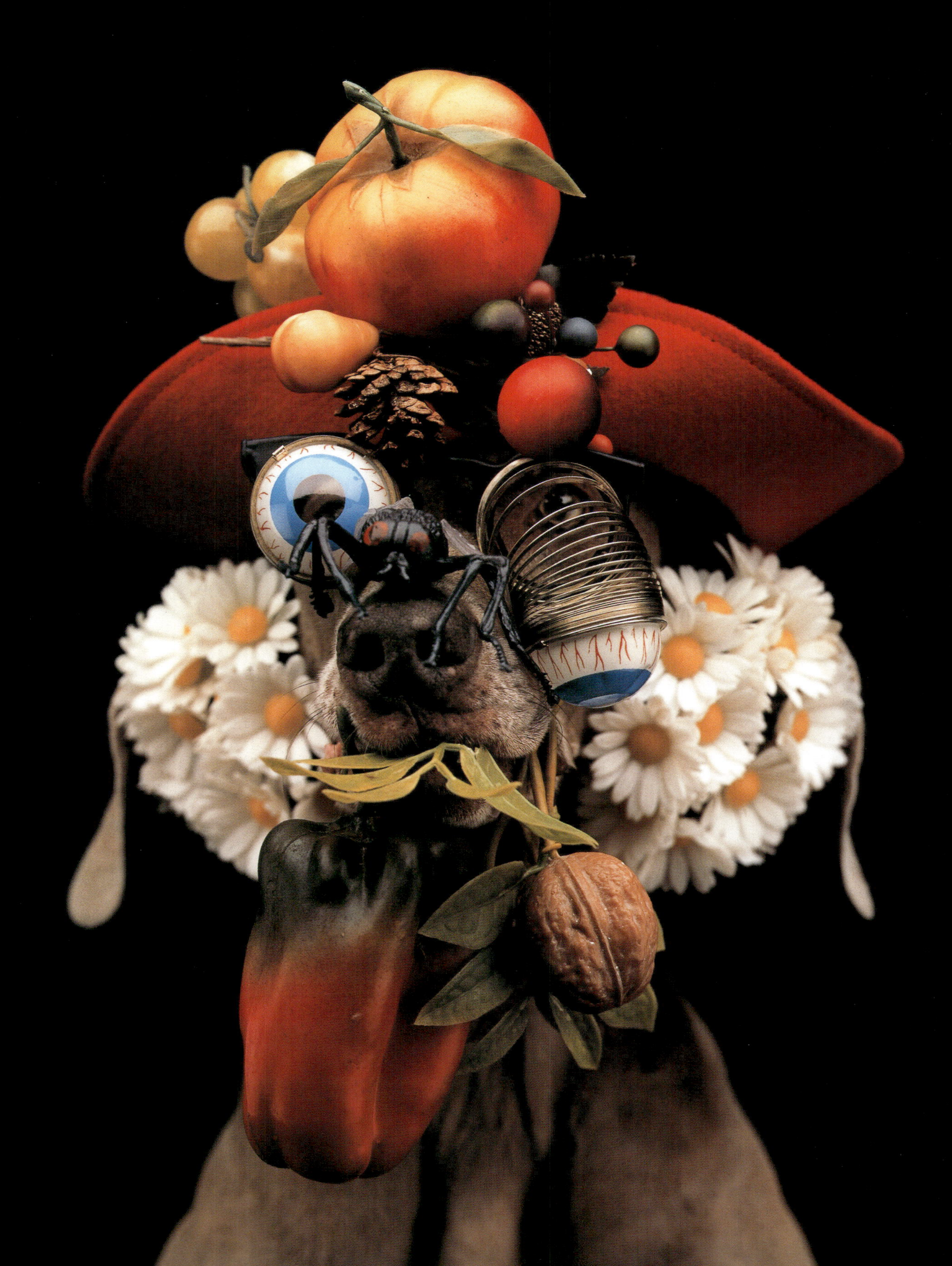

Opposite: ***Archimbaldo*, 1994**
Below: ***Eyewear*, 1994**

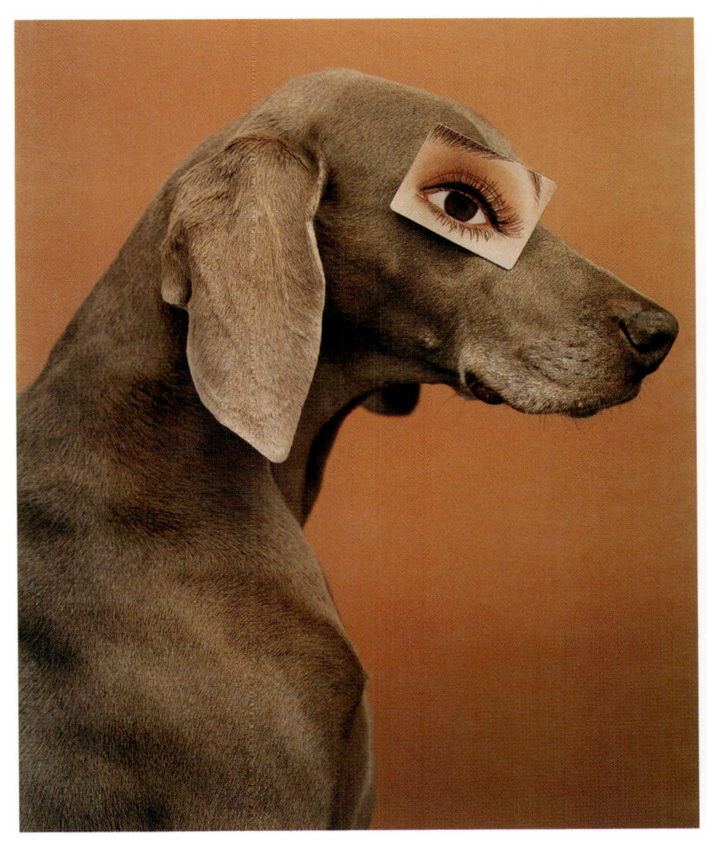

Fay loved to show off her ability to hold difficult positions.

If the pose was too easy for her, she got bored. She required a challenge to keep her intensity. You could see it in her eyes.

At the Polaroid studio, she developed the spooky habit of looking directly into the lens (not at me), anticipating the snap of the shutter by listening for John Reuter's "Ready Bill" after he finished setting the camera.

In *Archimbaldo*, she's wearing a red felt hat and bulging eyeball glasses that anchor a conglomeration of plastic fruits, flowers, nuts, vegetables, and a big acrylic housefly. Because of the prop elements and the magnification of the image, Fay had to be very still. If she moved at all she would be out of focus or out of frame. Even behind all that stuff I could still feel her penetrating gaze.

Plaiderpiller, 1994

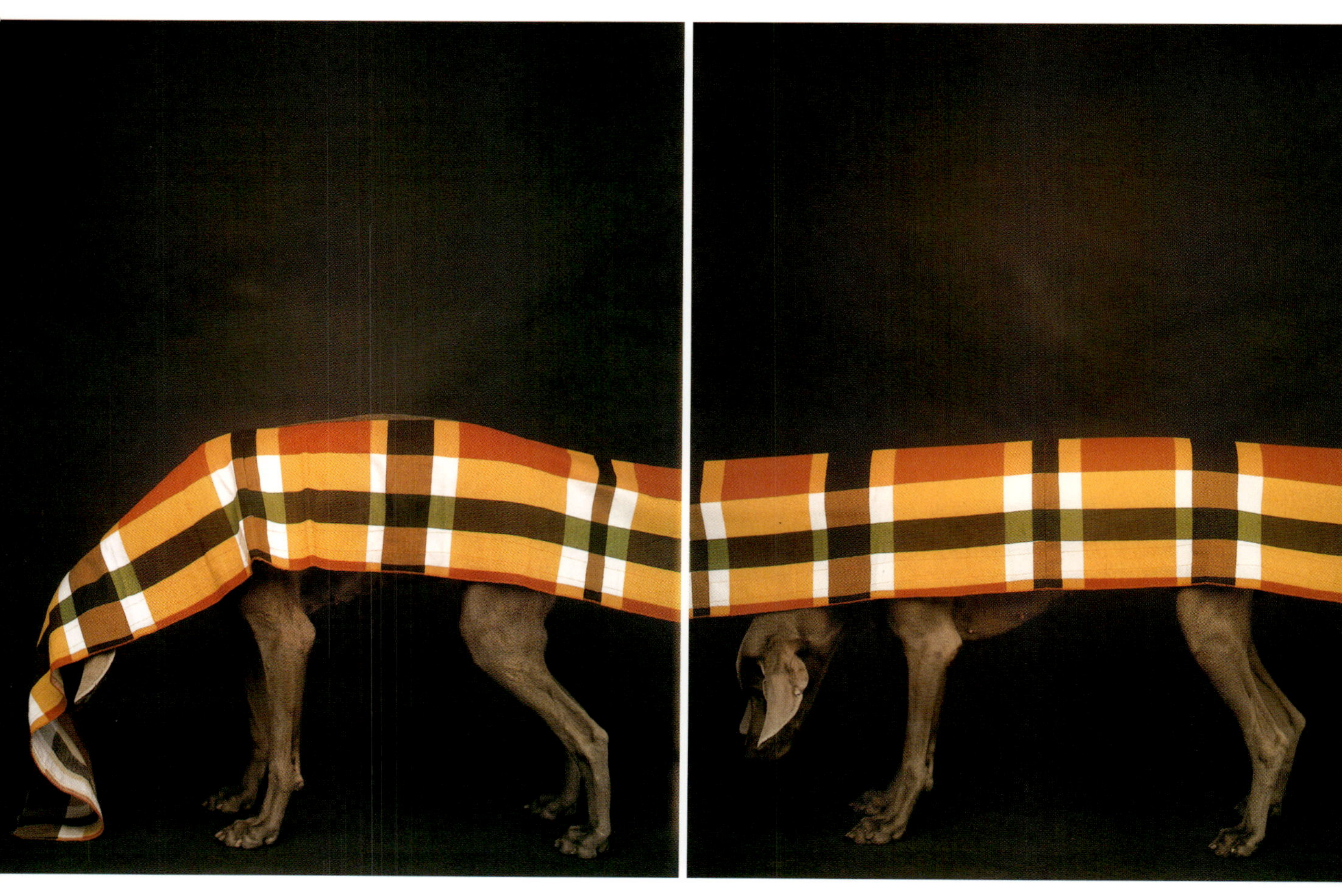

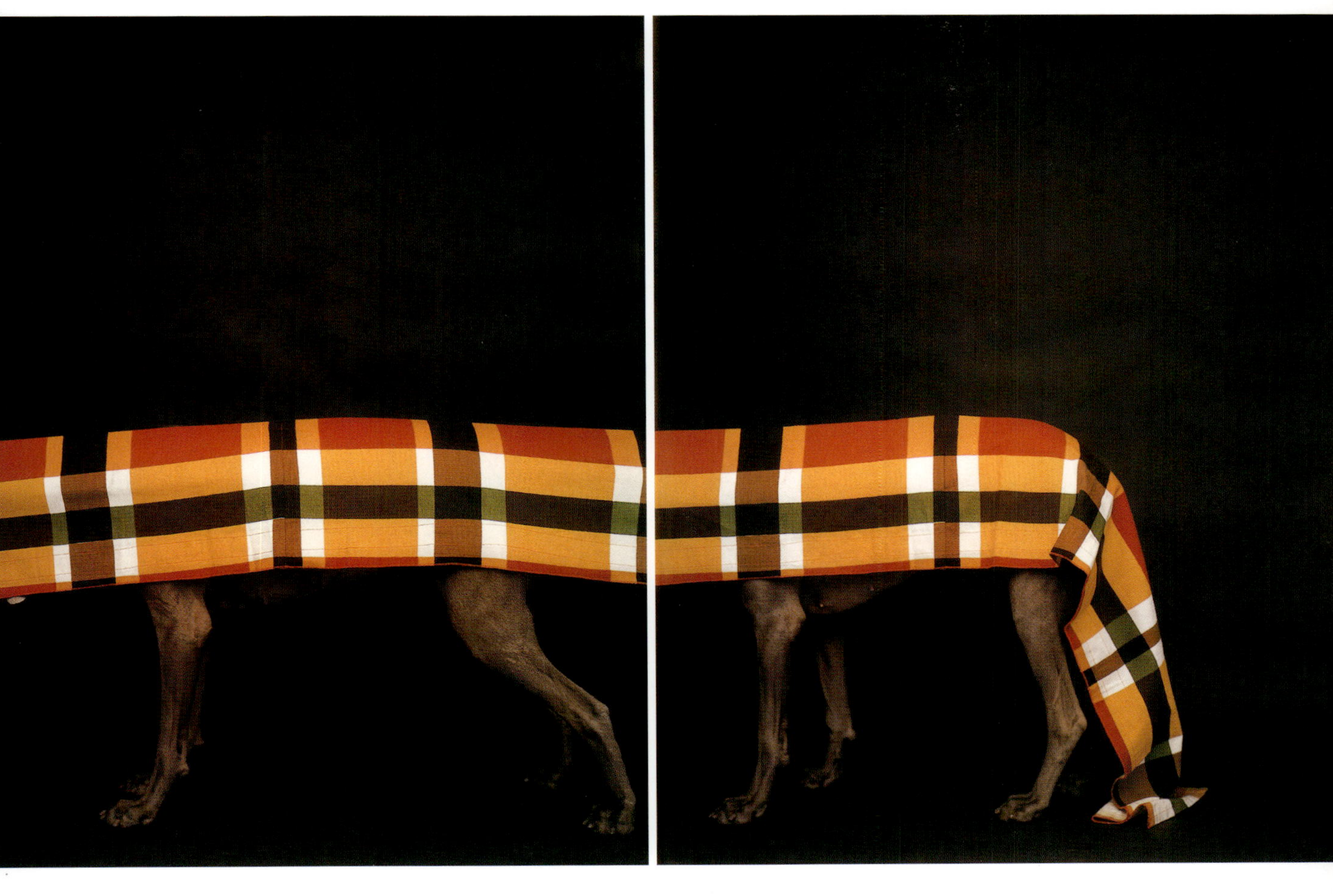

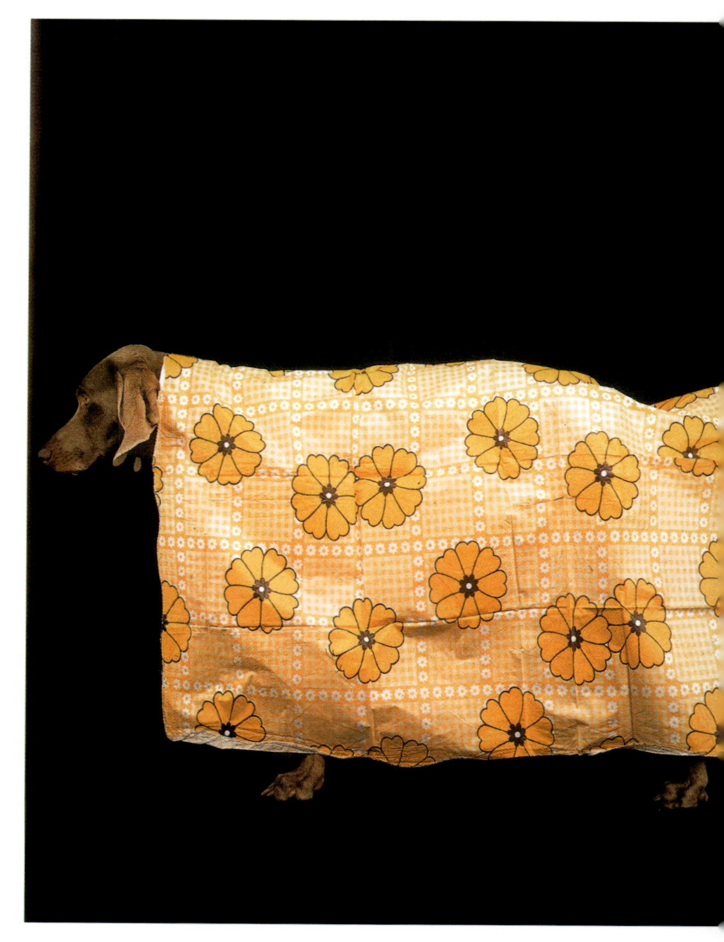

Caterpillar, 1994

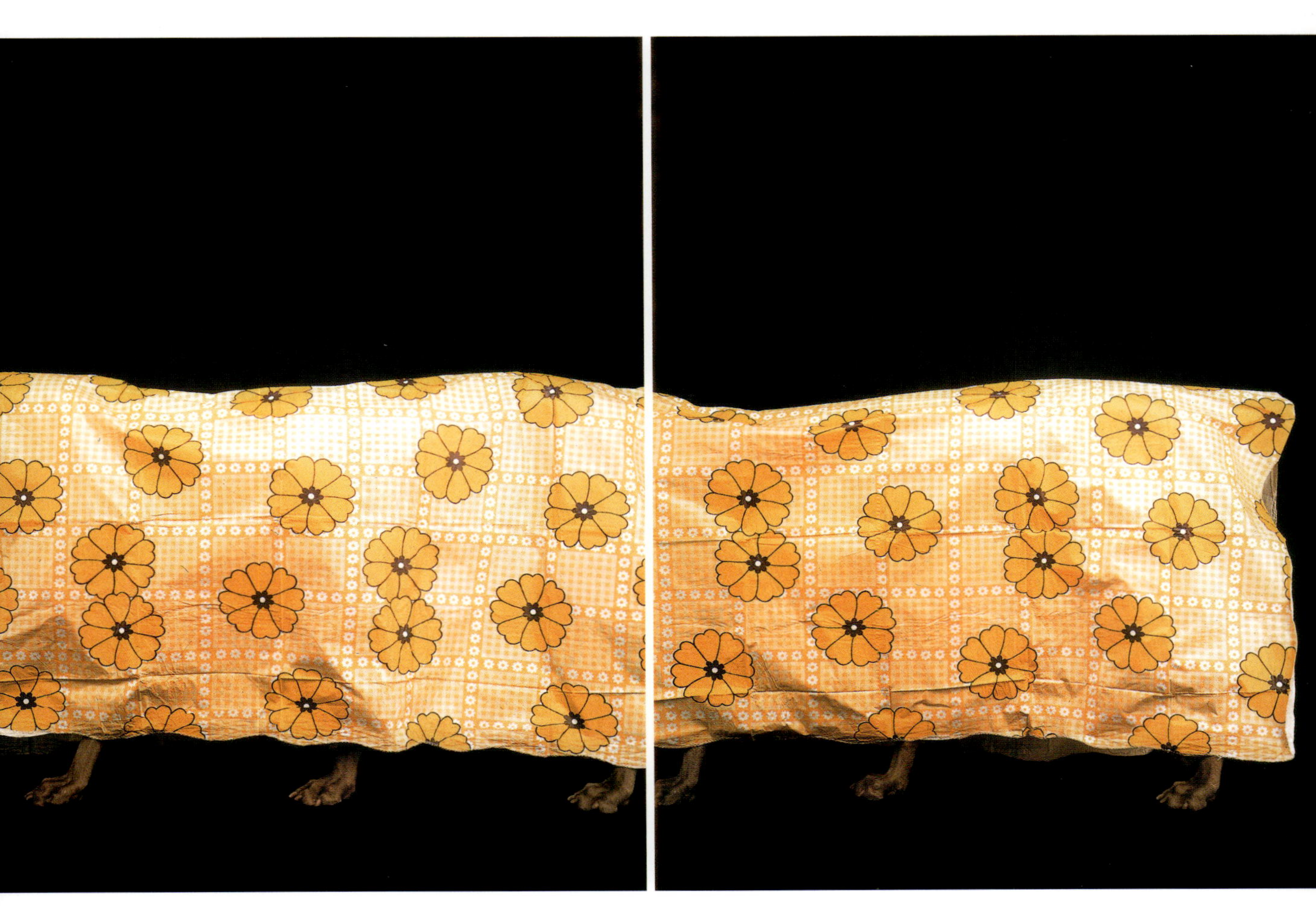

Times Square, 1995

Fossil, 1995

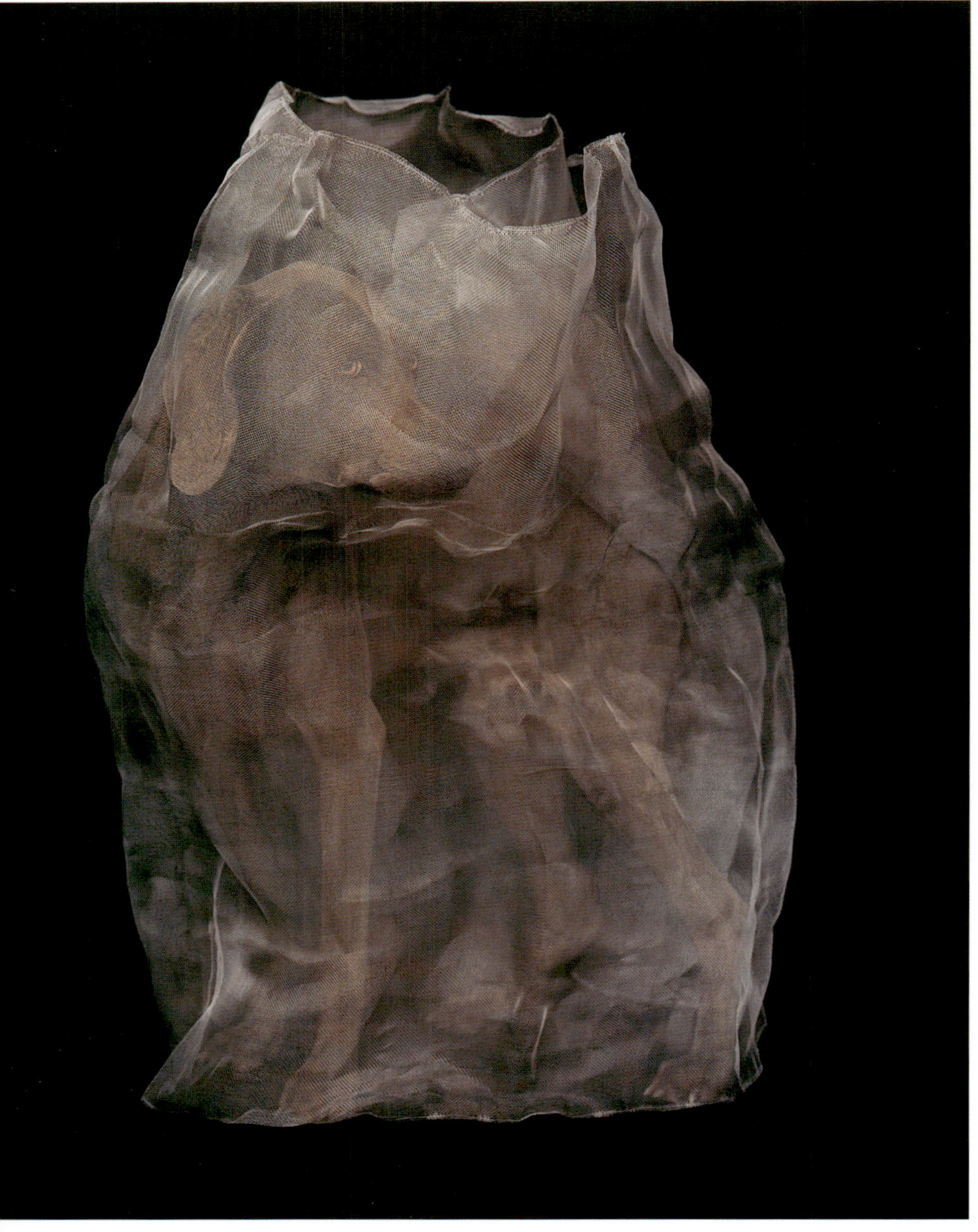

Left: ***Severini*,** 1989
Right: ***Cloud*,** 1988

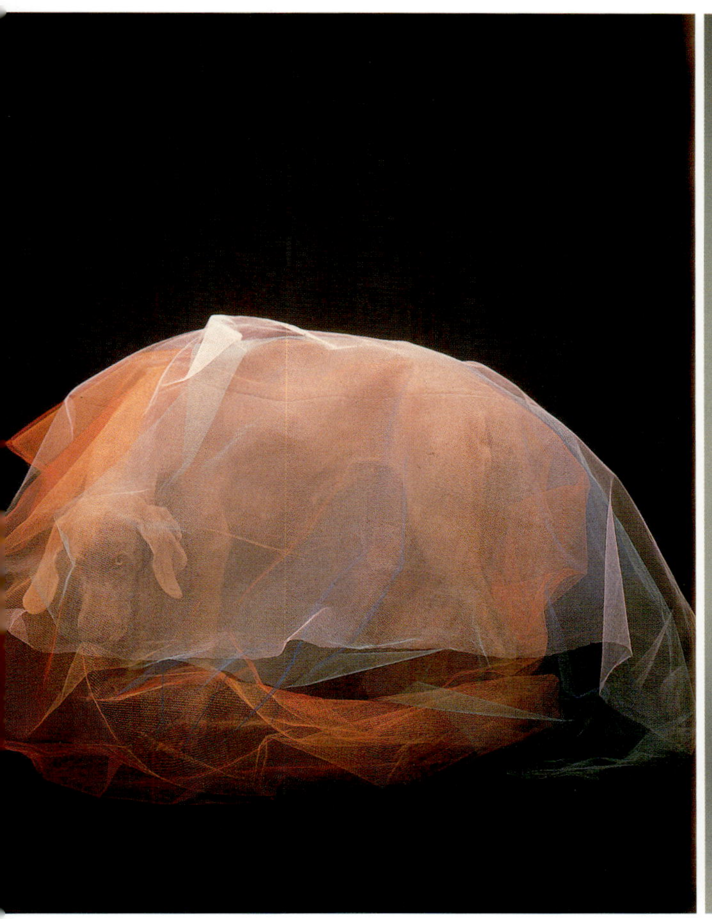

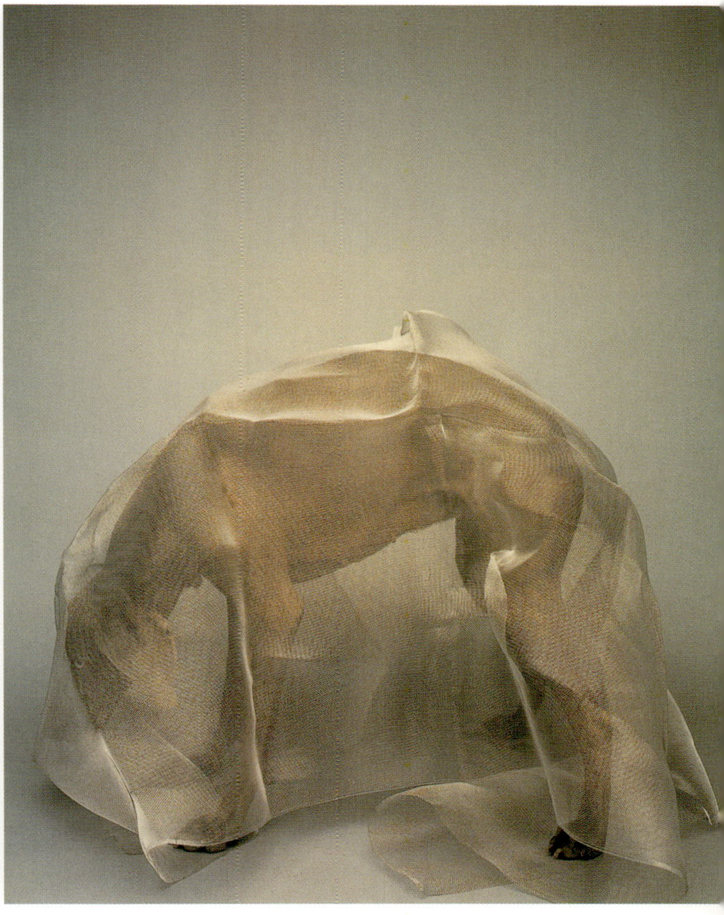

Dressed for Ball, 1988

The format of the Polaroid camera forces
you to think in terms of its vertical frame,
ideal for what it was designed for,
photographing people.

Dogs are not so easy. Unless in sitting position, or in a tight close-up, their form is not so accommodating. Over time this factor became a compositional challenge. I began to think of ways I could get Fay up into the frame.

With that in mind, I came across a little round pedestal table and brought it to the Polaroid studio one day. I lifted Fay up and sat her on the table facing the lens. John pulled back the camera to include Fay and the table without cropping either. Foraging around the room for something else to add, a striking polyester gold-ochre dress and jacket ensemble on a garment rack caught my eye. It was still on the hanger when I slipped the dress over Fay's head, allowing it to hang in front of her, draped to the floor. From the front she appeared to be wearing the dress, a society lady out of a John Singer Sargent painting.

Holding a yellow tennis ball in my hand to get her attention, I tossed it to her. Just before she caught it in her mouth I took the picture. The result made me giddy.

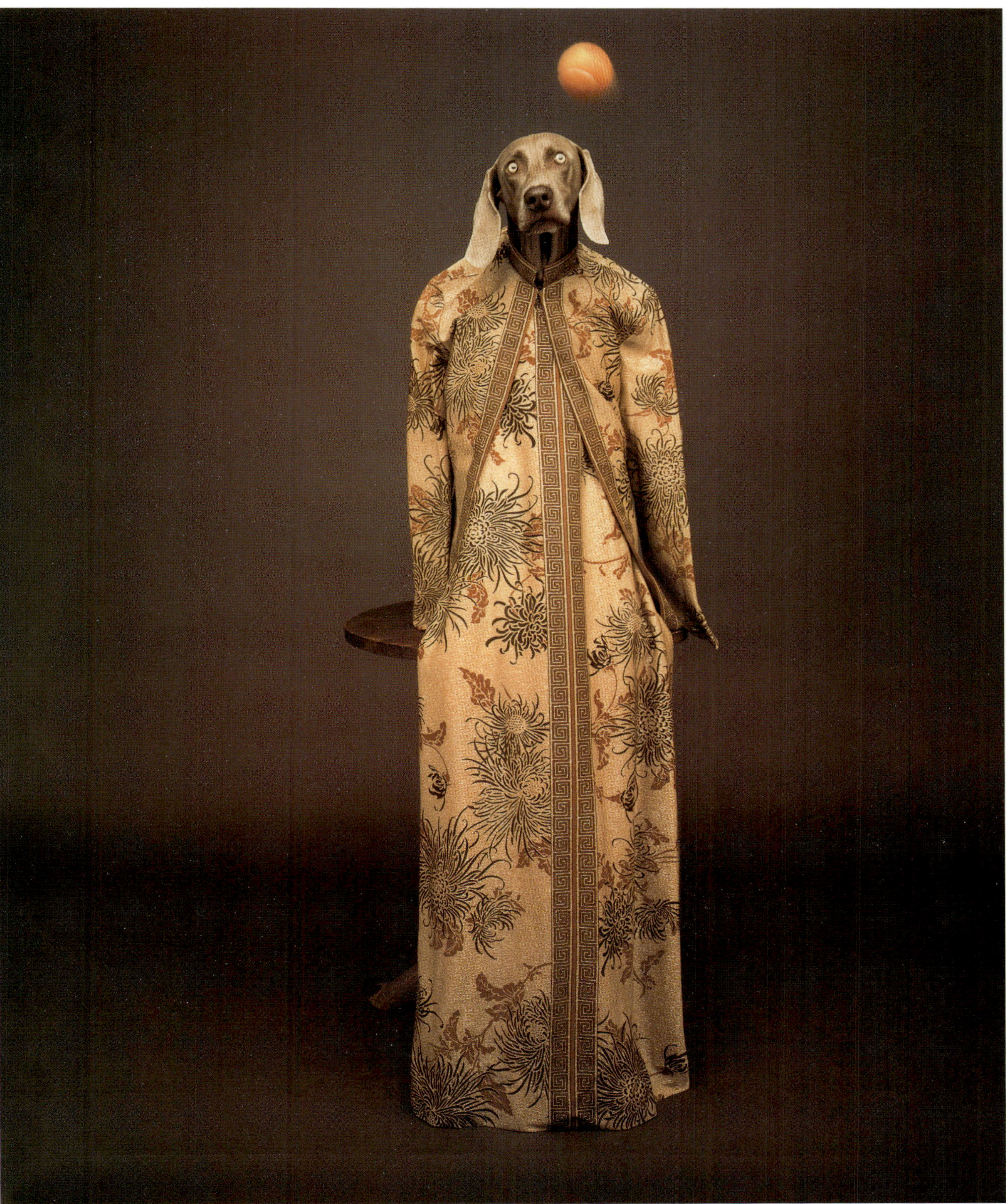

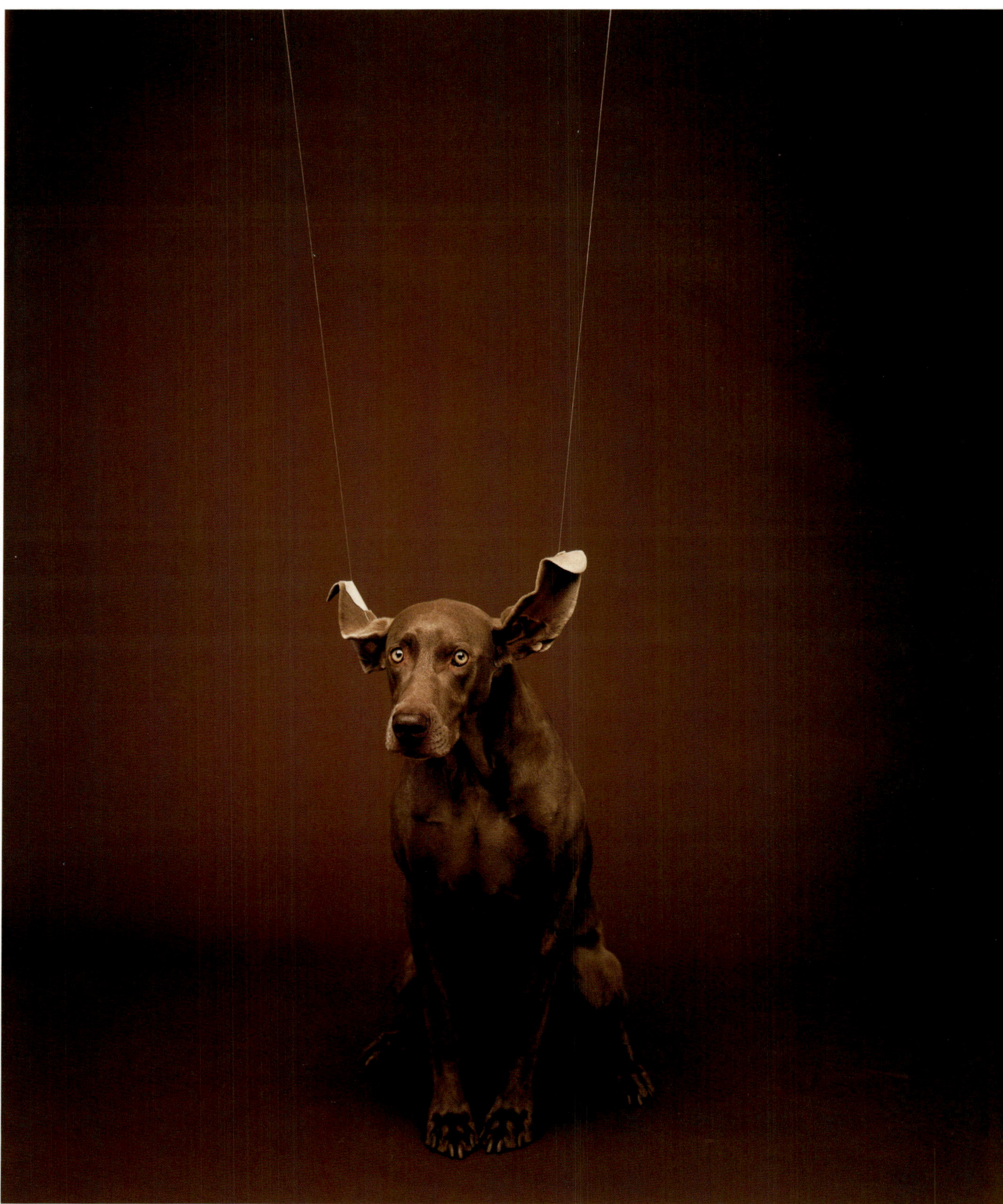

Opposite: ***Puppetry,*** 1989
Below: ***Red Dress,*** 1989

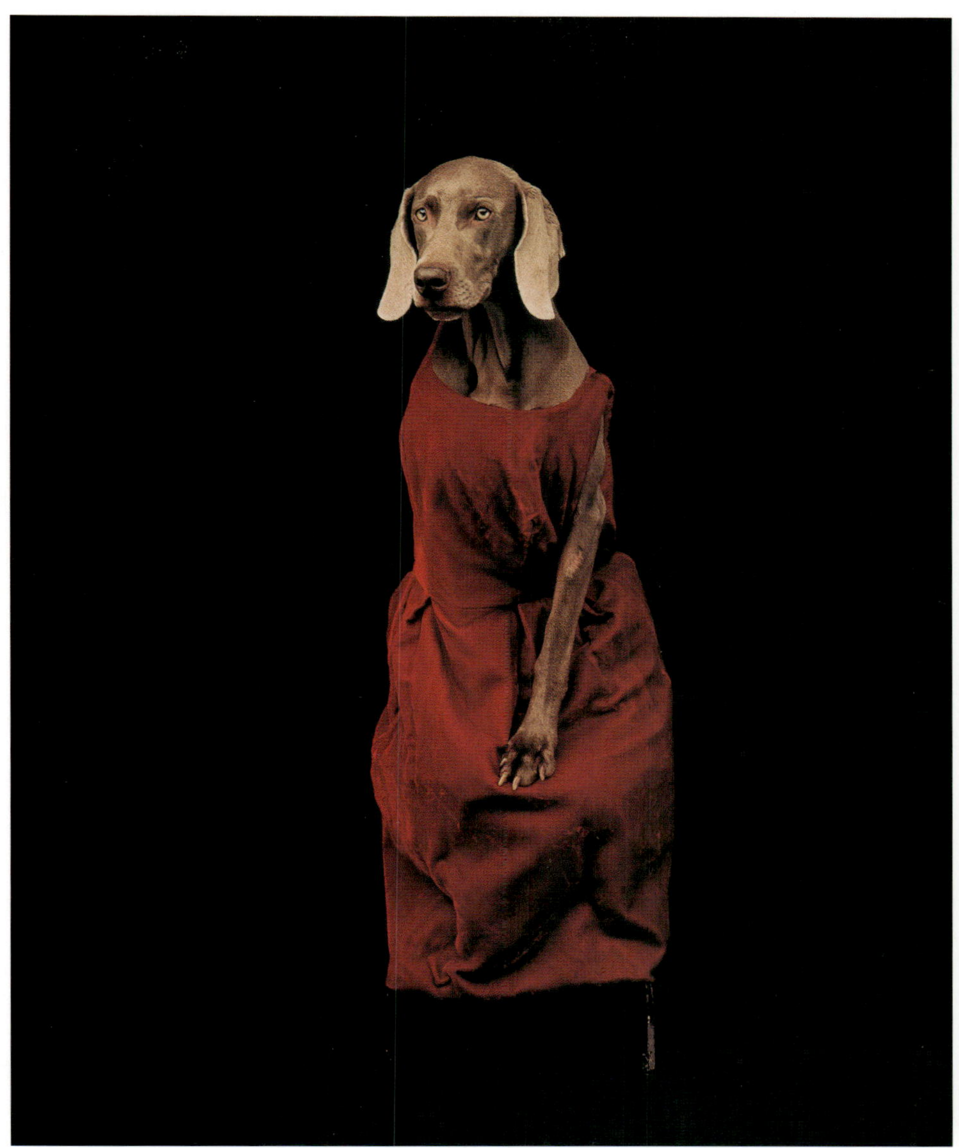

Becoming, 1990

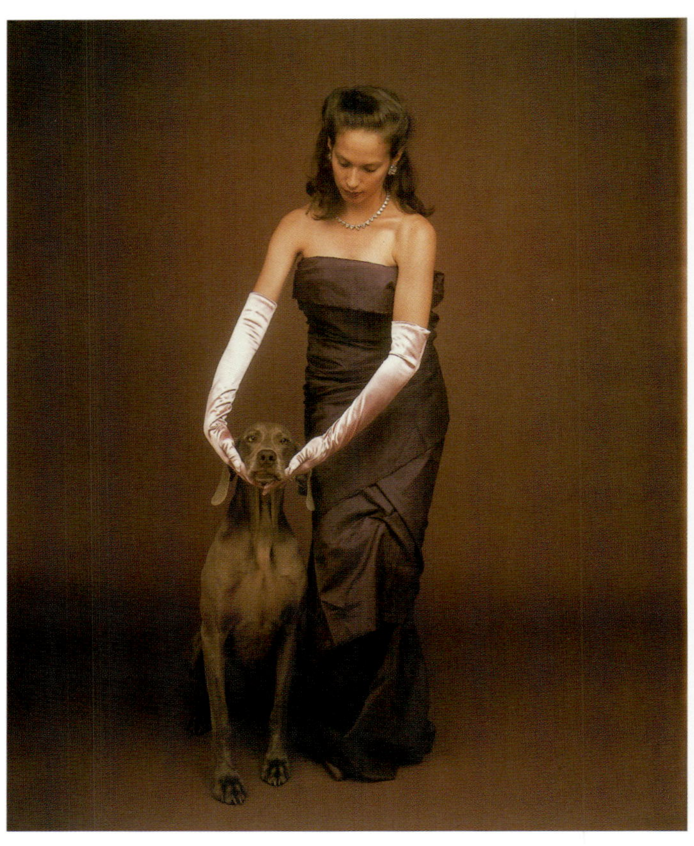

Subsequent dressed images revealed a shortcoming. Arms . . . or lack thereof. Fay seemed to be an amputee.

One day at the studio, as Andrea was helping me dress Fay on the set, she gestured to me from behind Fay. I had to laugh. It seemed that Fay was making the gesture.

I asked Andrea to slip her arms into the sleeves of the dress, extend them as far as she could around Fay, and duck. I snapped the shutter. Now Fay was speaking through Andrea's gestures. Andrea's gestures and Fay's expression combined almost but not quite seamlessly into one character. You could still tell that the character was constructed.

I decided it was good to show the process, to make clear that the effect was not made through digital Photoshop or other post-production means. It has always been important to me that the viewer is aware of the cooperation involved between the human and canine in my work.

The appearance of arms raised an issue I could no longer evade. In *Becoming*, I finally came to terms with anthropomorphism in my work. Fay, posing with a glamorously attired Andrea, is transformed in a sequence of three pictures. Fay becomes Andrea (or Andrea becomes Fay).

No other breed that I am aware of is as conducive to the illusion of transformation as weimaraners. Weimaraners are called "gray ghosts." Their fur gives off an almost iridescent glow. They inhabit their forms in a strange way, never appearing to solidify into themselves as, say, a Lab, a collie, or a bulldog does. When you photograph a collie you get collie. (That's why Lassie can be played by any collie.) Andrea's body with a collie's head would be . . . a collie's head combined with Andrea's body.

After *Becoming*, I began to cast Fay as an array of bewitching figures and characters.

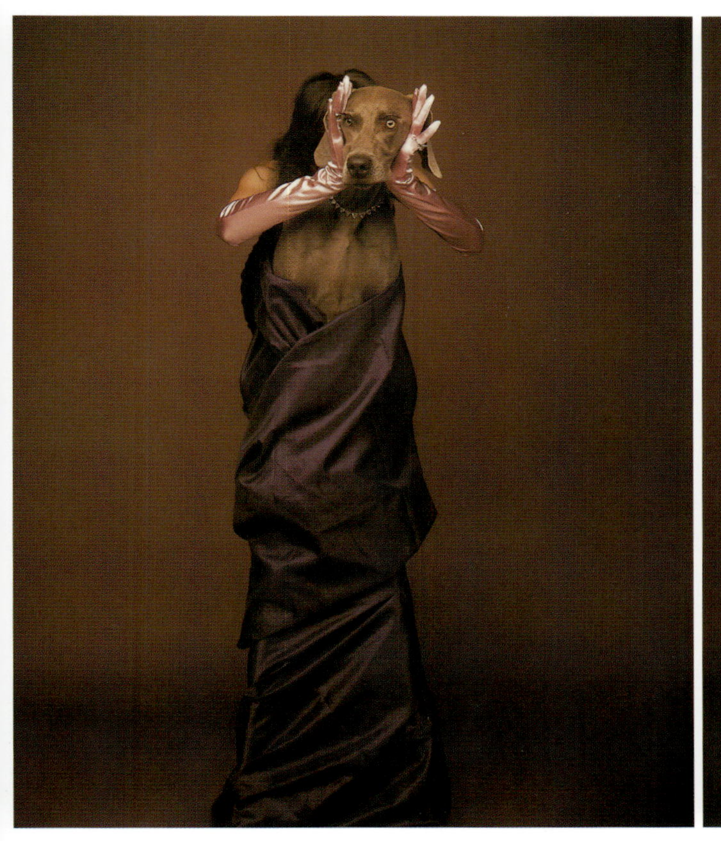

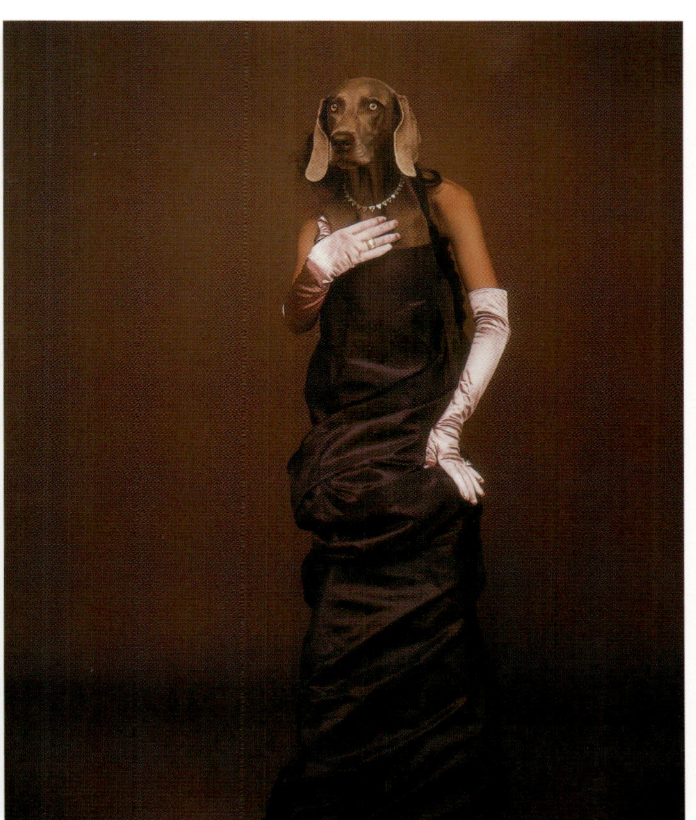

Below: ***Shiva Fay*, 1994**

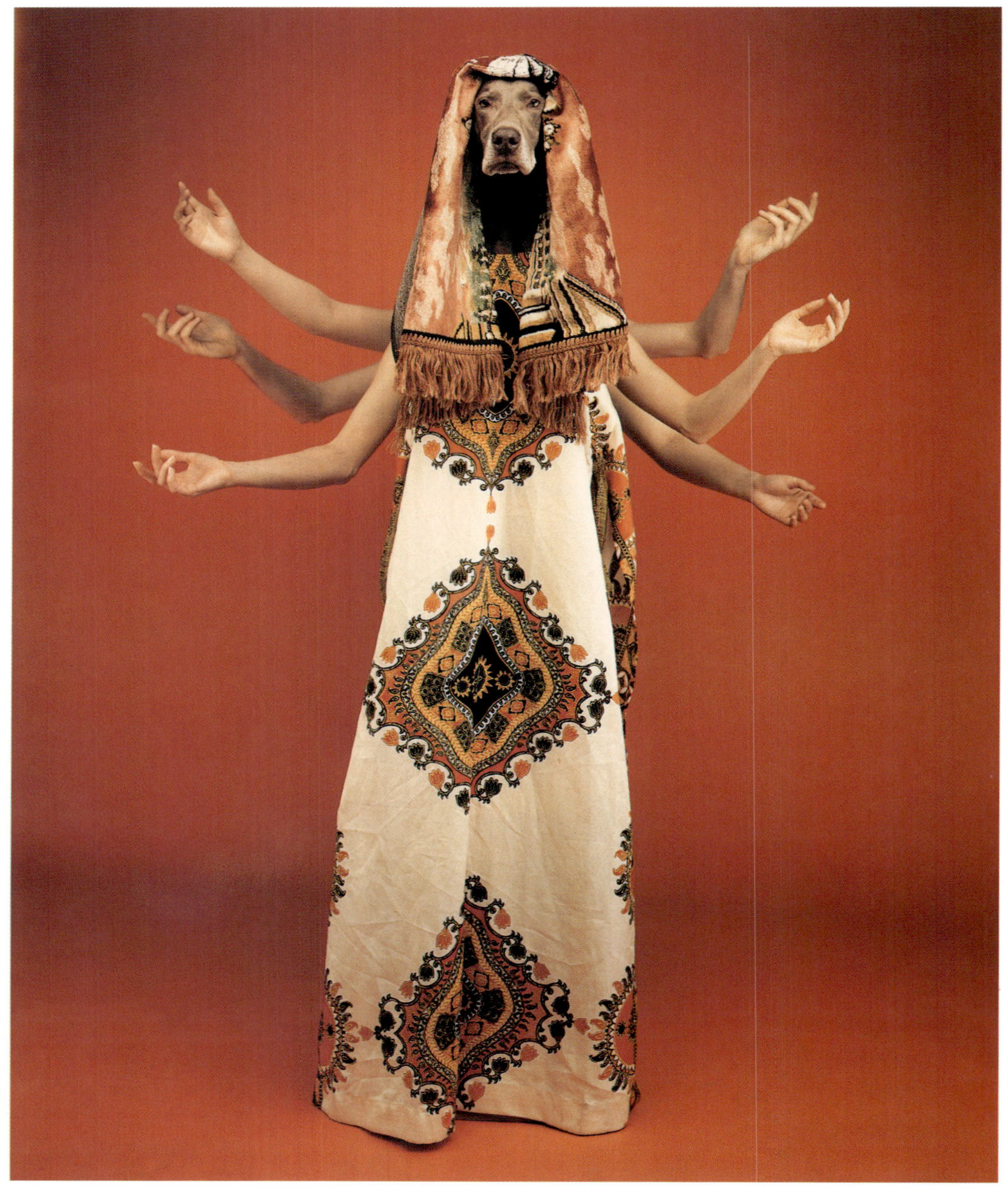

Top Left: ***Daisy May*, 1991**
Top Right: ***Anxious Traveler*, 1990**
Lower Left: ***Colonial Maiden*, 1991**
Lower Right: ***Lap Dog*, 1989**

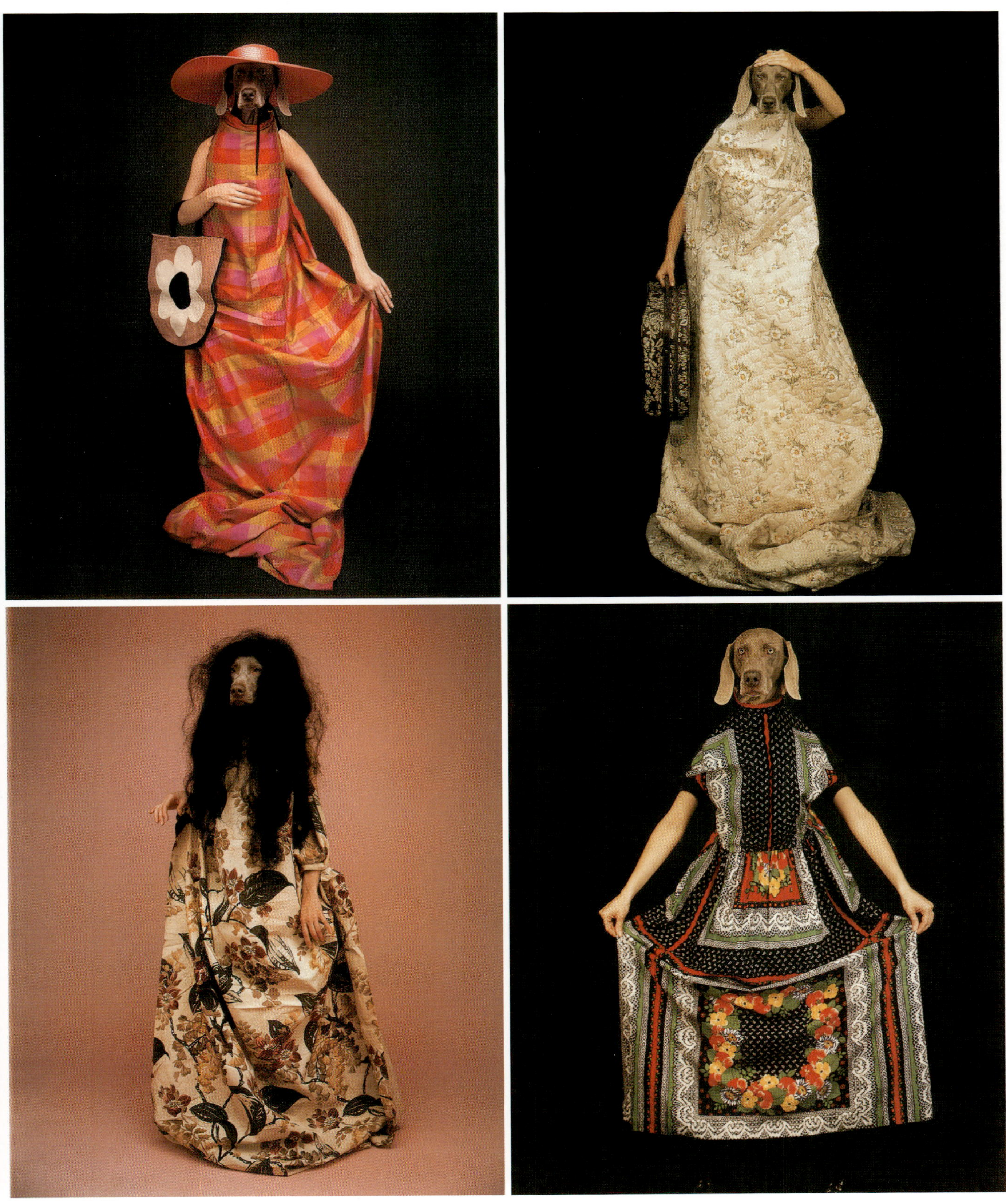

Below: *Lolita,* 1990
Opposite: *1/2 Packed,* 1989

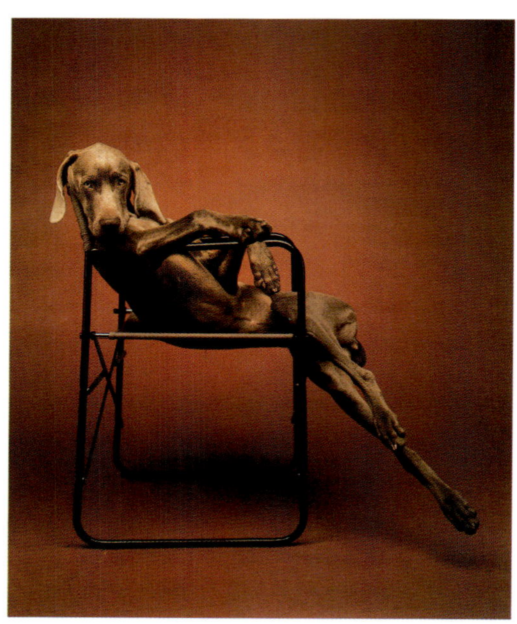

In June 1989, one week ahead of schedule, Fay gave birth to eight puppies.

The sire was Arco belonging to Virginia Alexander of Reiteralm Kennel. This development was to alter the direction of my work and change my life significantly. The first three, Chundo, Battina (Batty) and Crooky, named at the moment of birth, were to become, along with Fay, the central characters in my work. Multiple weimaraners multiplied pictorial possibilities exponentially, leading to a myriad of new directions, from formal experiments to narrative fairy tales and children's stories.

I kept Battina (the little bat) with Fay. Fay dominated Batty and that was fine with Batty. She accepted her position with grace. Batty was trained just like Fay, on the job, but Batty had the advantage of being born to it. As Fay worked in front of the camera, Batty watched from the couch. So when it became Batty's turn to perform, it was, like, no problem. She was very relaxed on the set. The two models gave me contrasting personalities as well as body types to work with. Fay's body houses an inner struggle and Batty's houses none.

It amused me to see how differently Fay and Batty approached certain familiar objects in the set: the ochre chair, the white cube, the rectangular box. Where Fay powered herself into positions, Batty poured herself like syrup from a bottle into hers, then fell asleep. Serenity to the point of recklessness, I thought.

Mother/Daughter. Good /Evil. Young/Old. Over/Under. The two gave me lots of contrasts to play with.

I soon became very charmed by Batty. She was dreamy, comic, and seductive, a genuine Lolita. As she worked she seemed to be off someplace else. I enjoyed daydreaming about her.

Although I began to work more and more with Crooky, Batty, and Chundo, Fay remained the center of my work. Her psychological weight held the group together and gave it order. Children loved Fay. Perhaps it was the name. Whenever I asked children which of my dogs they liked the best, they invariably named Fay—even when the dog they were looking at was Batty. Art dealer Holly Solomon, however, preferred Batty. She thought Fay looked suburban.

Fay's illness in 1995 took me by surprise. Acute leukemia, rare in dogs, is always fatal. She didn't suffer long. Her demise came swiftly, two short weeks from diagnosis. During this time, Batty changed. She became Fay-like.

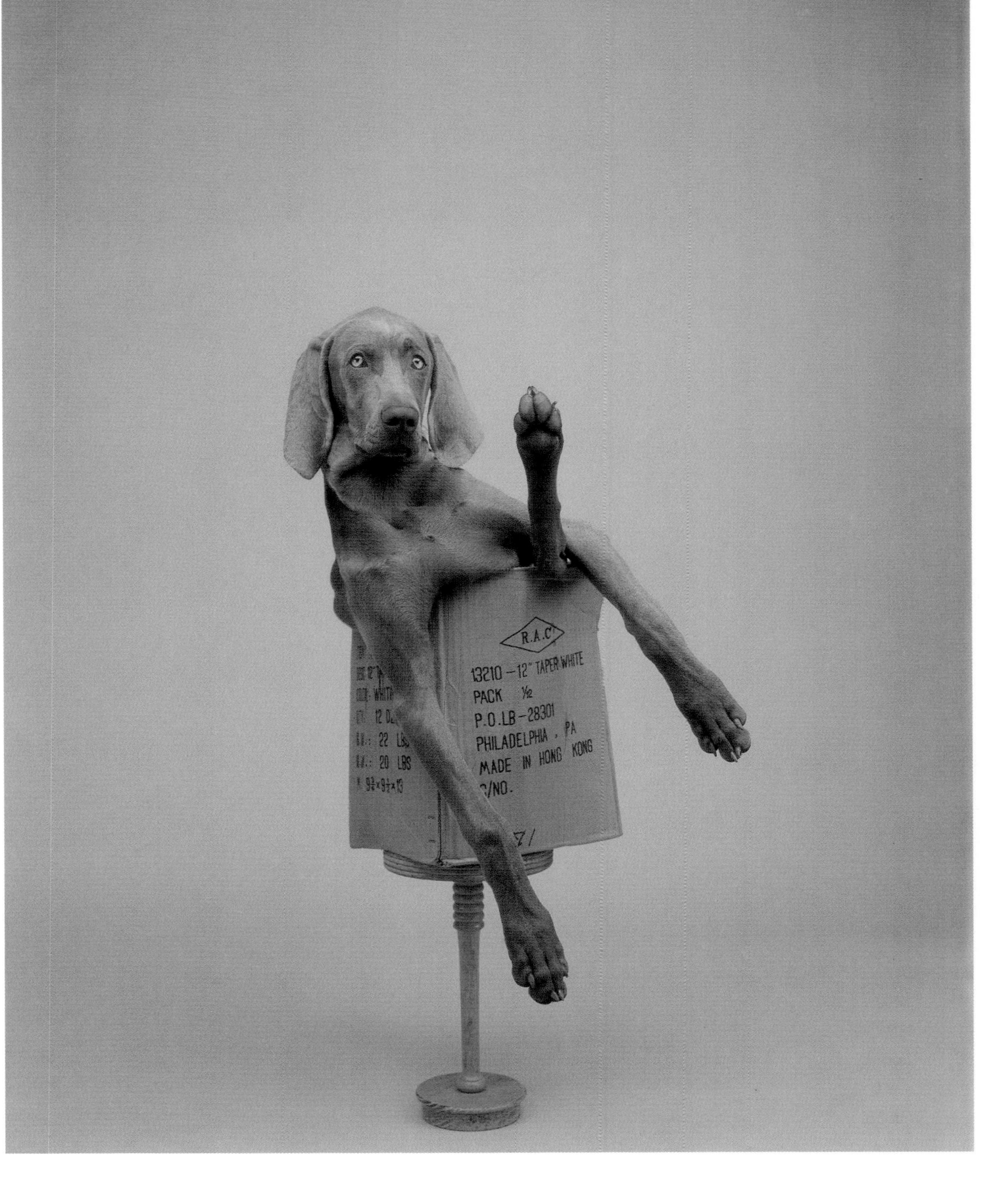
R.A.C
13210 – 12" TAPER WHITE
PACK ½
P.O. LB-28301
PHILADELPHIA , PA
MADE IN HONG KONG
C/NO.

Below: ***Oxygen***, 1990
Opposite: ***Slumber Party***, 1991

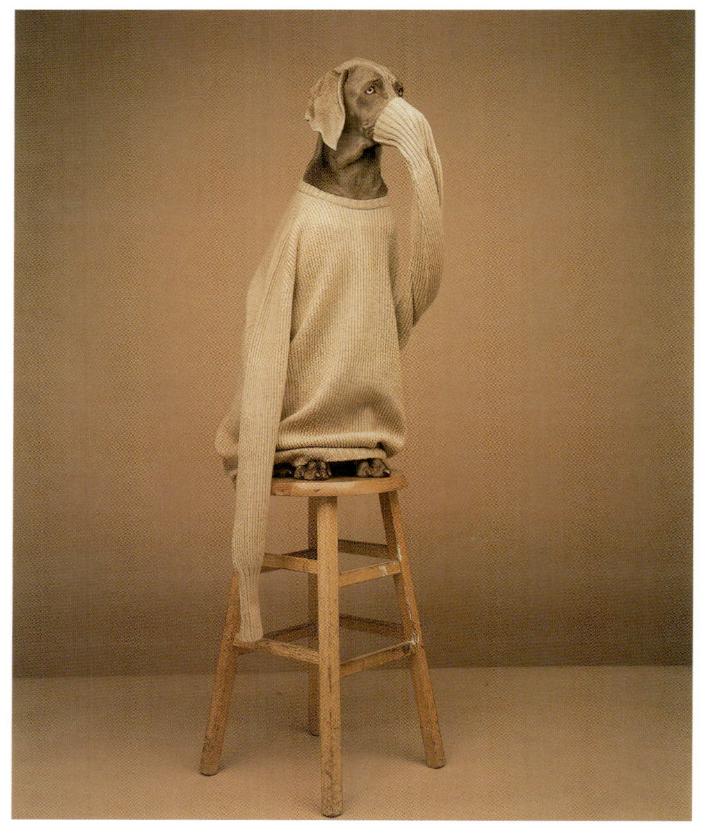

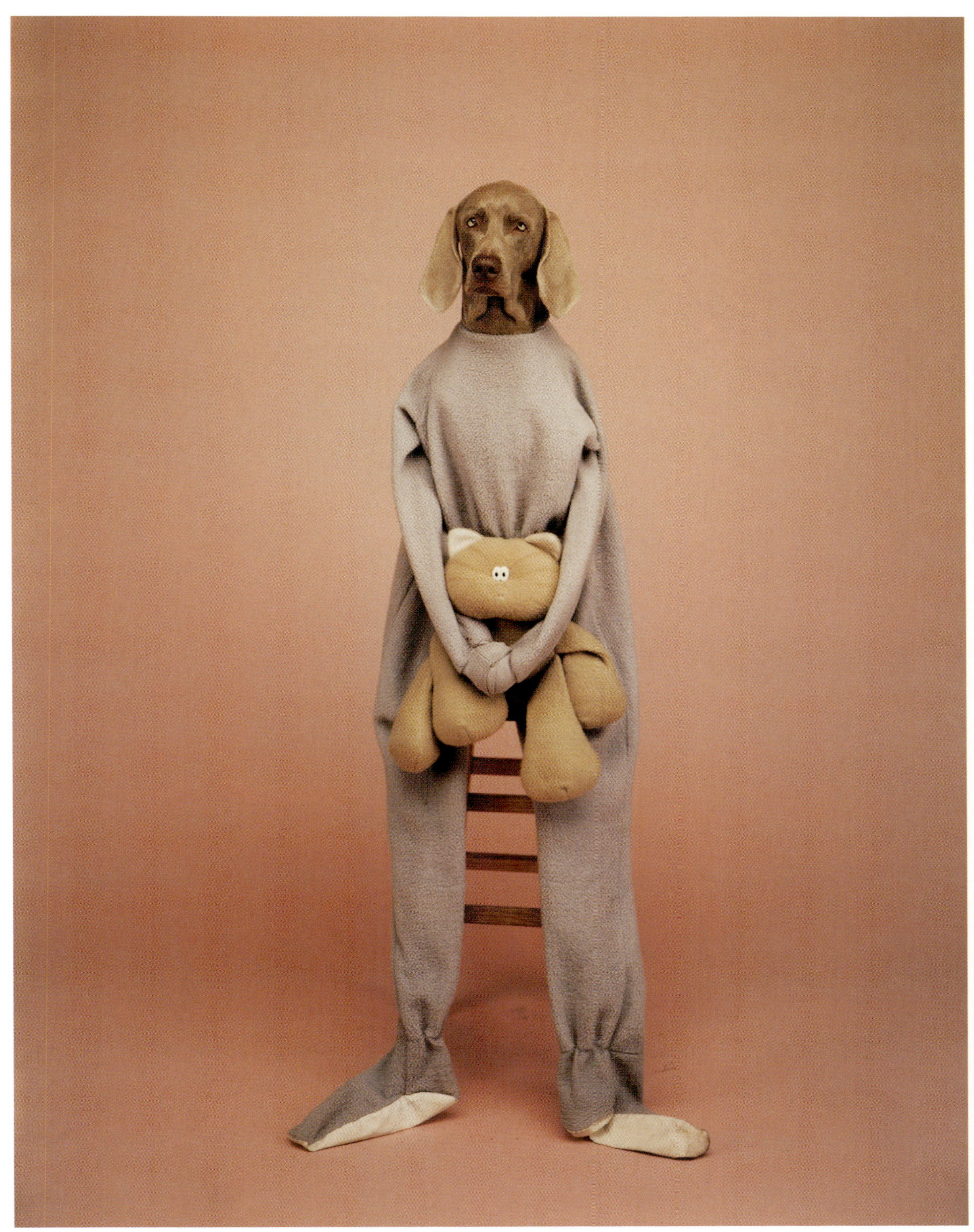

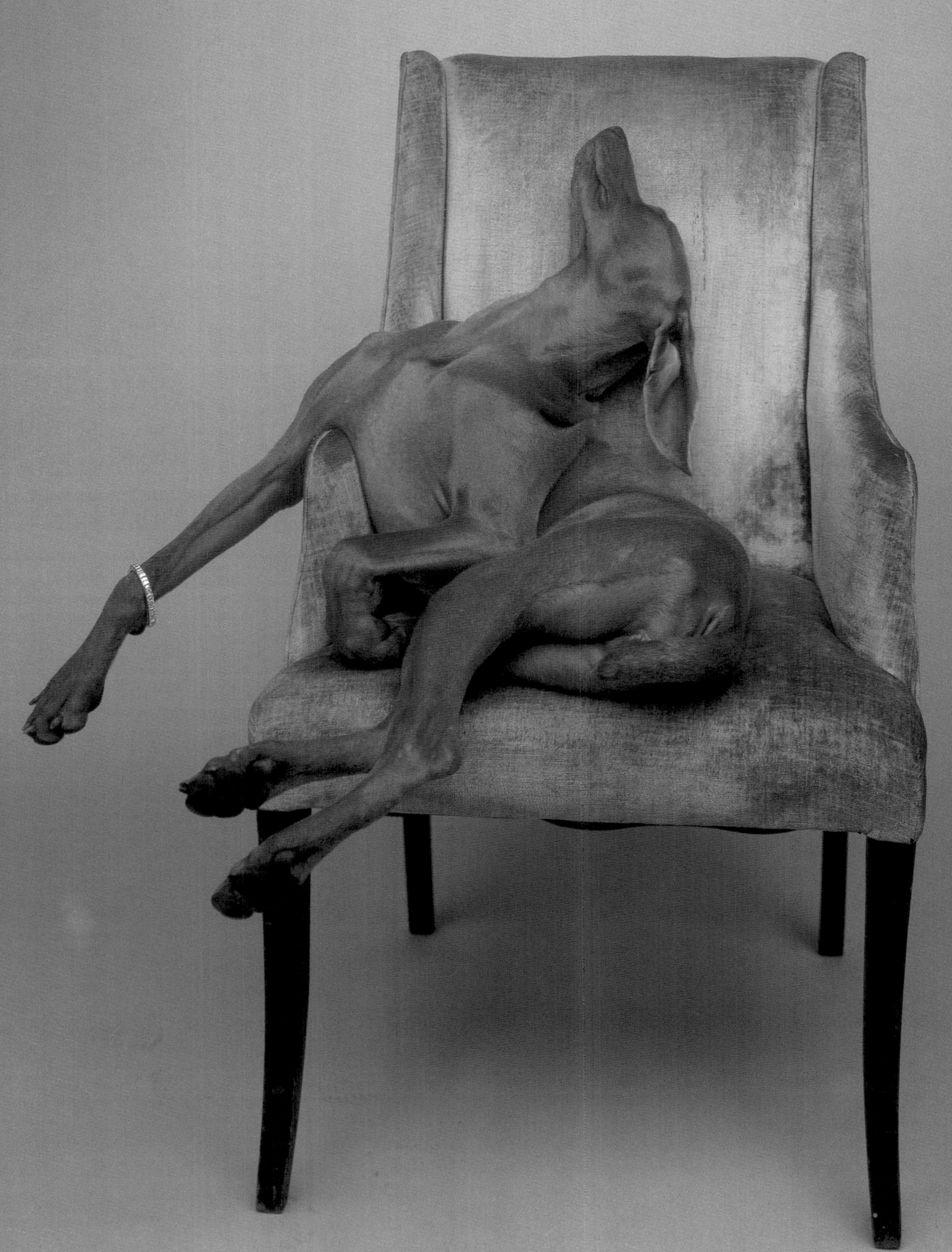

The Bracelet, 1990

Left: ***Arc,*** 1990
Right: ***Innocence and Guilt,*** 1990
Opposite: ***Underdog,*** 1989

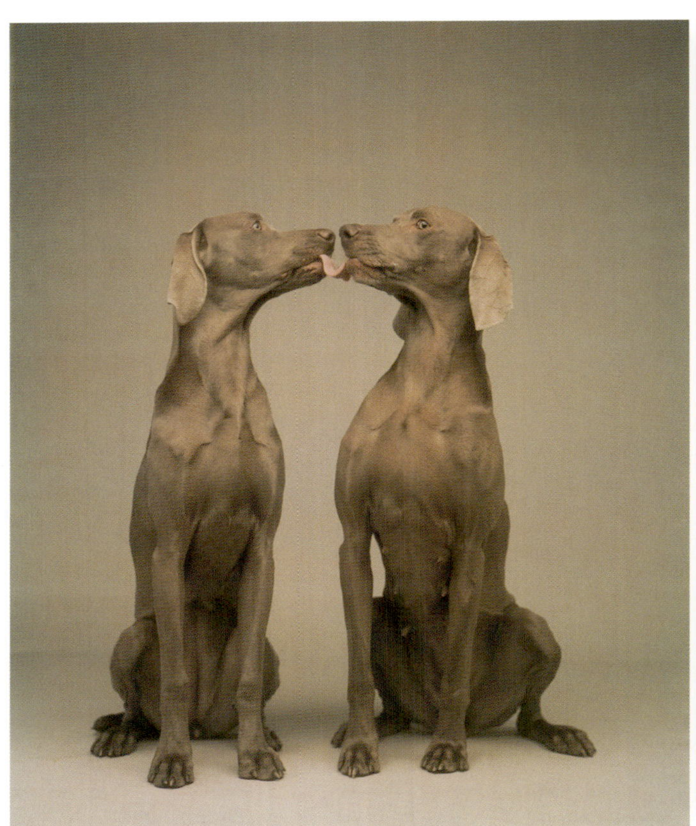

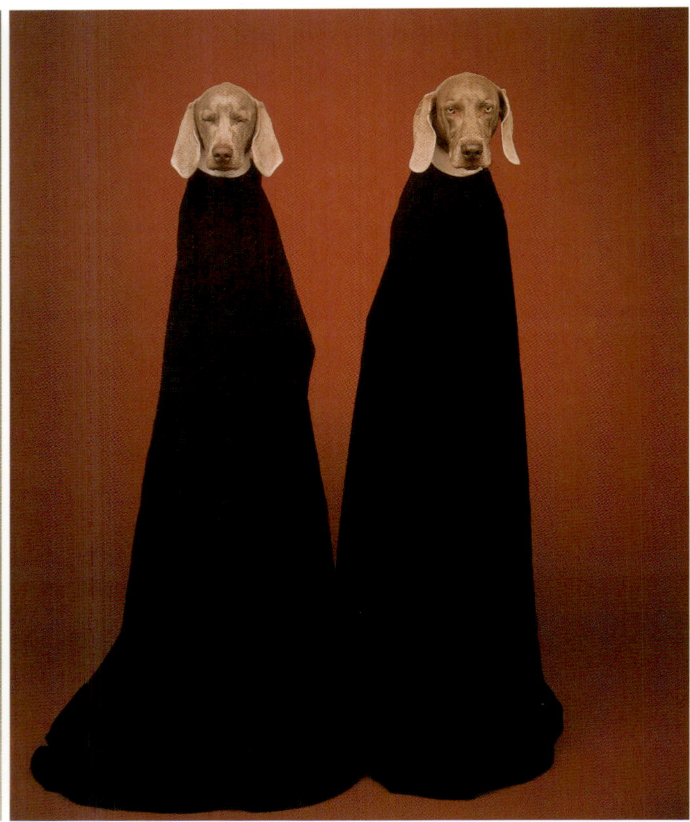

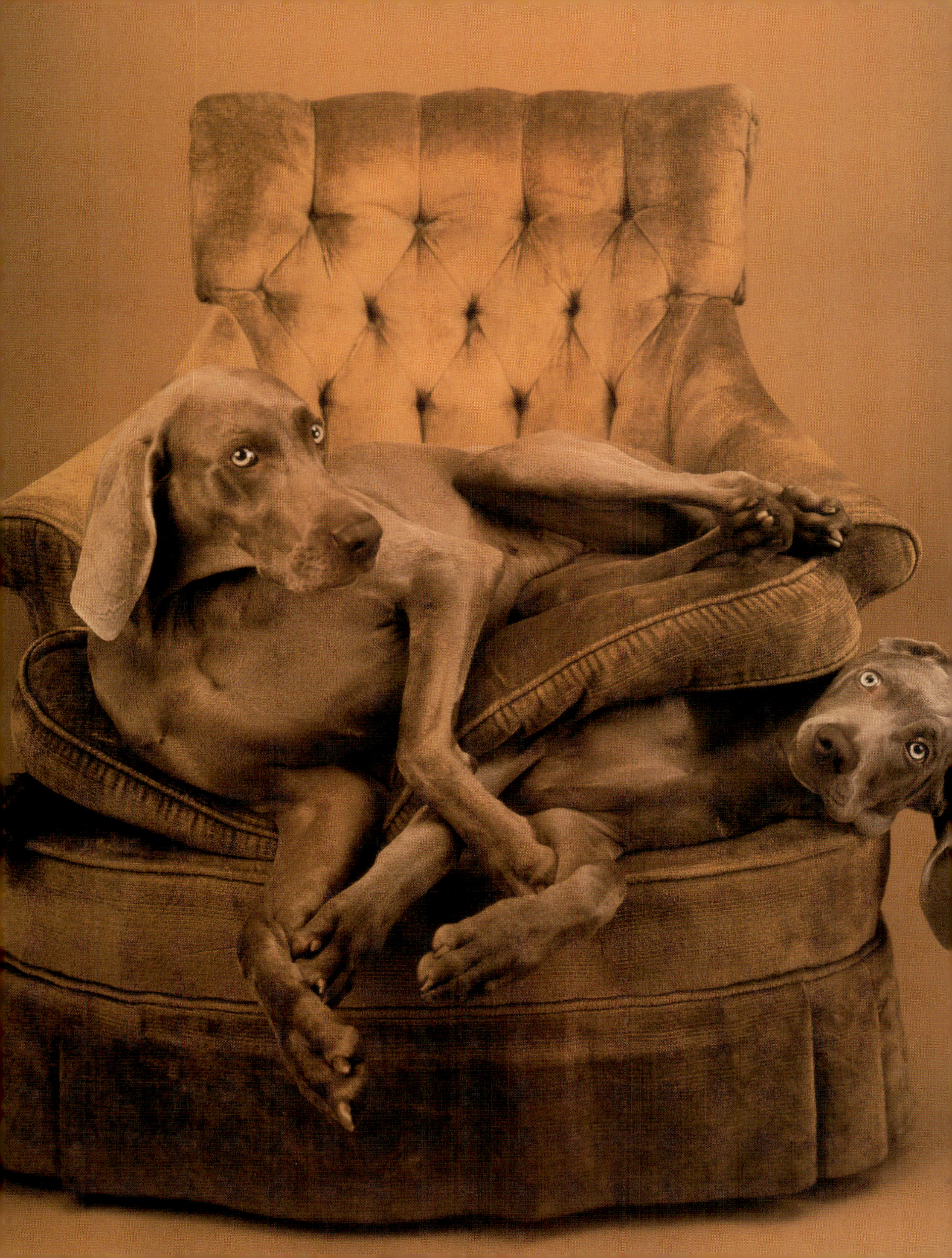

Winter Walk, 1990

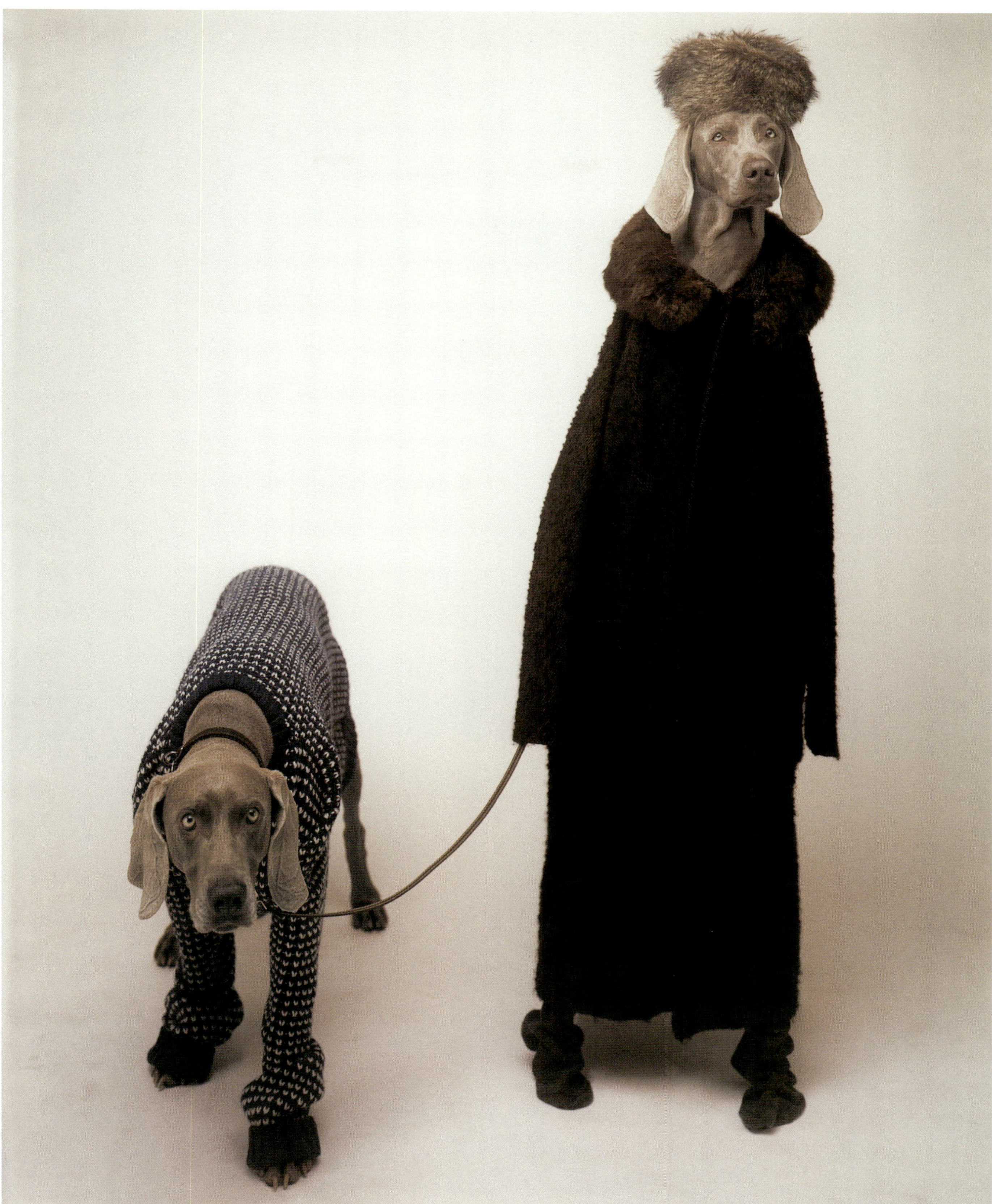

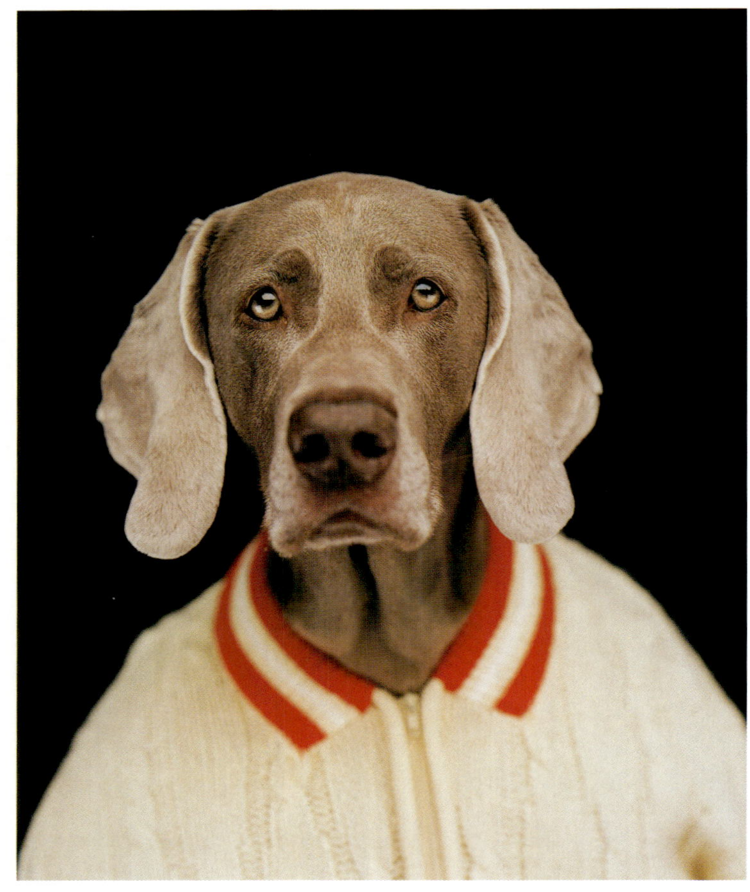

Chundo, Fay's first born male,

who lives with my sister Pam in Maine, was the lion of the litter. Named after the biggest person I ever saw, Chundo grew into a big dog whose expressive features filled the frame of my photographs, videos, and films with earnest masculinity. Without Chundo, there would be no stories. Chundo is the prince, the king, the wolf, the woodsman, the man. His masculinity anchors every picture he is in.

I found Chundo to be more expressive than Man Ray, but not as stoic. He is an eager worker whose limits are expressed in fidgety appeals. Jason Burch, my assistant since 1989, has worked particularly well with Chundo, like Andrea with Fay, to create memorable hybrid characters such as "Mr. Hardy" and the "evil caretaker" in the Hardly Boys project. Chundo also has a lot of magazine and calendar covers in his portfolio—more than any of my other dogs, past or present.

Crooky, so named for her crooked tail (cropped at day three), is another eager worker. She lives near Chundo in Maine with Dave and Kerry McMillan, my athletic Rangeley friends. In appearance, Crooky

Sally, 1995

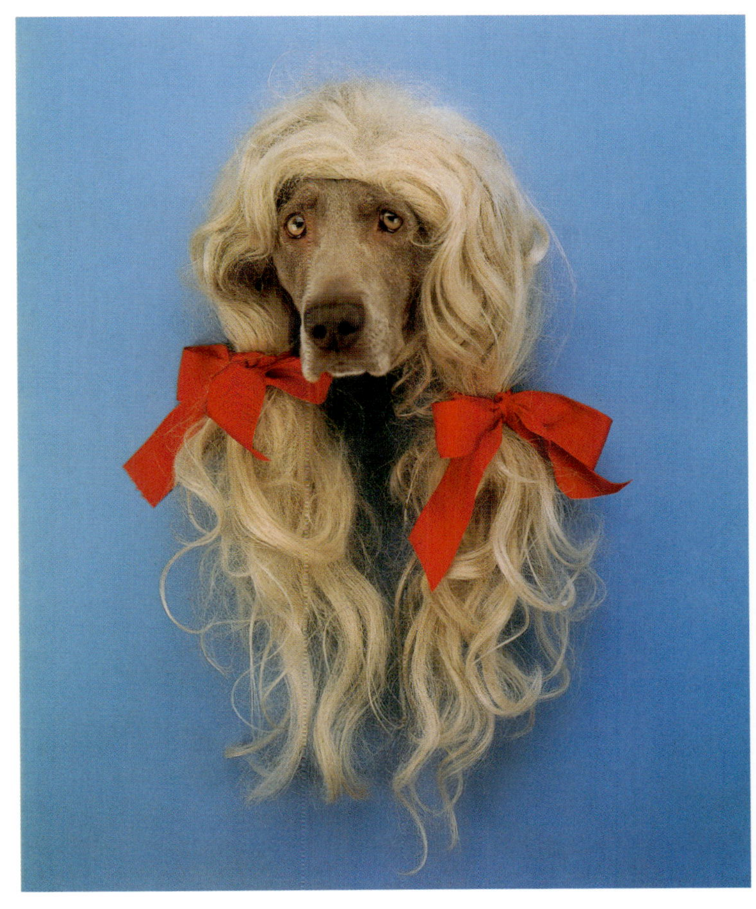

is a miniature Fay. Her wild look and substantial ears fuel a sparky charisma. Crooky easily out-hustles all the other dogs, both in the field and on the set. I found her wide-eyed looks and quizzical expressions particularly interesting in tandem with Batty's dreamworld narcolepsy.

One of my favorite pictures, the Vermeer-inspired *Side Entrance,* was taken on our second Polaroid 20x24 Maine excursion, in 1990. The photograph, Crooky's debut, shows Crooky and Batty dressed in vintage waitress uniforms peeking out from a rustic doorway. After that picture, I started thinking about casting the girls in tandem roles, resulting in the McDoubles and the Hardly Boys series of photographs, films, and videos. That summer, assistant Lisa Martin provided Crooky with the perfect "hands" accompaniment, performing tennis forehand wonders as Crooky's right arm.

Crooky's enthusiasm for work created a new job, that of "weimaraner wrangler." The wrangler's job is to keep Crooky out of the other dog's scenes. Crooky really came into her own during this trip.

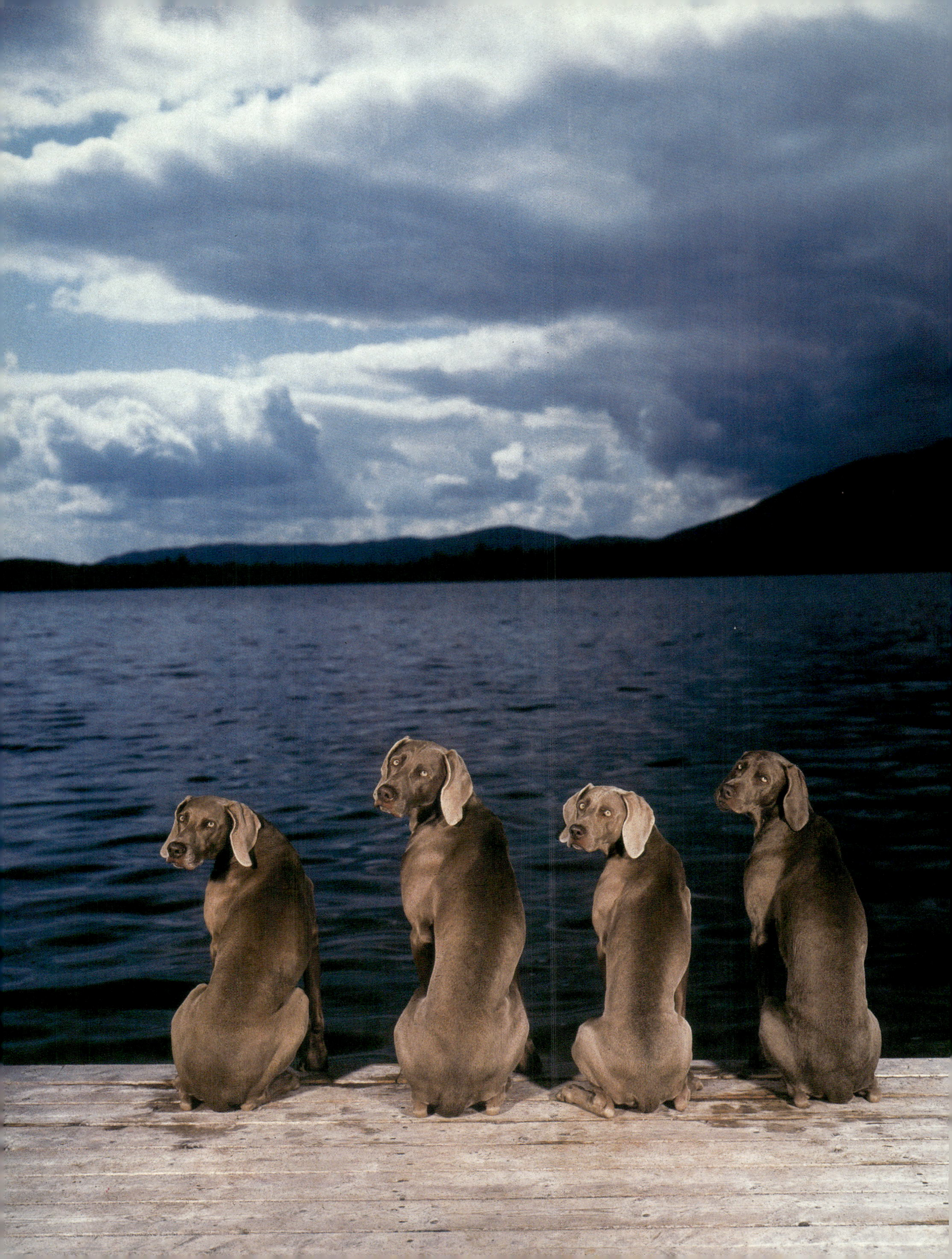

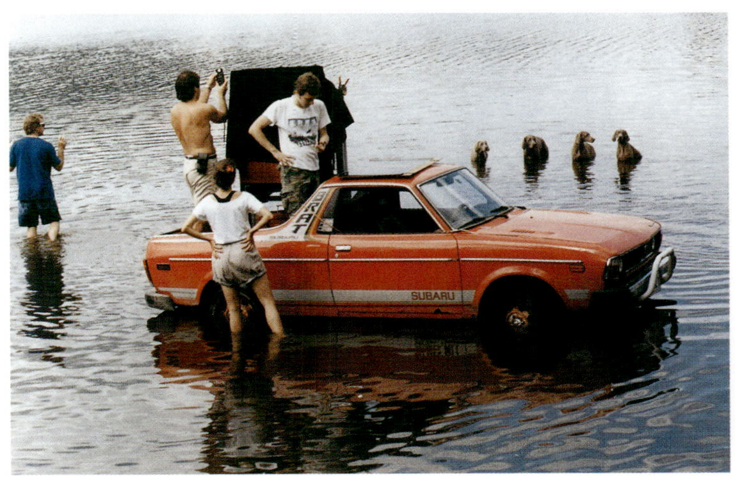

John Reuter assured me that we would be ready for anything on the third Maine excursion.

Along with Tracy Storer, operator of the Boston-based camera, which was the one that traveled, he had worked out the logistical problems of running the camera on location. John told me that a lot of his improvements came during a photo expedition to Death Valley with famous movie director Tim Burton, whose infatuation with the 20x24 stretched John and his crew to the limits. Wind and sand? Temperature extremes? No problem.

Richardson Pond is a shallow, rocky-bottomed lake bordered by scenic mountains—perfect for pictures, but lacking an accessible place for the camera to stand. "How about we drive it out into the lake in the pickup," suggests Dave McMillan. "Good idea, Dave," I said. After Tracy revived, we drove the camera and lights into the lake on the bed of a little Subaru Brat and lived to tell about it. I decided that, in addition to color, we would work in black and white Polapan film, an option I had only recently heard about with the 20x24. This film would give a greater depth of field but require coating, a tricky process that we could perform later inside my cabin.

While Dave, Tracy, and John figured out how to get the camera into the pond without spilling it, I concerned myself with the four dogs. Using empty milk crates filled with rocks, I built up a series of cribs, submerged anchorages that they could stand on. It should appear in the photo that the four dogs are floating magically on the surface. Compared to John's and Tracy's, my job was easy. Working with multiple dogs is no more difficult than working with one, as long as looking in only one direction is required. If you call one dog they all look: "What do you want with Fay?"

The Maine Polaroid enterprise became an annual summer rite performed eight times until 1999, when it was decided that the project was too costly. Sometimes strange things happened to the film. One year it turned purple.

Crossing, 1991

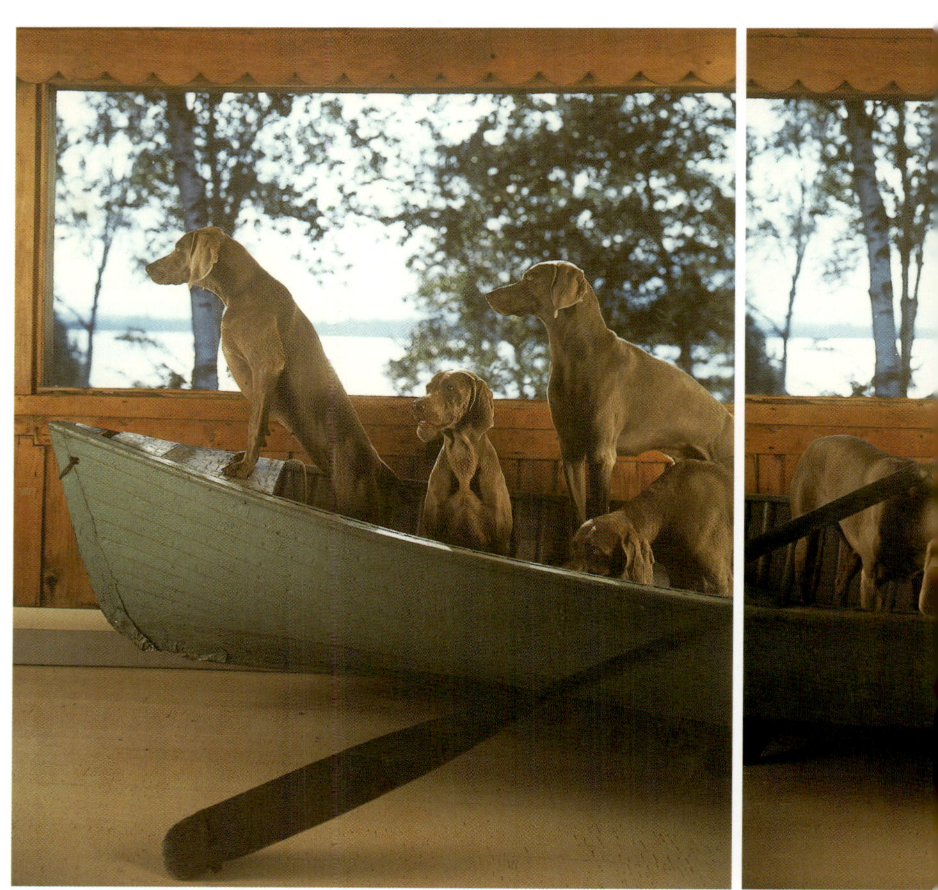

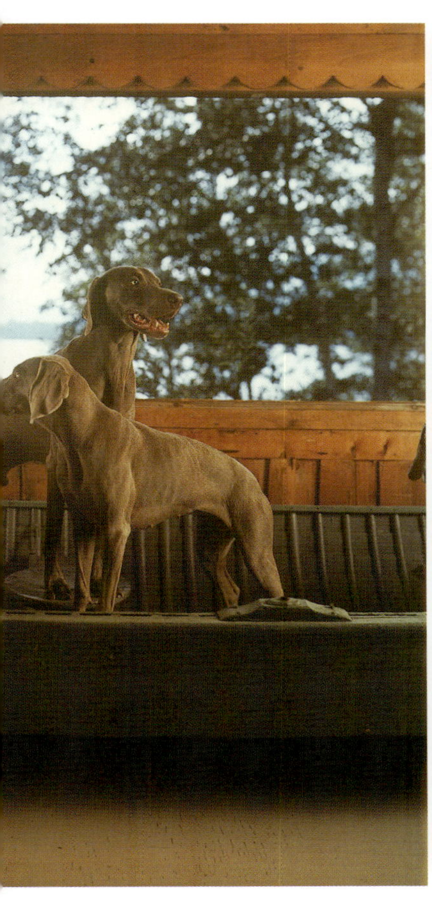
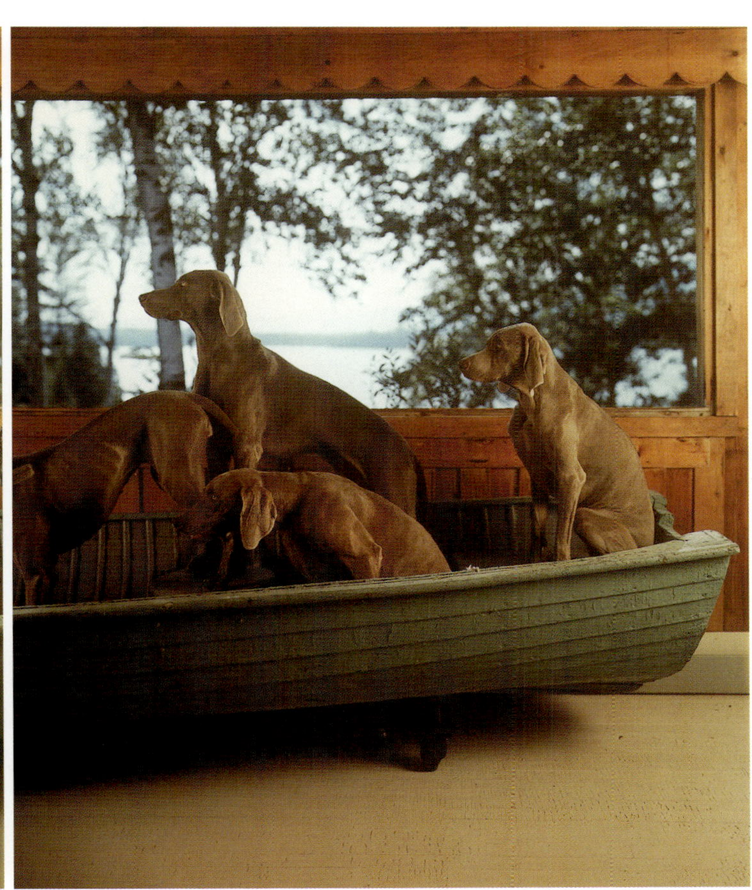

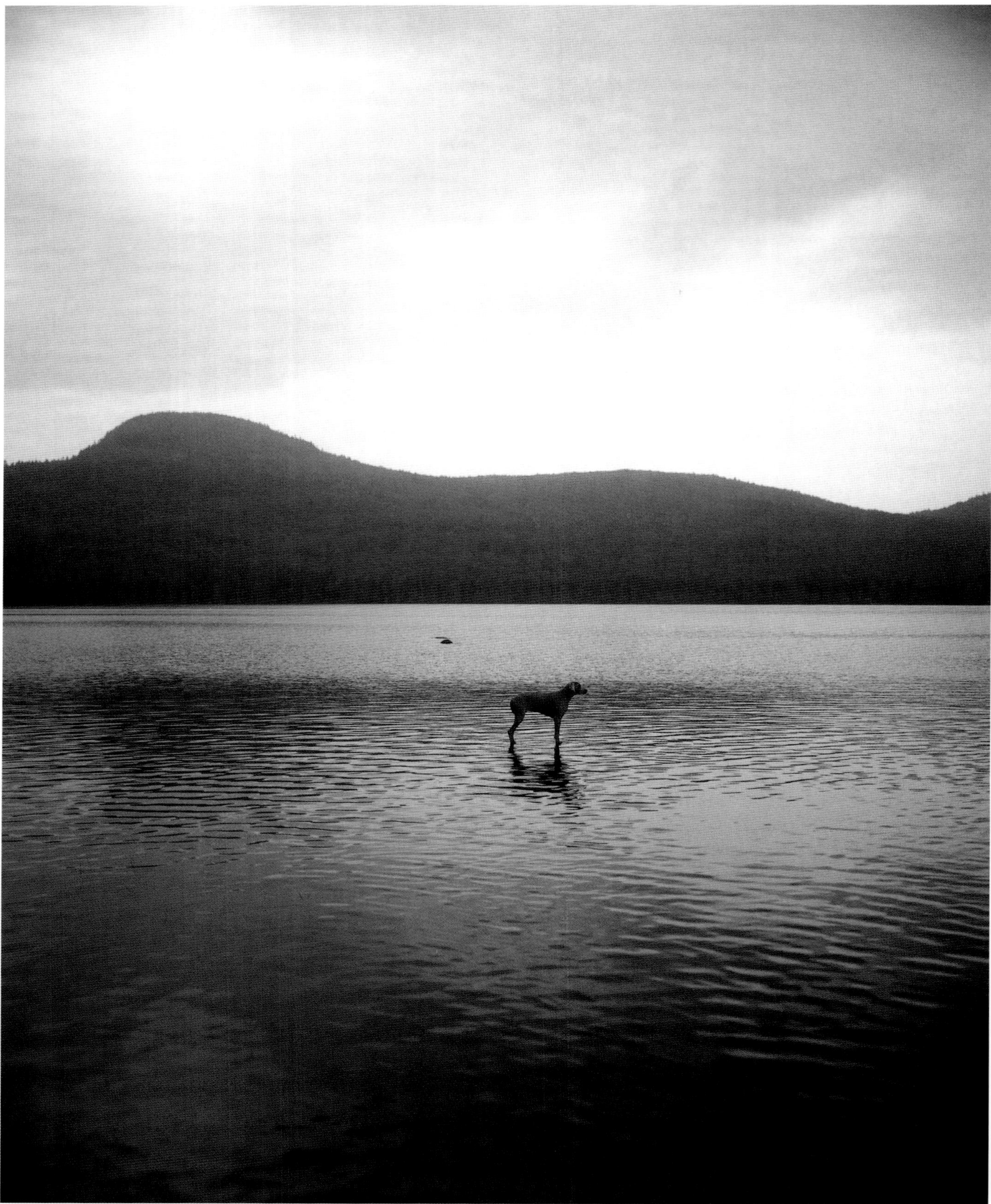

Opposite: ***Float,*** 1998
Below: ***Peak's Twisted Mass,*** 1994

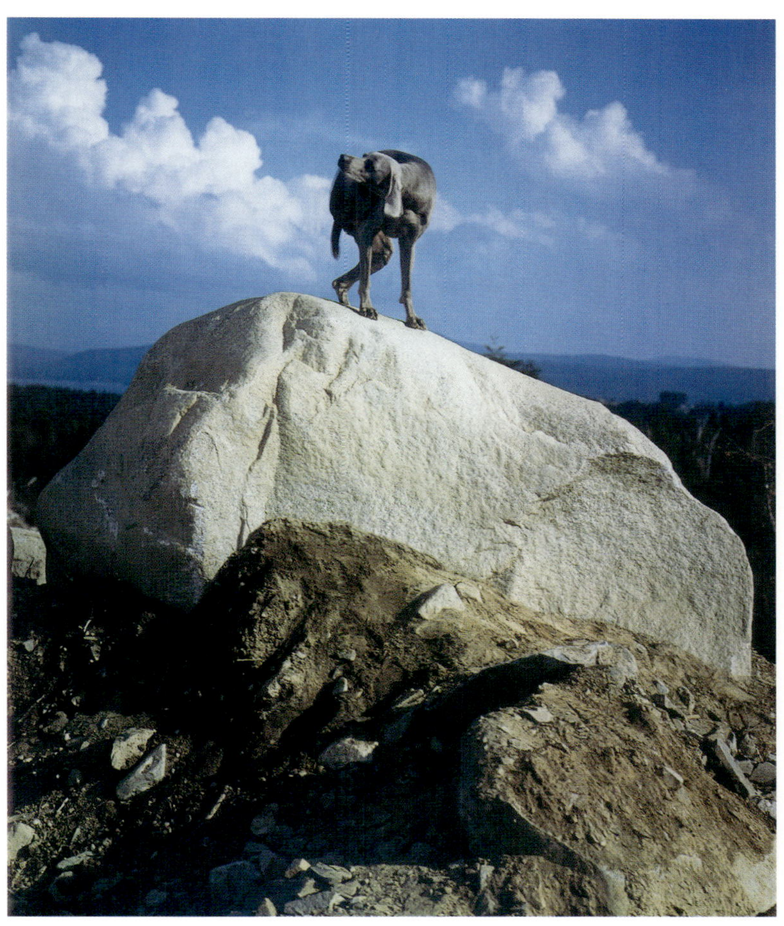

Country Road, 1990

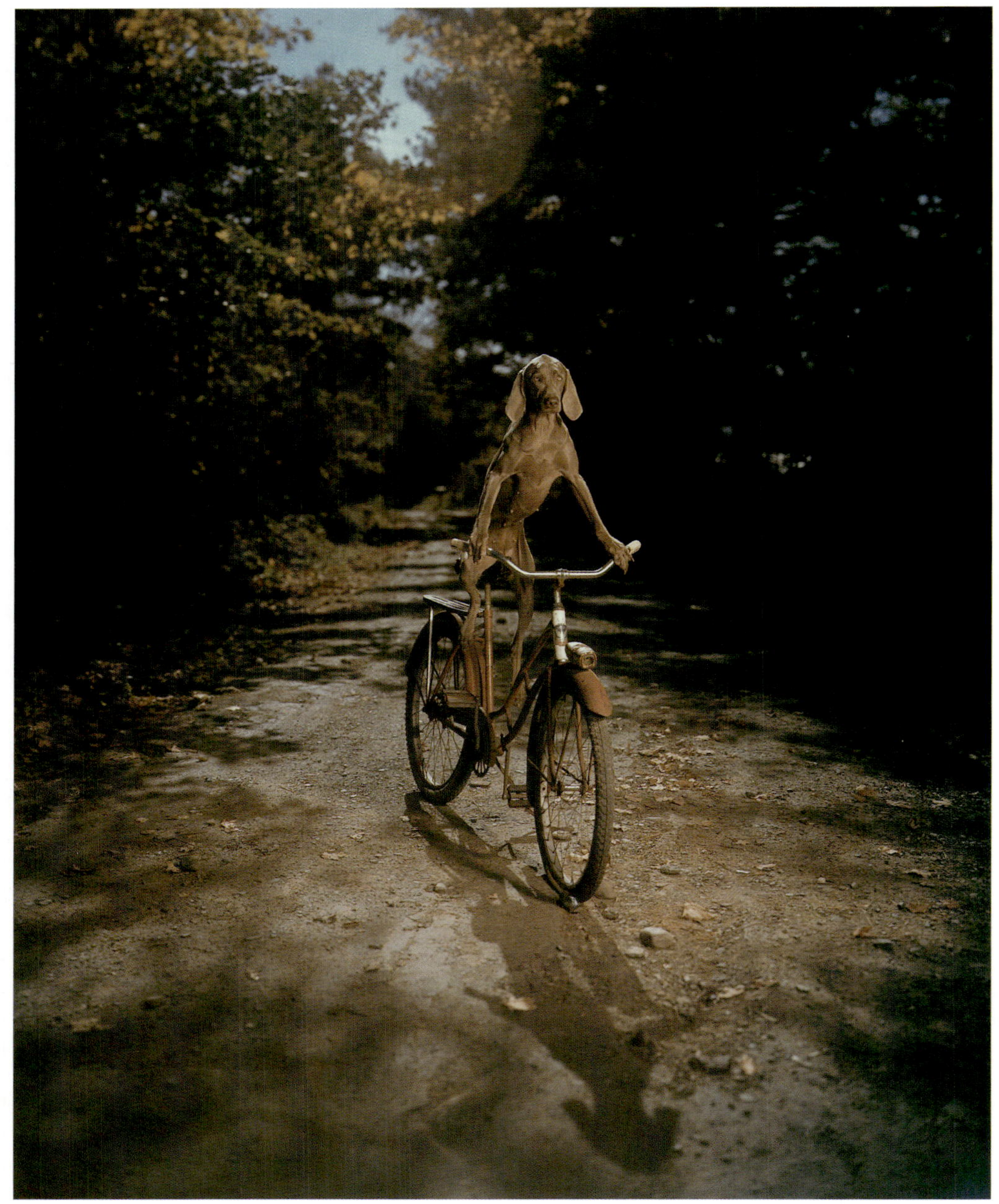

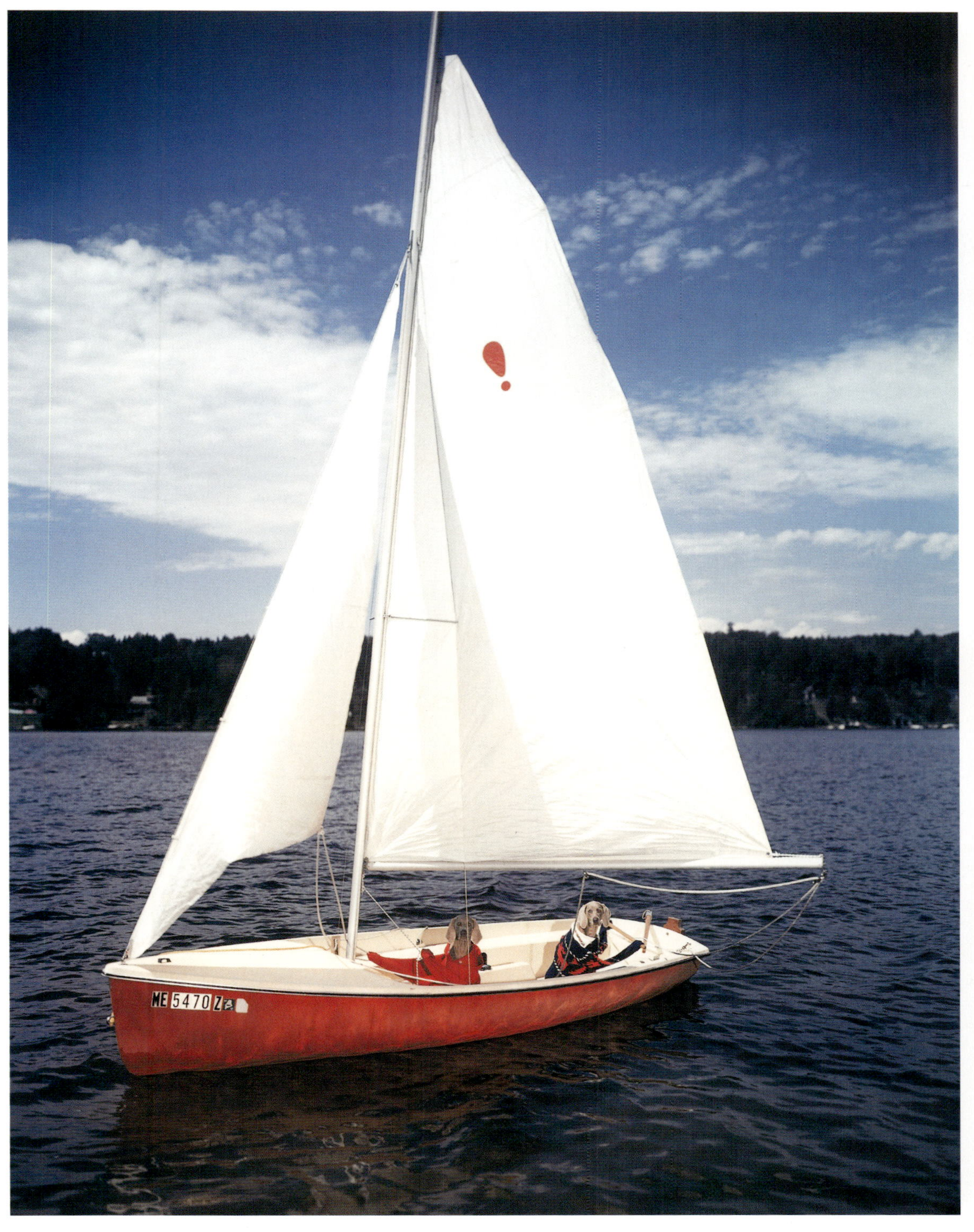

Vacation Land, 1993

Below: *Up to No Good*, 1994
Opposite: *Side Entrance*, 1990

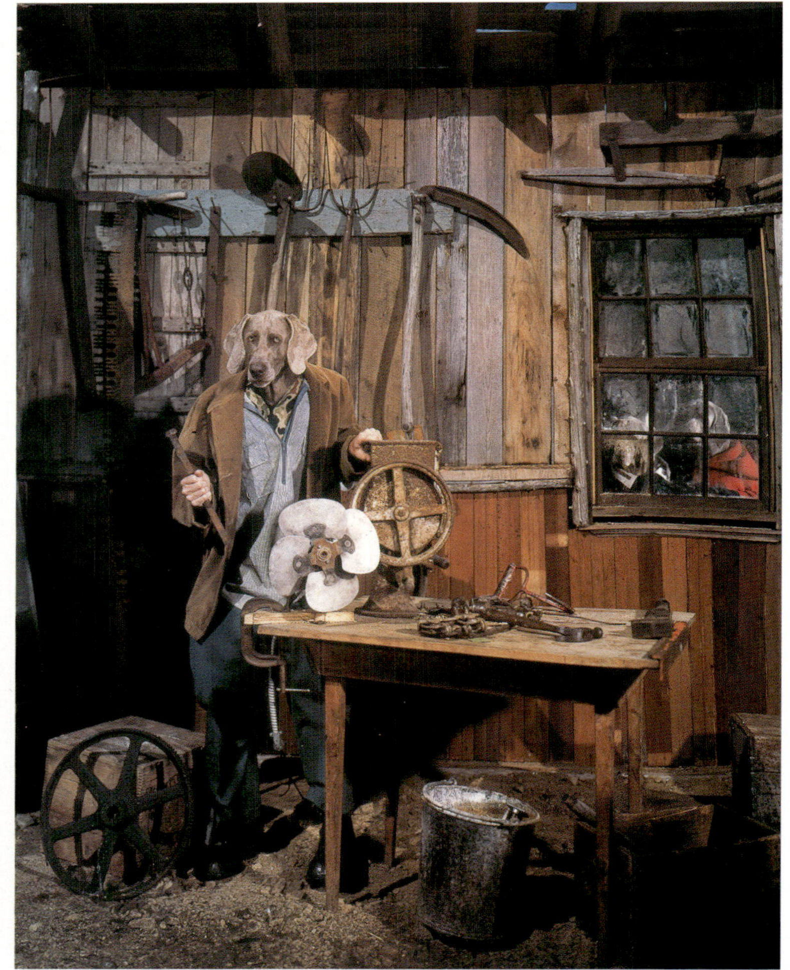

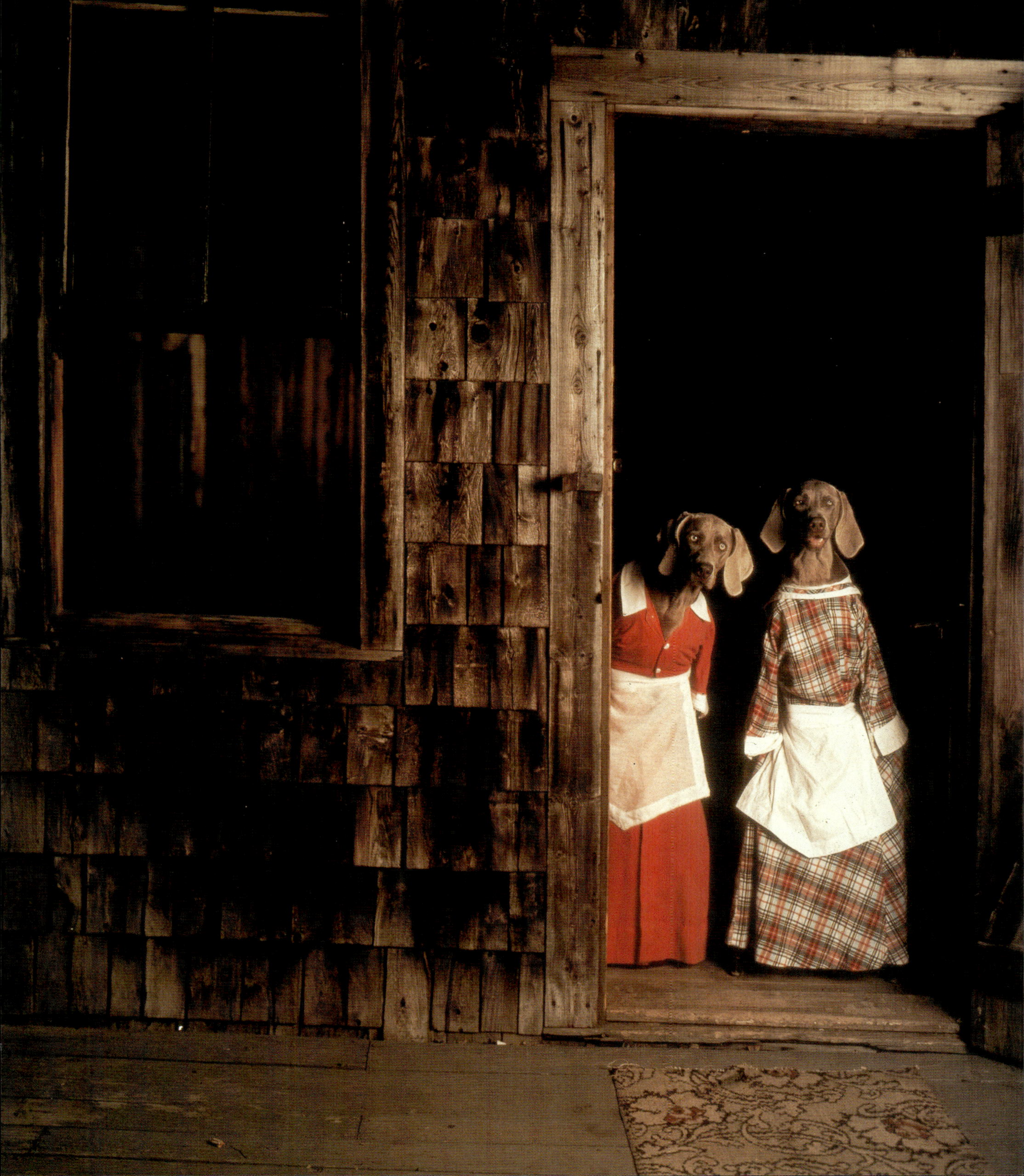

Ocean View, 1997

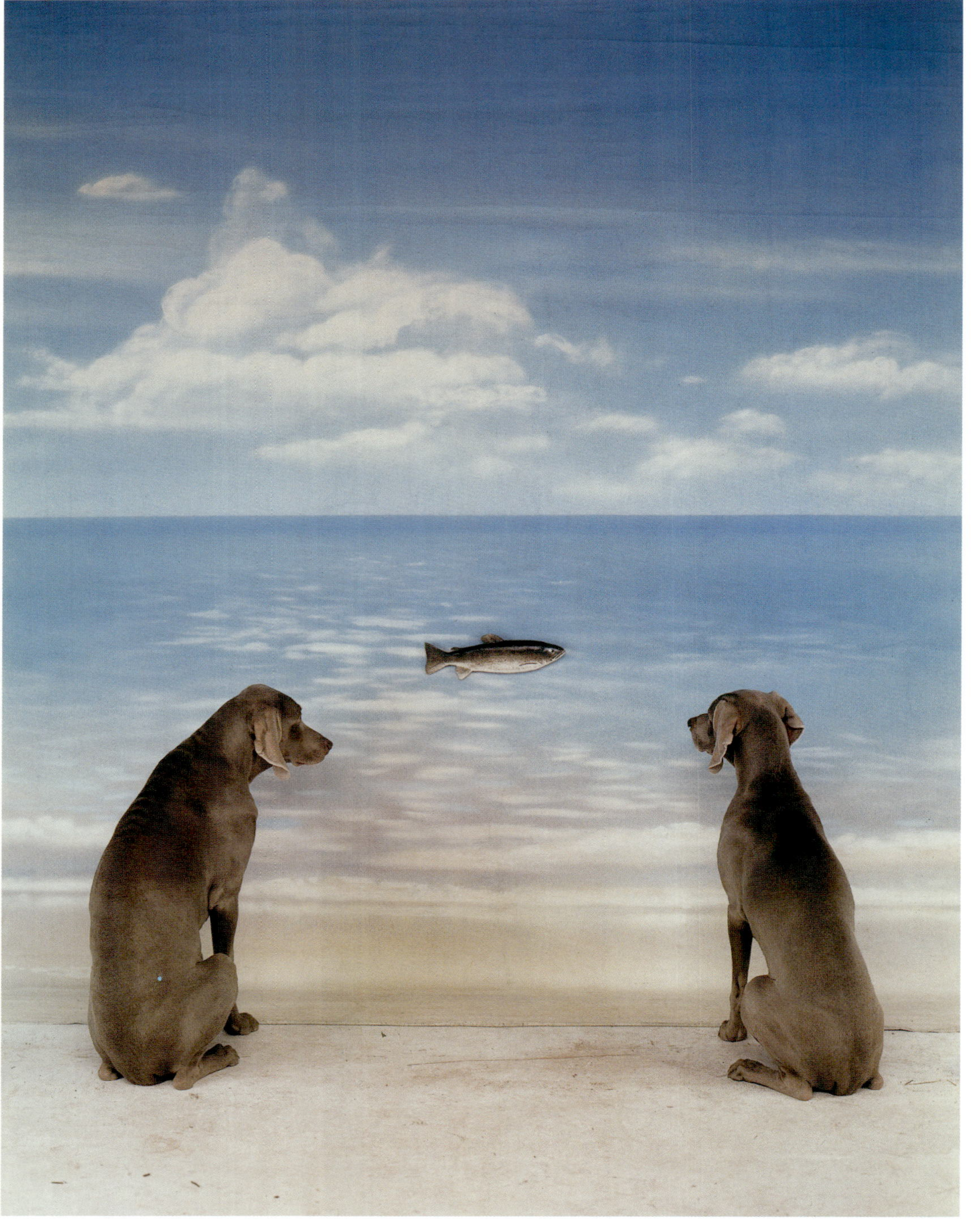

Left: ***Surfboard*****, 1992**
Right: ***Country Lane*****, 1996**

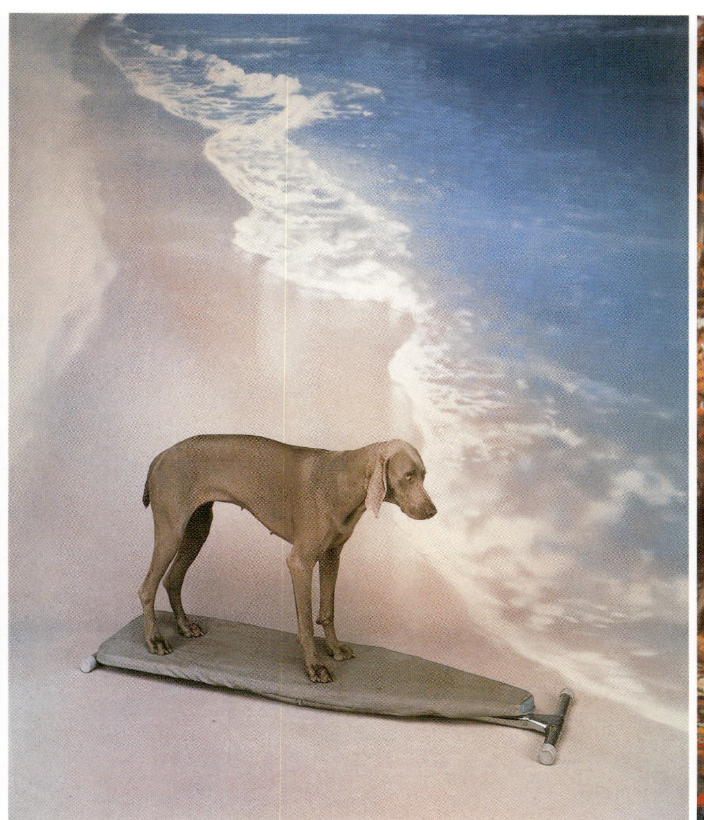

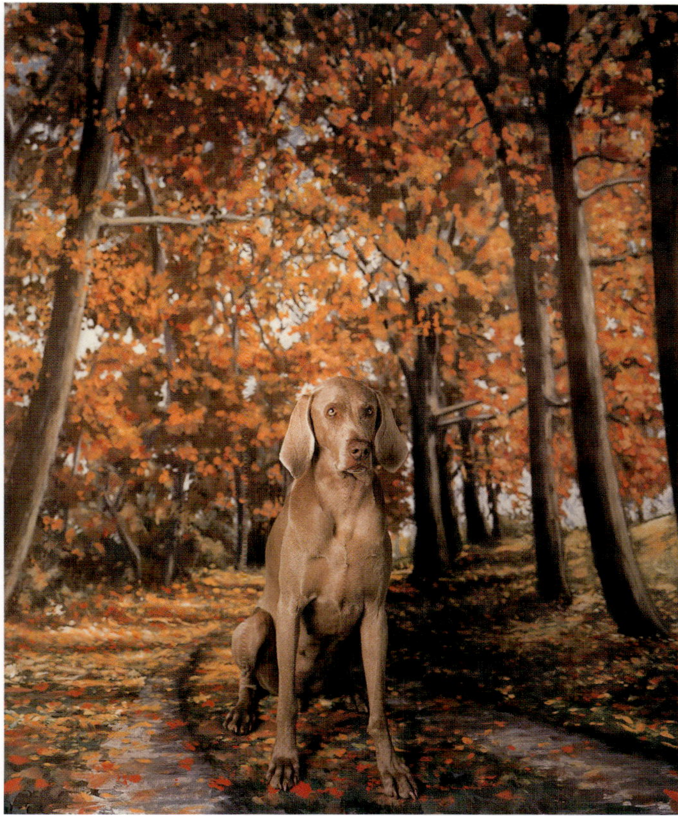

Opposite and Overleaf: ***Six Scenic Scenes*, 1997**

In portraiture, photographers have relied on painted scenic backdrops since the beginning,

and in the commercial world they are used extensively. I knew about their existence, but never used them until I went to Boston to photograph my dogs for a benefit project at Massachusetts College of Art. My friend, Jeff Keogh, Mass Arts' gallery director, introduced me to the scenic portfolio of Mass Arts alumnus, Mark Hunt, and an idea was hatched. I selected a few from a catalogue and scheduled a shoot to coincide with a return trip from Maine.

I was particularly attracted to a dusky sunset scene. My dogs are dusky. In real life you could never work with the 20x24 in anything but the bright light of midday. The large-format camera requires full sun at a nice moderate temperature. I don't live in San Diego.

Unrolling the backdrop, I was surprised at how crudely it was painted—nothing like what it looked like in the catalogue. After taking a picture, I was even more surprised at the convincing illusion of reality it elicited. Magic. Of course, I could never use anything the proper way, and before long, I found all kinds of alternative perspectives for the backdrops.

From this point on, I expanded my quest for scenic interplay. In the works that ensued, those depicting sky and/or water proved to work best. A major work of mine, *Six Scenic Scenes*, commissioned by the New Jersey State Council on the Arts for the Atlantic City Convention Center made maximum use of rented scenic backdrops. Covering what I thought were some of the state's highlights, I let the dogs slip from one scene to the next via a bridgework of connecting props and materials. Farming leads to gambling leads to fishing, camping, golf, football. Neither the dogs or the camera had to go to New Jersey.

In 1997 Jeff Keogh invited us back to Mass Art for a new project. An exhibition of vintage painted sideshow banners on loan from the Carl Hammer Gallery, Chicago, and by banner artist Johnny Meah spectacularly filled the Mass Art gallery spaces. I could choose any and all to work with. I was like a kid in a candy store. But the candy was sourballs. Nothing that I hoped for worked. The banners were not backdrops, they were assertive, the opposite of receptive to my subjects. If my dogs were in focus, the scenes were not, and a many of the scenes had words painted on them which when out of focus appeared out of focus. This project really provoked some serious rethinking. Ultimately I found ways to work with them.

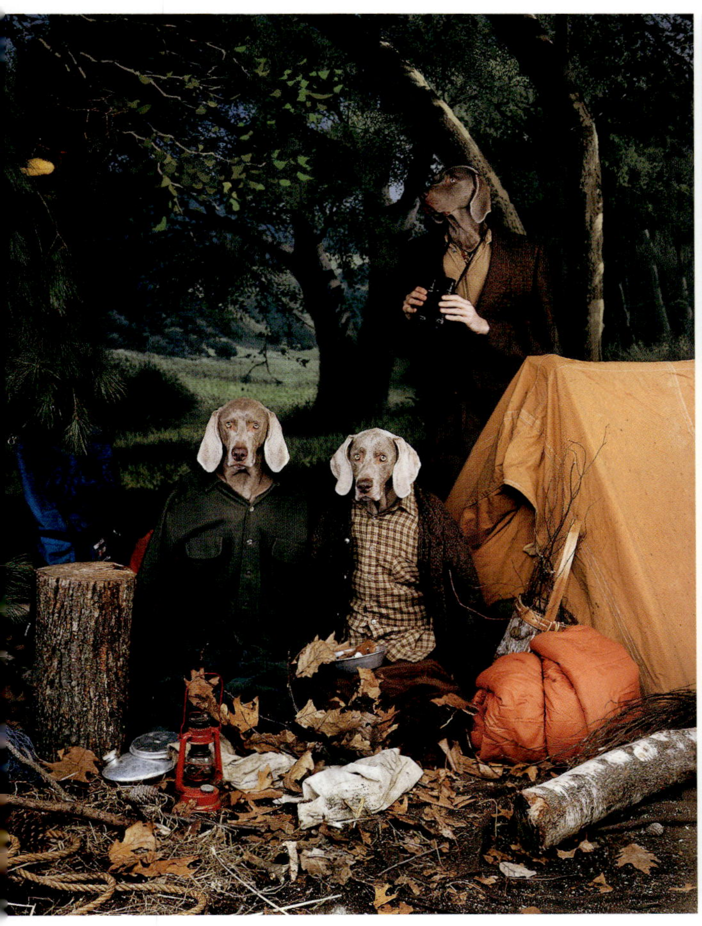

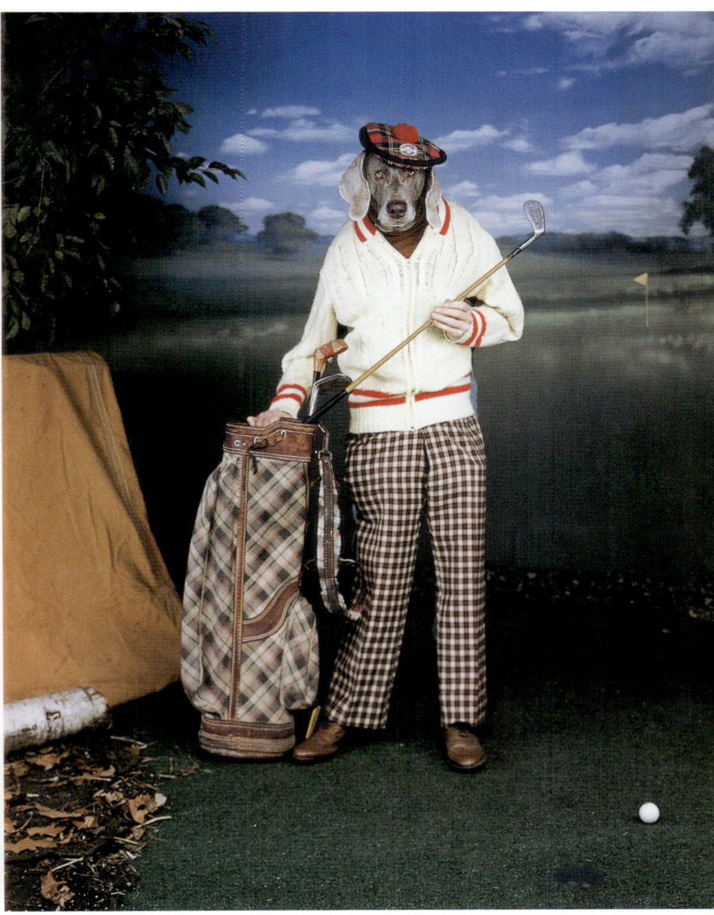

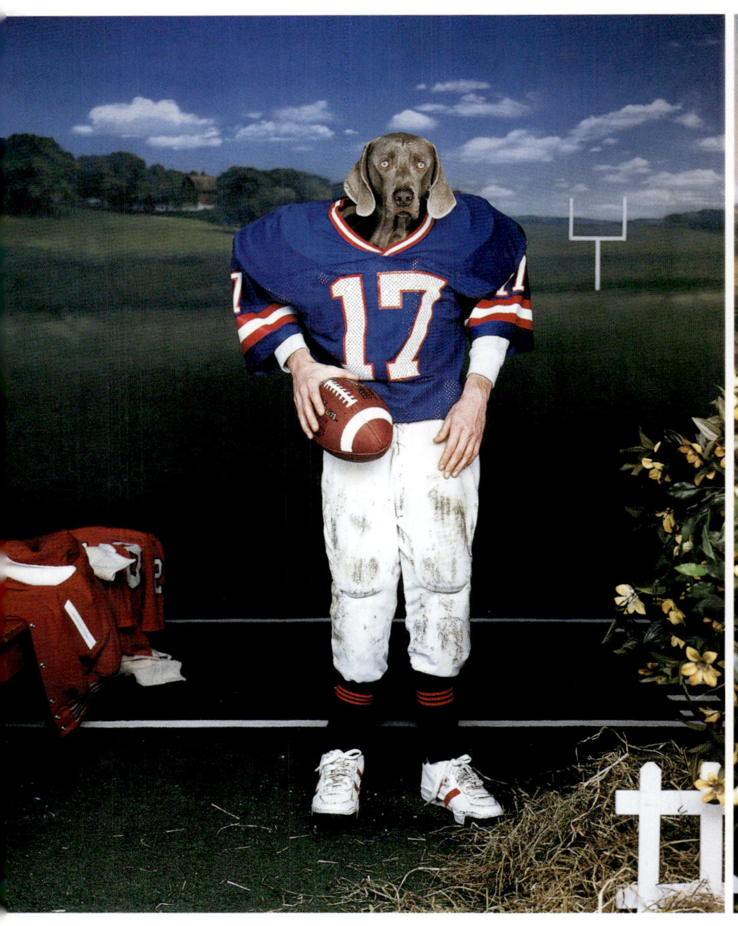
17

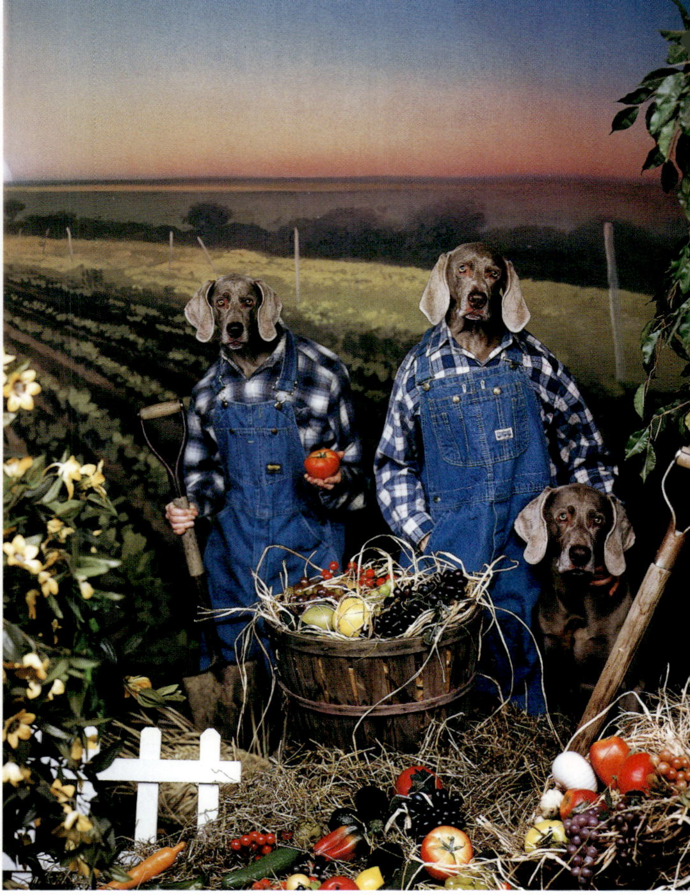

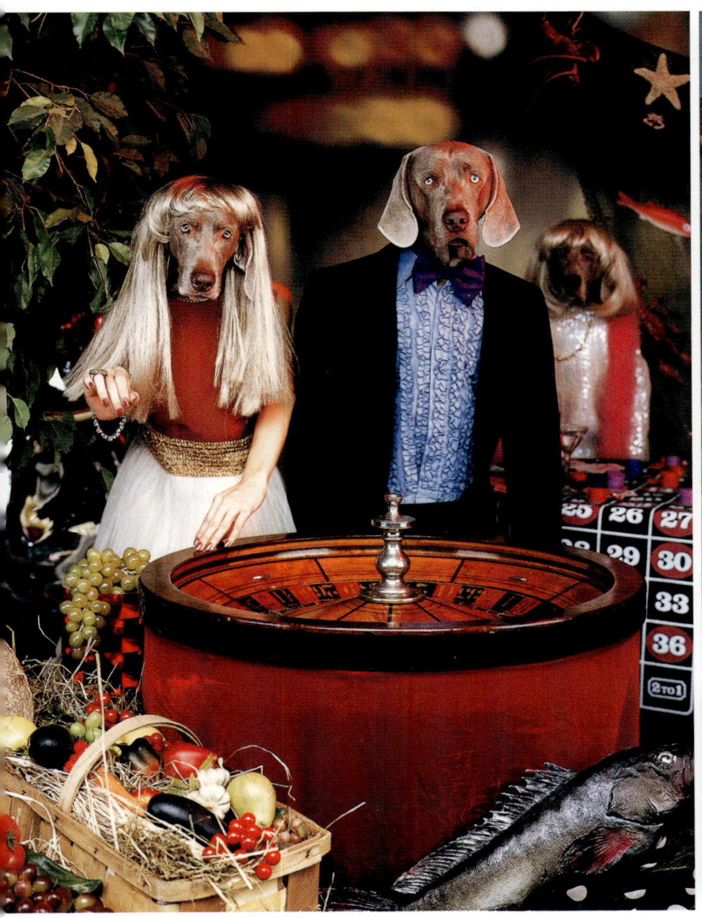
26
27
29
30
33
36
2TO1

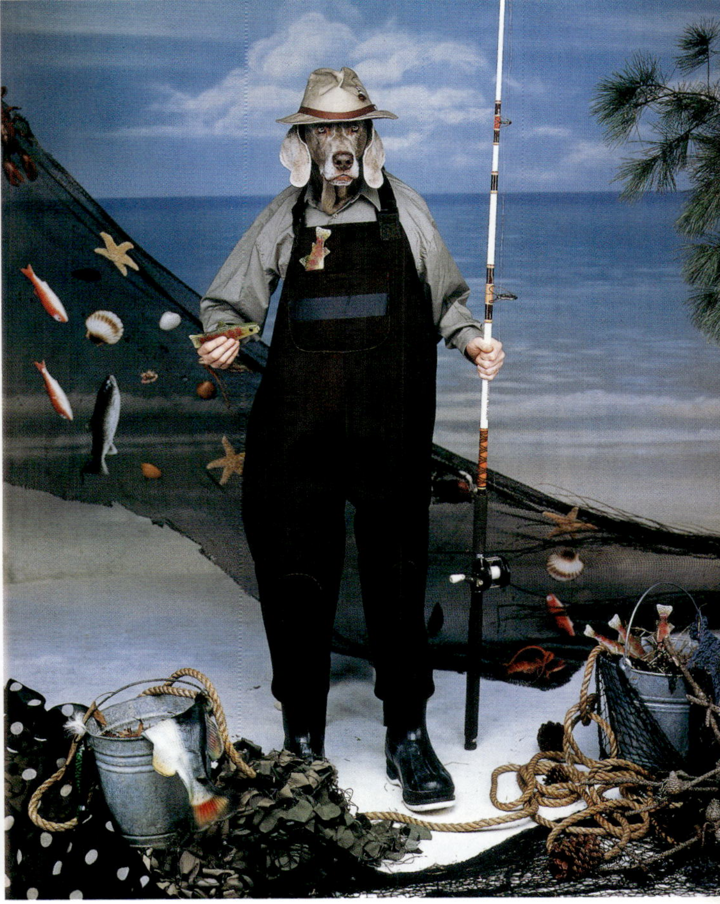

Opposite: ***Skyward,*** **1997**
Overleaf: ***Flock,*** **1997**

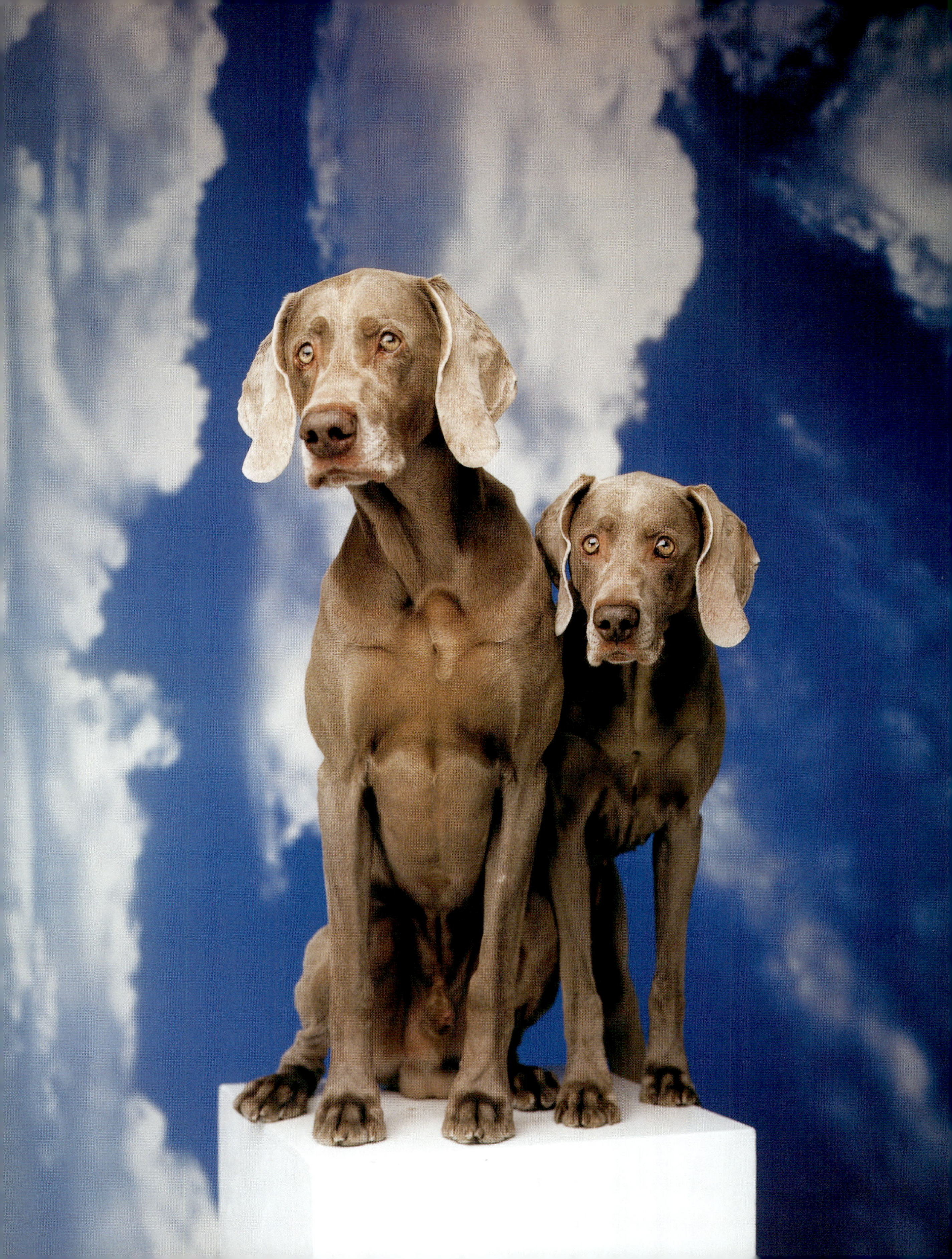

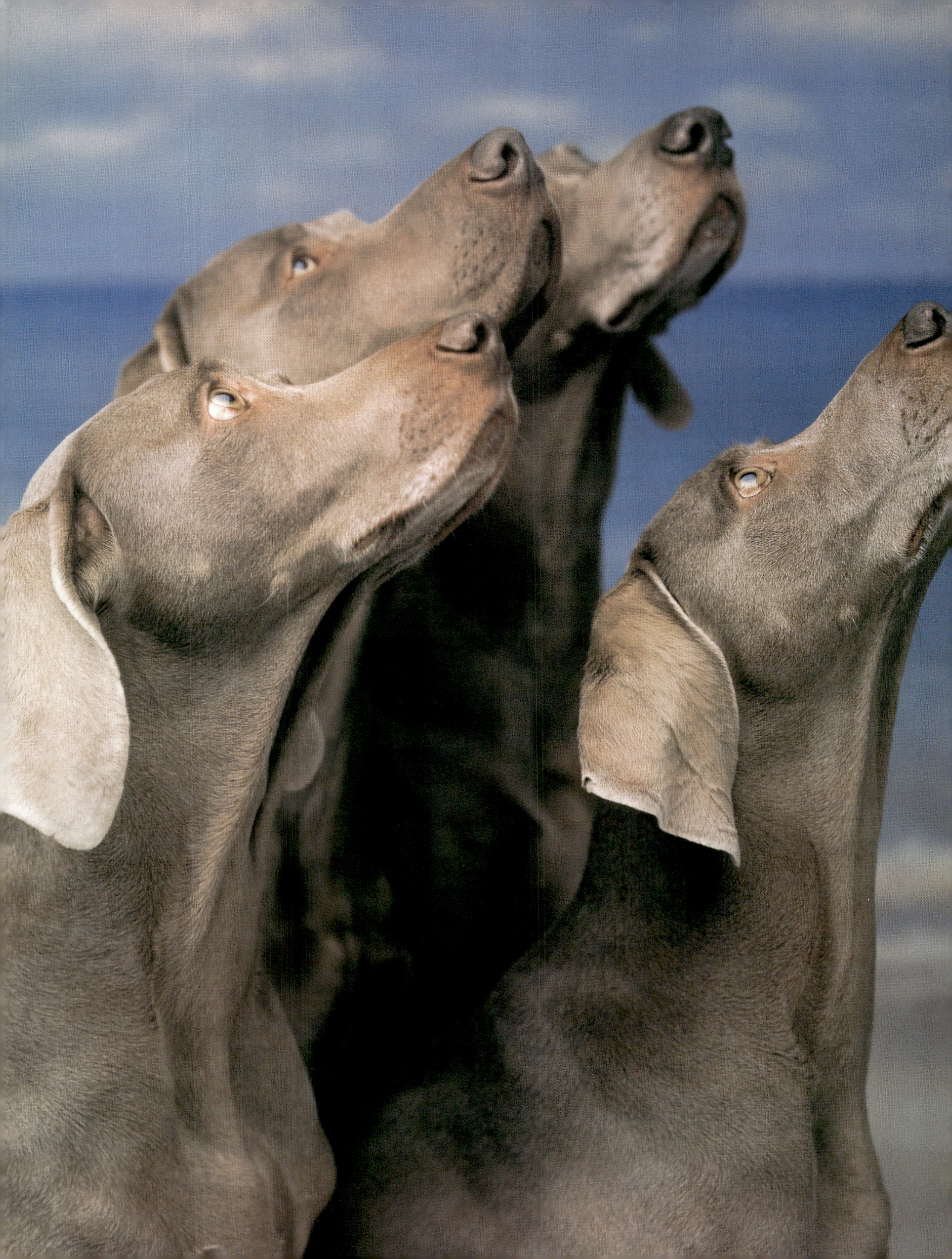

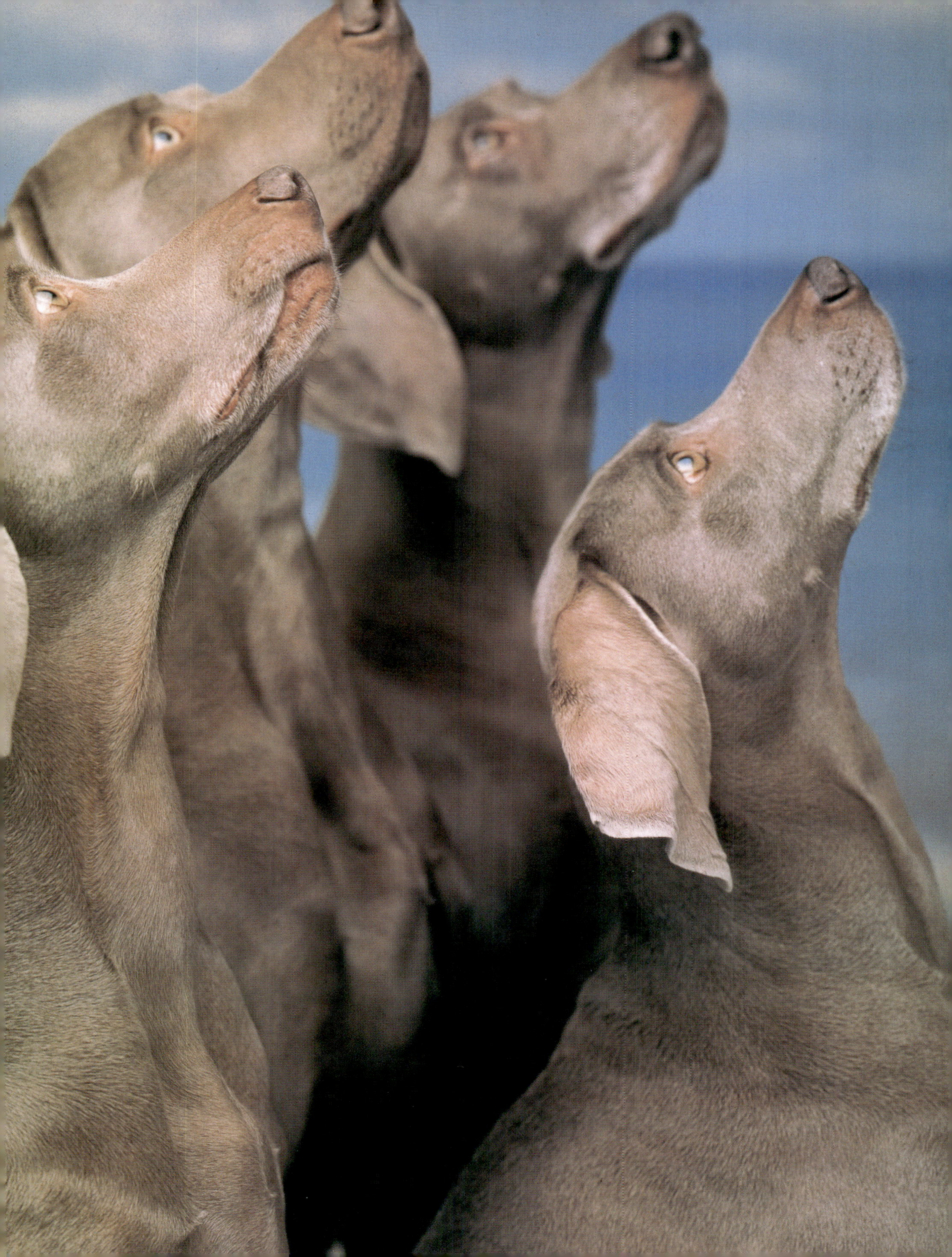

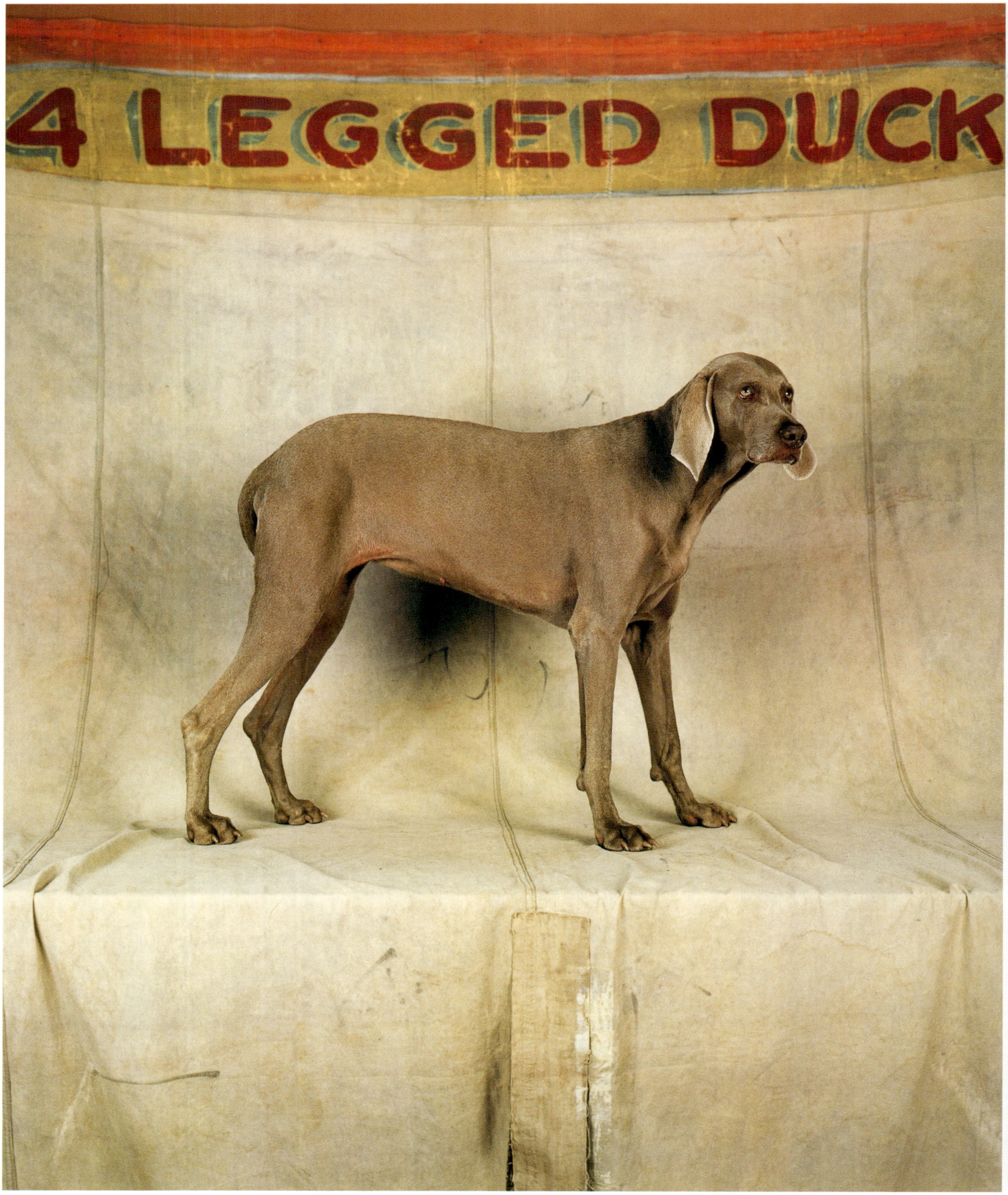

4 LEGGED DUCK

Opposite: ***4 Legged,*** 1998
Left: ***Facsimile,*** 1998
Right: ***Stand In,*** 1998

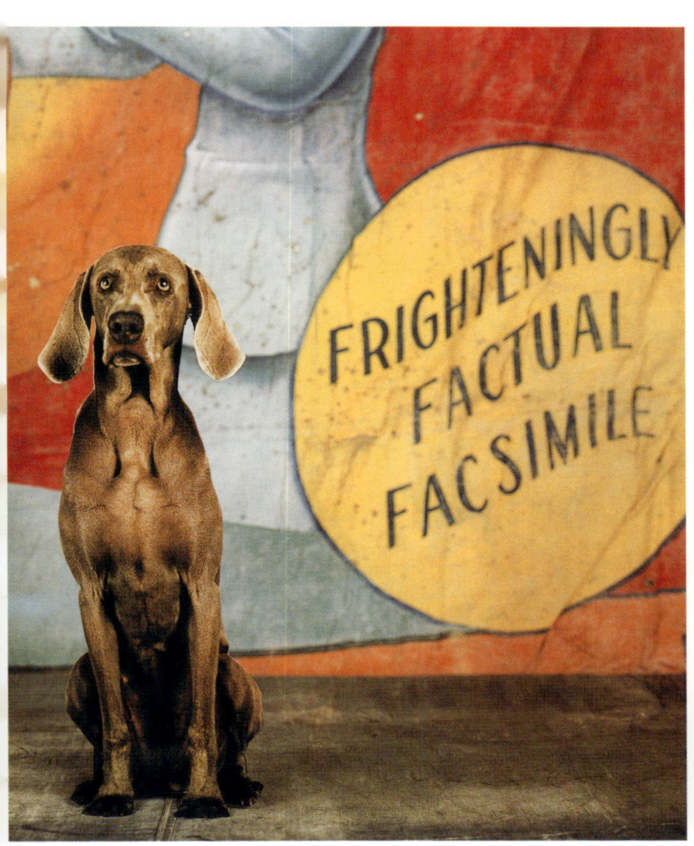

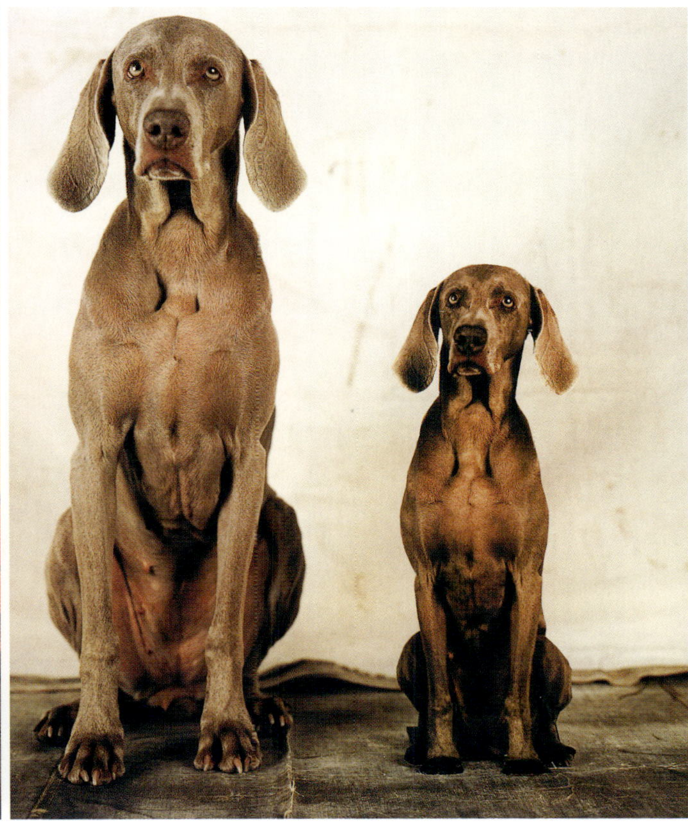

Cast Shadow, 1993

Left: *Manual Transmission*, 1992
Right: *In the Box*, 1987

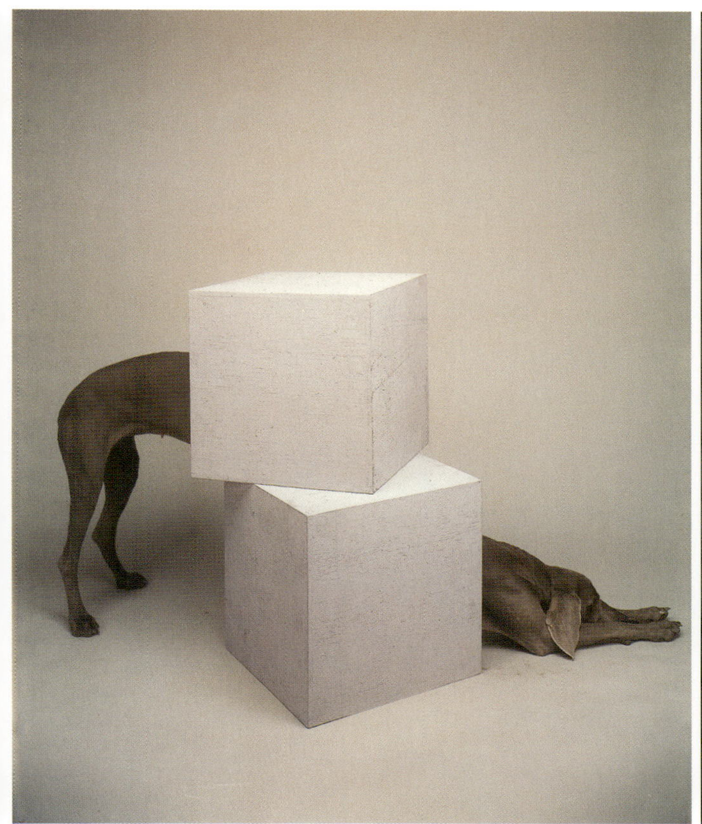

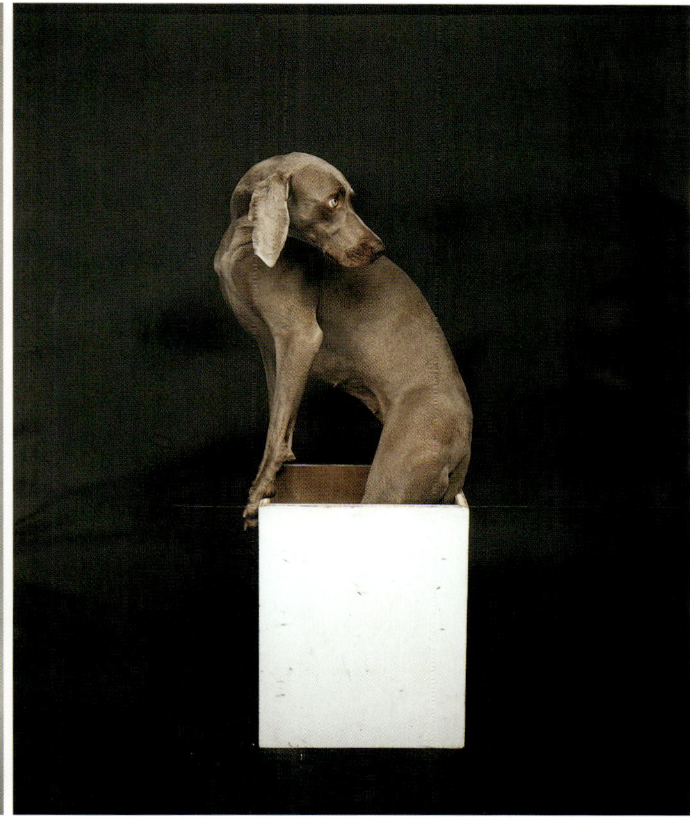

Left: ***Under Cover*, 1993**
Right: ***End Paper*, 1996**

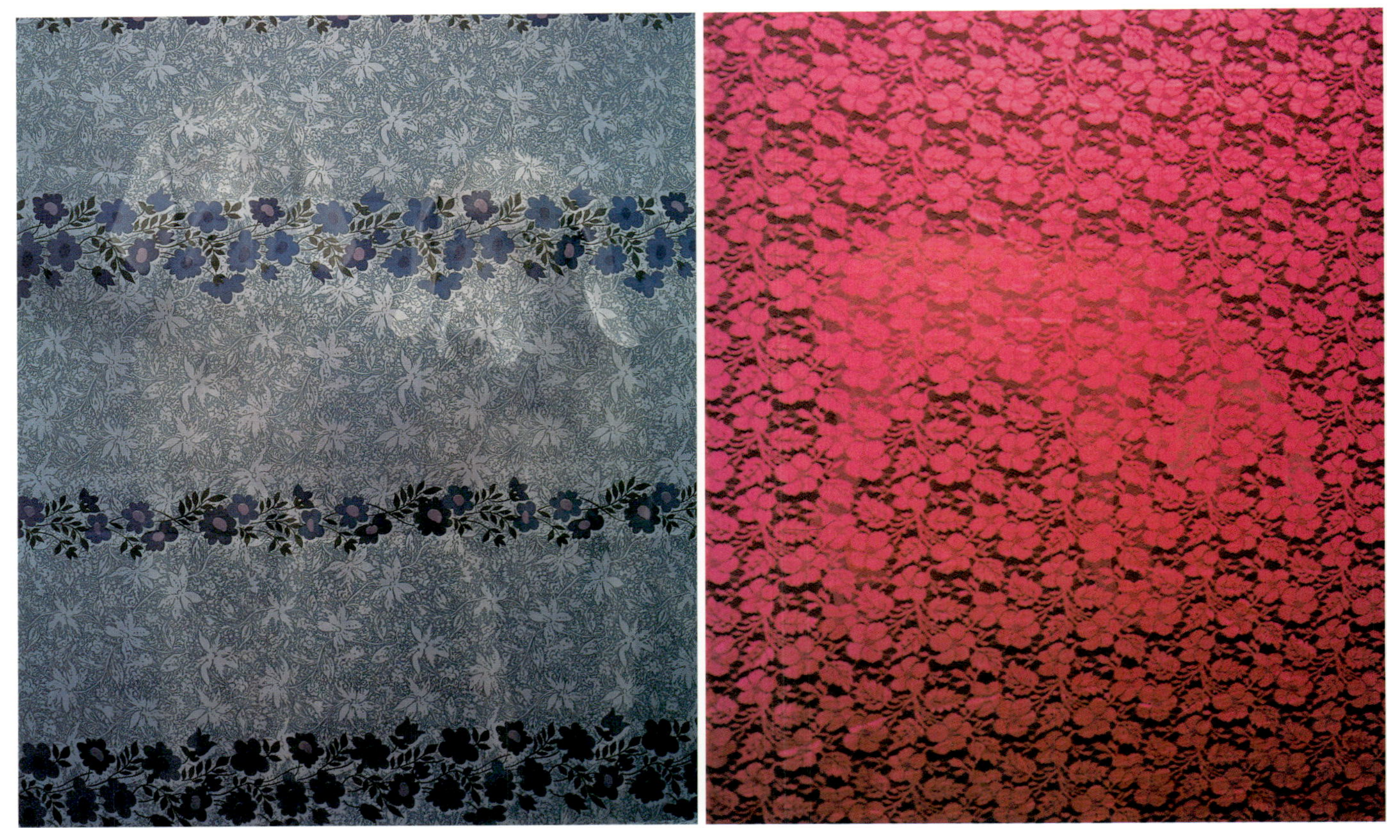

Left: ***Camouflage*****, 1993**
Right: ***Ghost Garden*****, 1991**

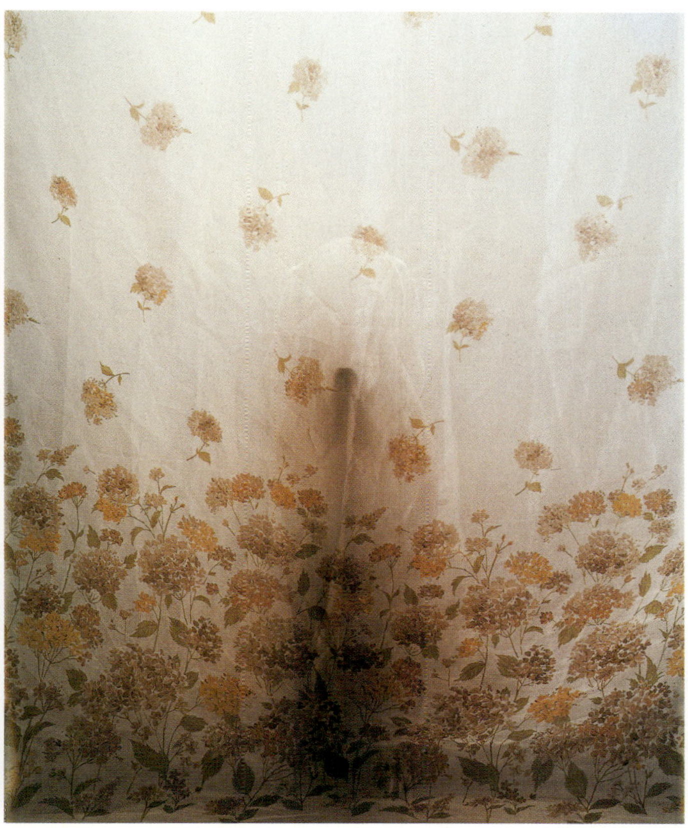

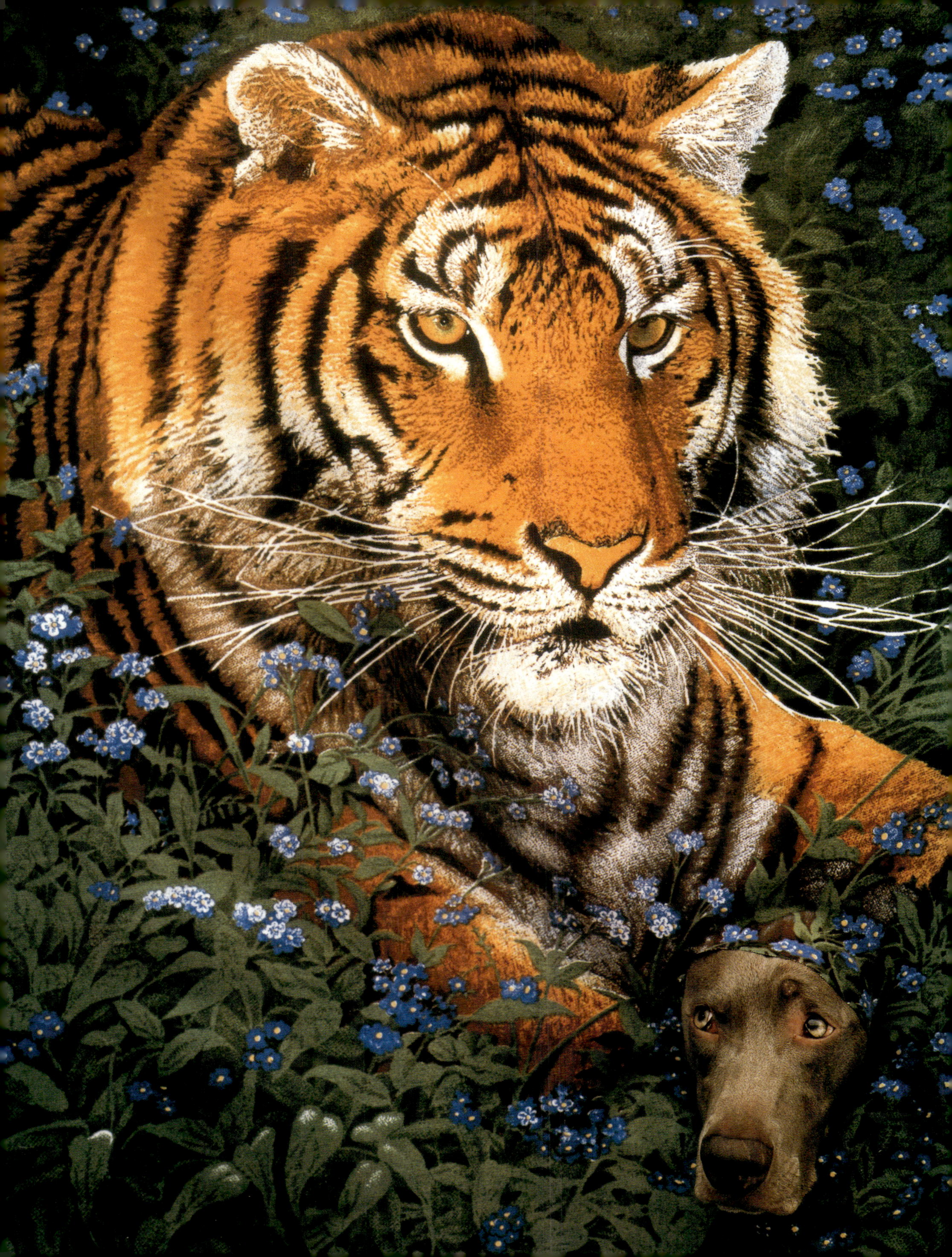

Tiger Field, 1992

Below: ***Evil Stepmother,*** **1991**
Opposite: ***Serrated,*** **1994**

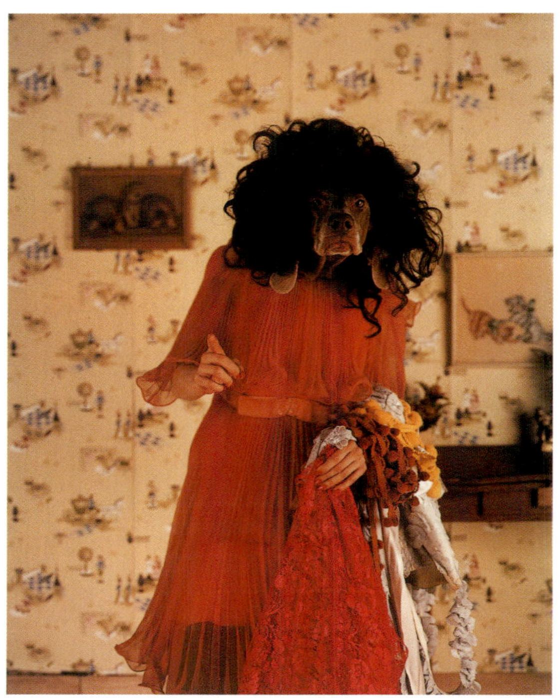

In my Cinderella, Fay was cast as both Fairy Godmother and Evil Stepmother.

With appropriate costume and lighting, she was equally convincing in both roles. The malevolent stepmother was the role she relished. Her domination over Batty/Cinderella was not far from their relationship in real life. After Fay's evil stepmother picture, I began to ask myself, "Is Fay really evil?" It was a theme I continued to muse about.

But perhaps it was me, the director and acting teacher, who skillfully elicited Fay's convincing characterization of evil. My interest in expression and gesture in the Polaroids went back to 1980, when Man Ray was ten years old and no longer svelte. In terms of poses, I didn't have many options. Athletic spans and gymnastic stunts were out. We were left with the basic five: Sit, Stand, Down, Shake, Roll Over. By covering his body with fabrics and using flattering camera angles, I tried to mask his physical deterioration, but I also had to look beyond the body for inspiration.

And so, in turning away from the corporeal, I began to explore his expressiveness, something I only sporadically considered as a vehicle in the past, more often seeking a detached, business-as-usual look from him.

I was inspired by a book that I came across in a New York dumpster. It was a vintage edition of a volume by François Delsarte, the nineteenth-century teacher whose system of dramatic expression was popular among actors of the era. Misunderstanding Delsarte, to be sure, I concocted several photographs, including *Broken Hurt,* and video works involving dramatic gestures and expressions from his teaching. In Man Ray's advanced years, I began thinking of him as a great actor from the silent screen era, and Delsarte gave me something to work from. I found I could elicit certain looks from Man Ray by uttering words like "cat," "park," "out," "bone," "beach," "walk, "bike ride," and so forth. To make a work based on expression seemed daring to me at the time—against the grain of cool.

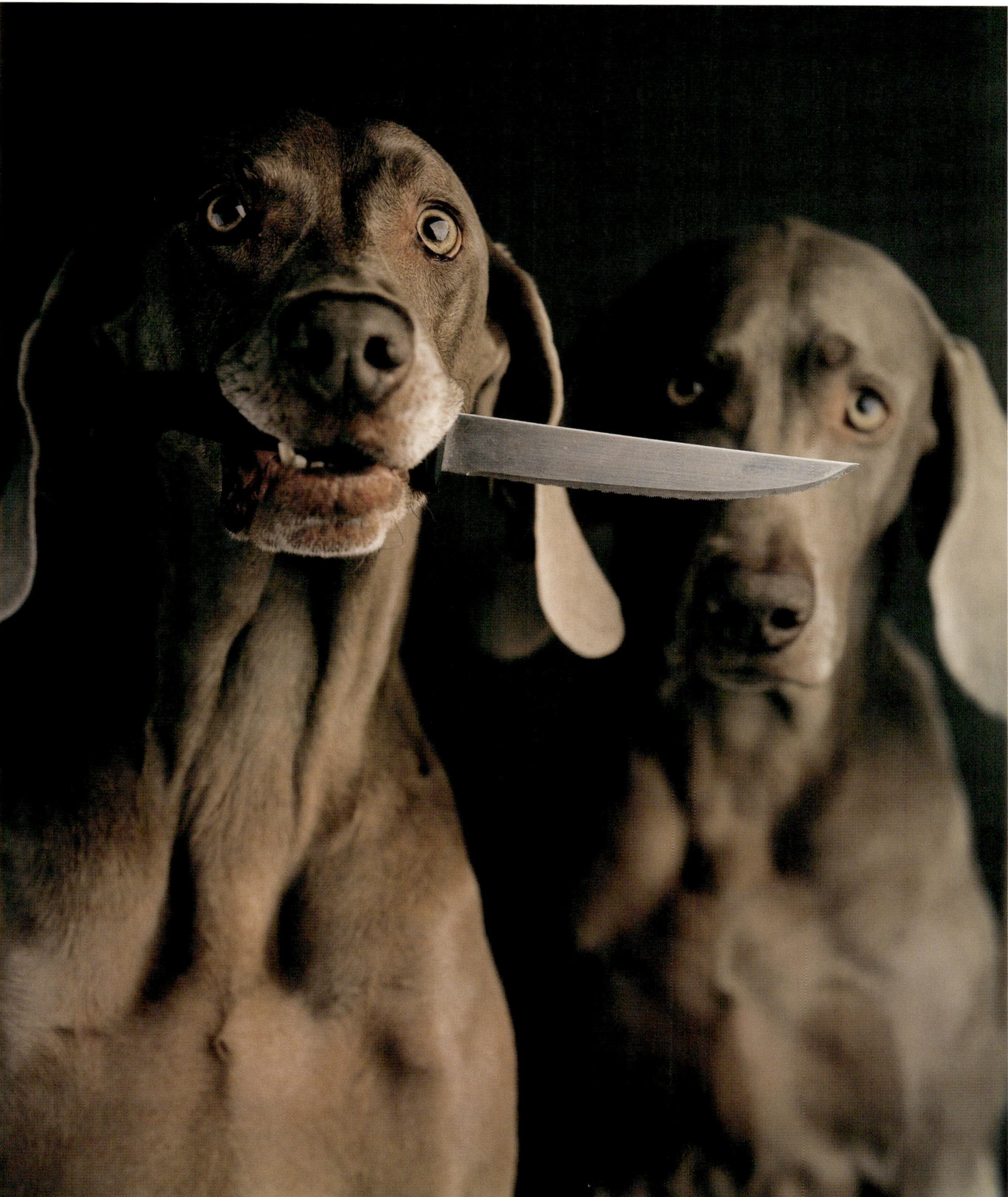

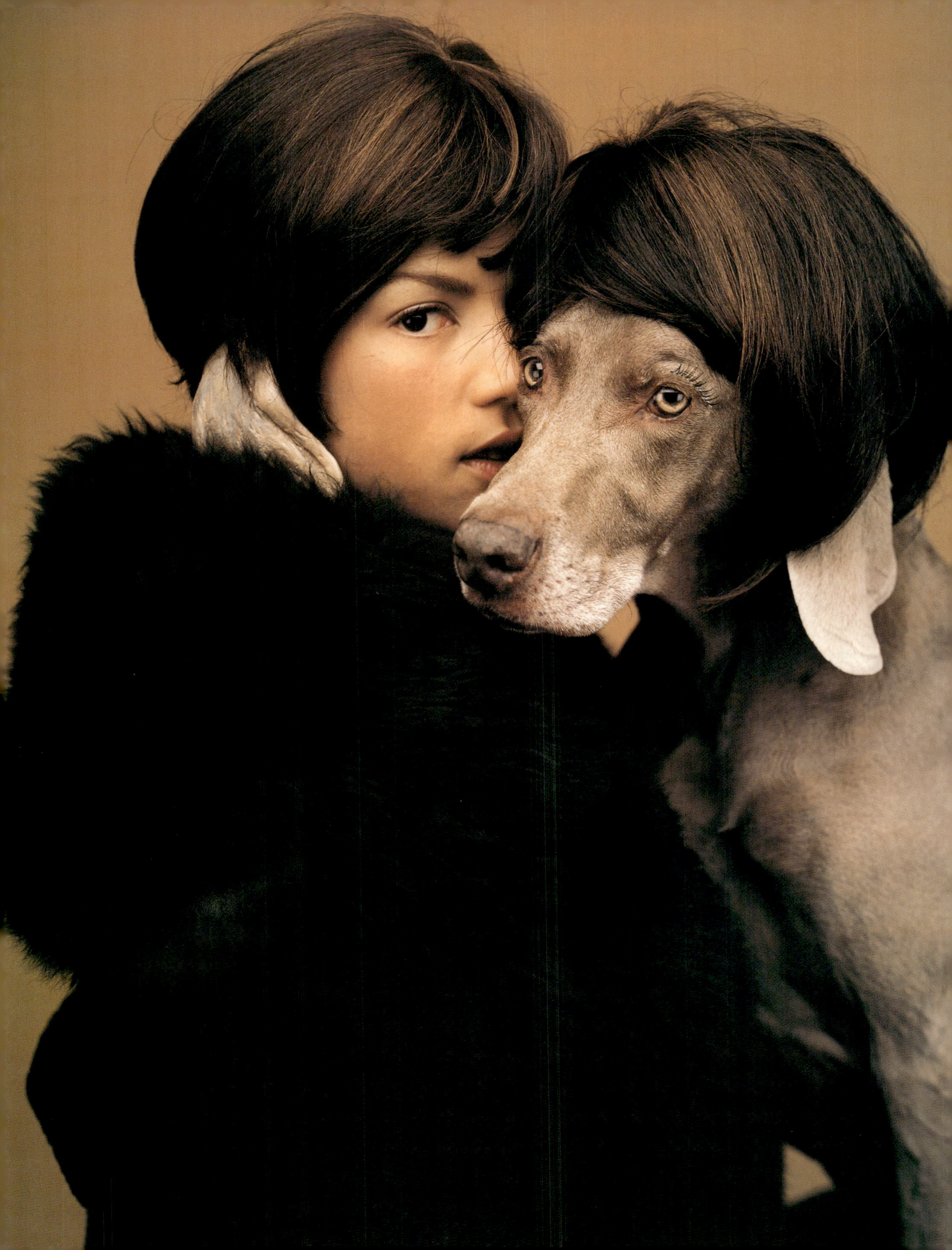

Opposite: ***The Secret*, 1994**
Overleaf Left: ***Bikini*, 1999**
Overleaf Right: ***Reader*, 1999**

I hadn't thought much about the world of fashion

until it was brought to my attention that supermodel Veronica Webb named Fay her favorite supermodel in *Vogue*. Soon after, I received a call from Veronica proposing a photo op. "Wouldn't it be fun to get together?" Veronica arrived at the Polaroid studio with a makeup guy and a bag of extremely fluffy items from designer Todd Oldham. Then she and the makeup guy disappeared into the dressing room for an hour. When she came out, she was wearing Fay's ears. She looked gorgeous. I took several photos of her with Fay and with Batty, who, it turns out, she was really thinking about when she was quoted in the magazine.

The clothes were beyond anything I had used before—definitely not yard sale. Other brief fashion encounters ensued, including an AIDS benefit involving photos with fashions from Moschino and a few encounters with Anna Sui. It was fun but exceptional . . . isolated dots in a galaxy of hundreds of pictures. It wasn't until several years later, after a project for Saks Fifth Avenue windows, that the dots began to connect.

In the Saks window project, I used my own found clothes and displayed them alongside photos and videos of my canine models adorned in them. As I was shown all around the store, I became especially intrigued by the industrious artists who toiled deep in the subterranean depths of the store, the window dressers whose responsibility it was to create a new show every few weeks. I was attracted to some pretty outrageous wigs that had just been retired from a display and impressed by the variety of mannequins and unique display armatures at the dressers' disposal.

Through the auspices of Mary Dinaburg, acting as liaison with Saks, I was able to get my hands on some amazing props—almost anything I wanted from the store. This connection culminated in a traveling exhibition and a book: *William Wegman Fashion Photographs*. More than fashion, the work denoted a compromised interface. Do the dogs wear the clothes, or do the clothes wear the dogs? I'm not sure.

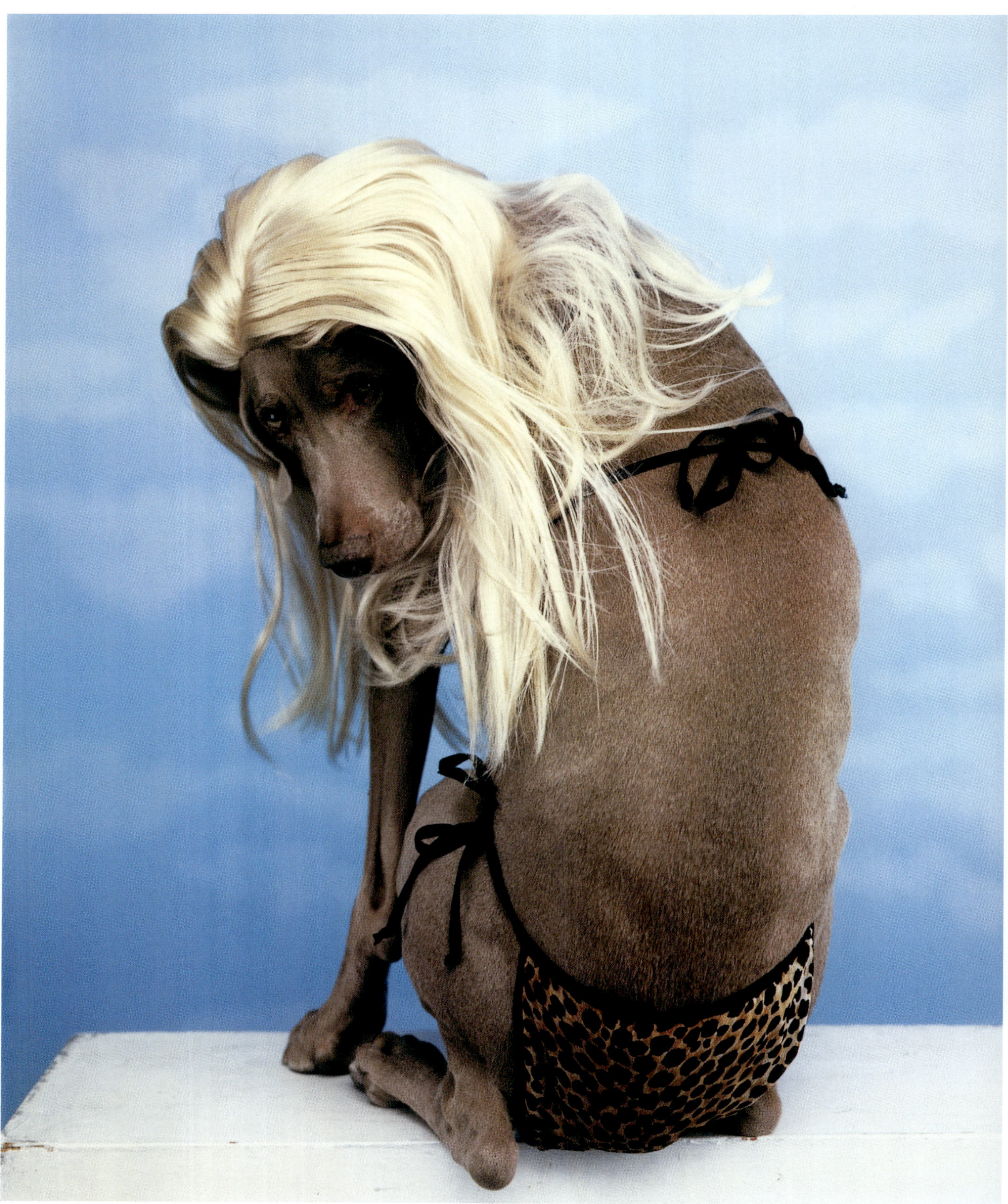

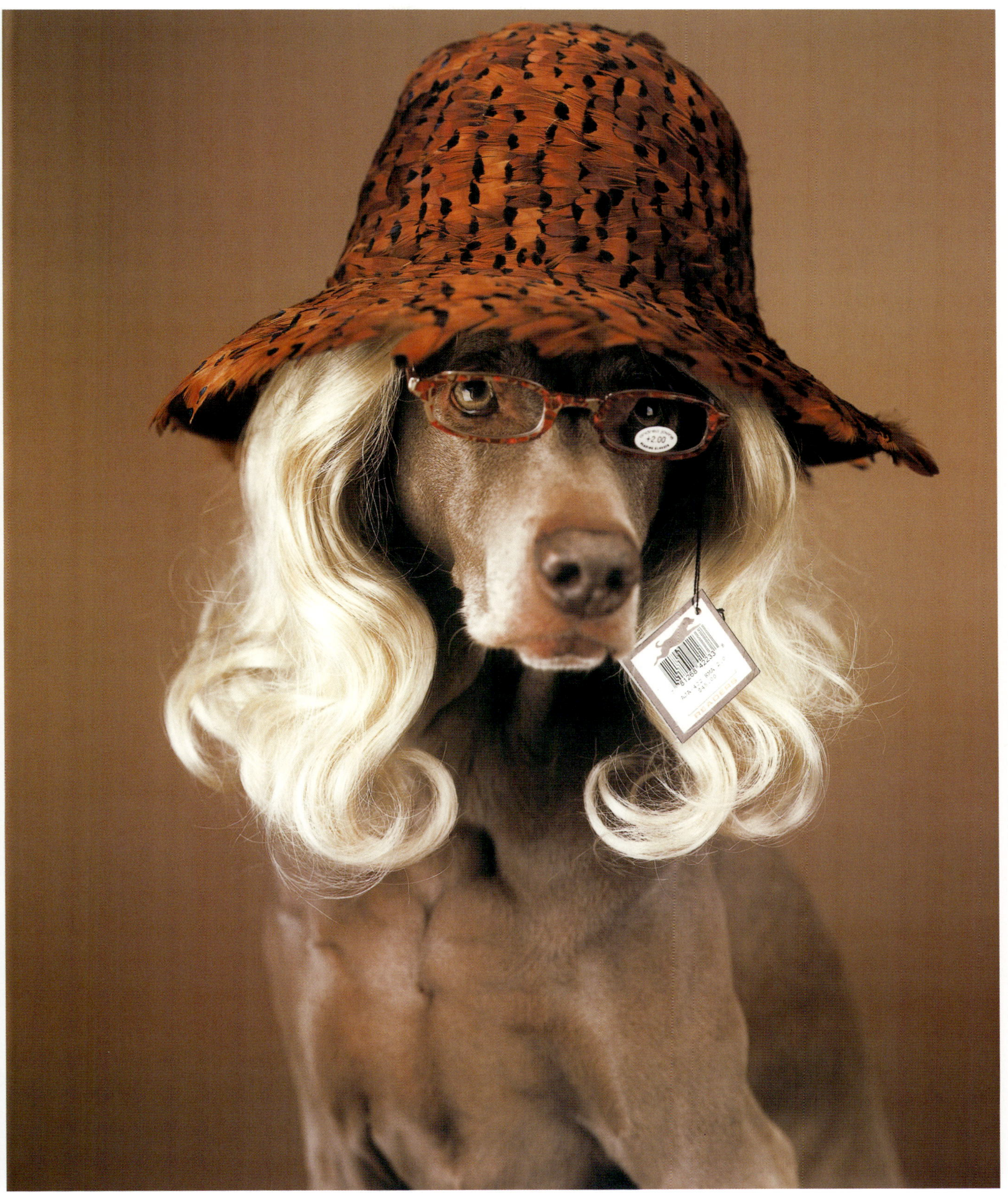
+2.00
81268 42233
READERS

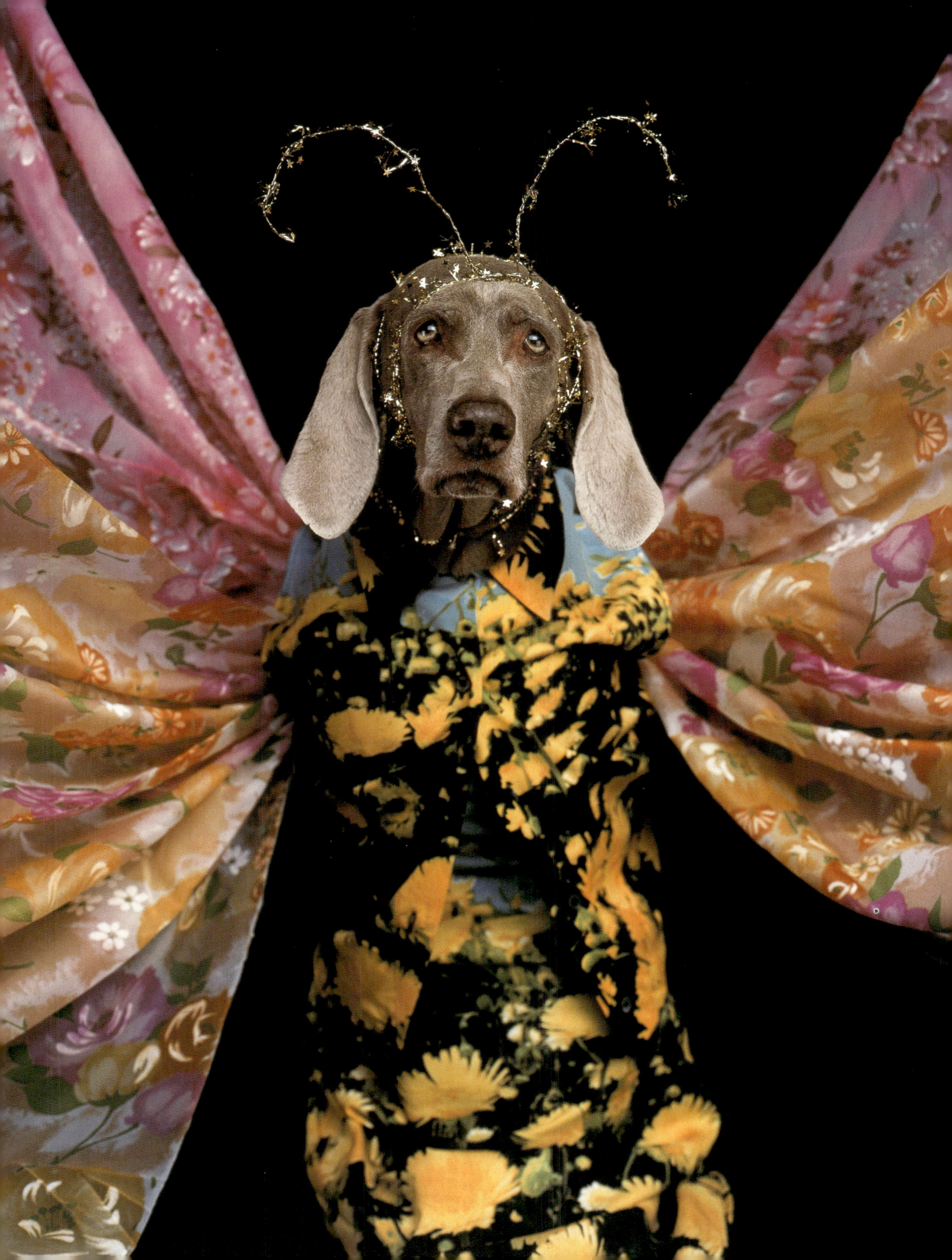

Midsummer Night's Dream, 1999

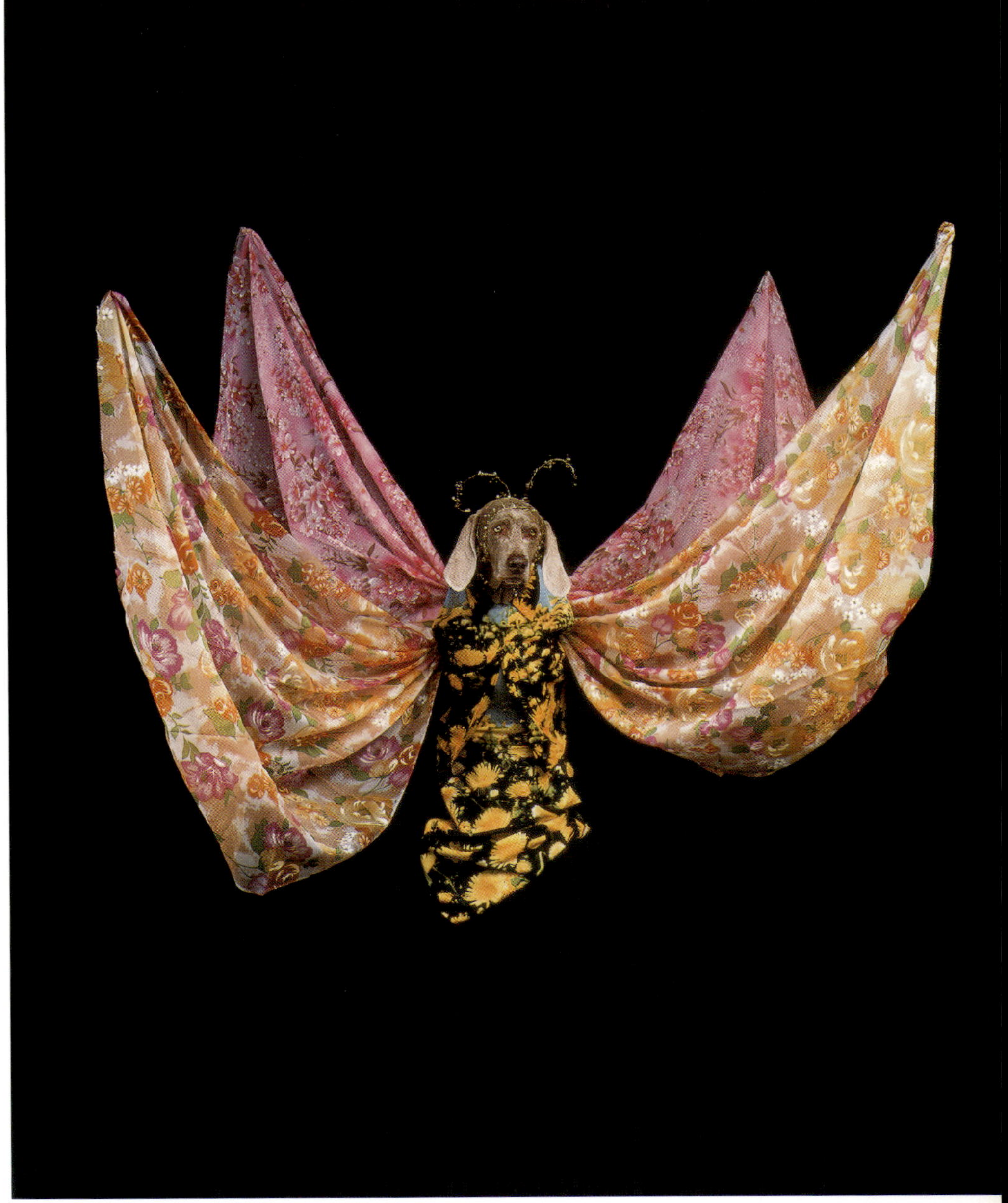

Below: ***Sign language*, 1999**
Opposite: ***Feathered Foot*, 1999**

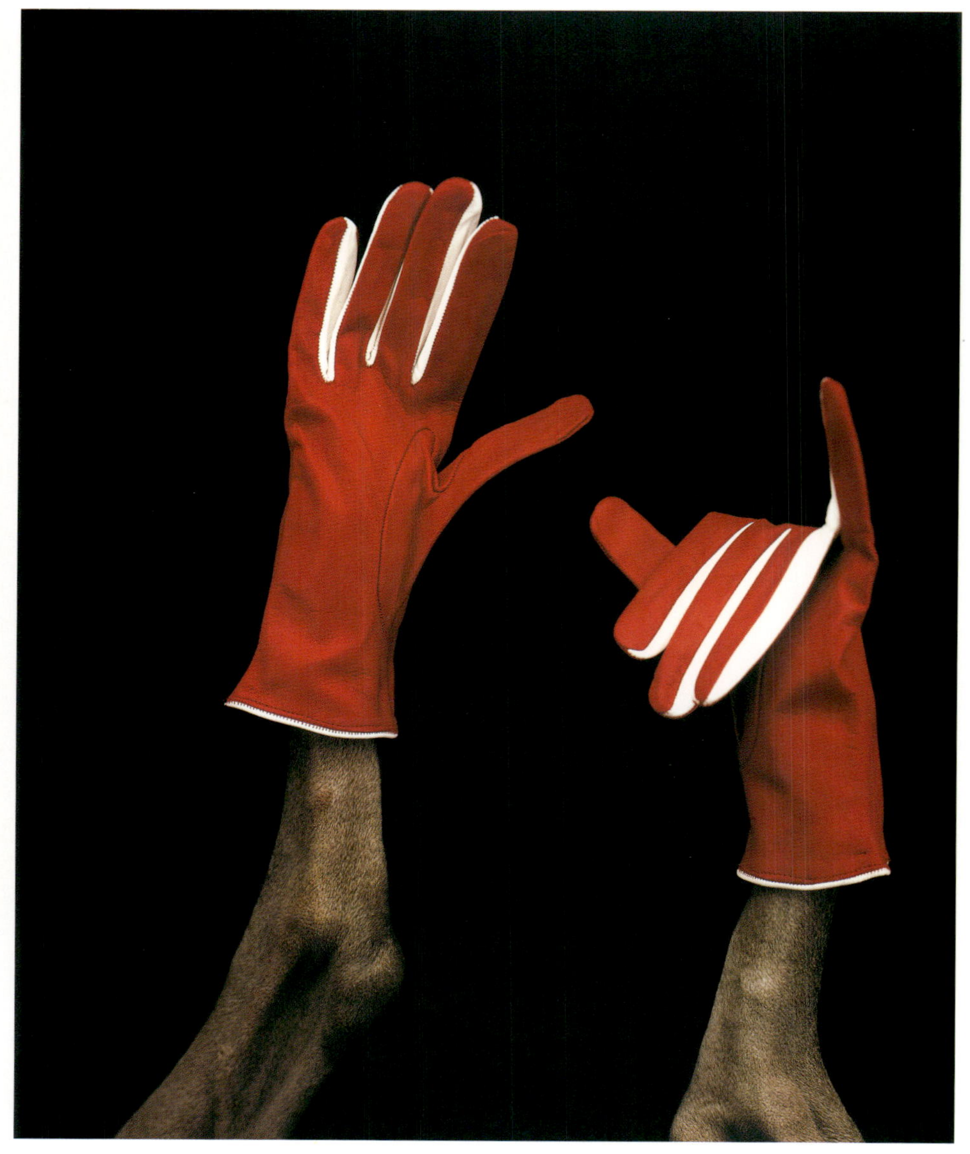

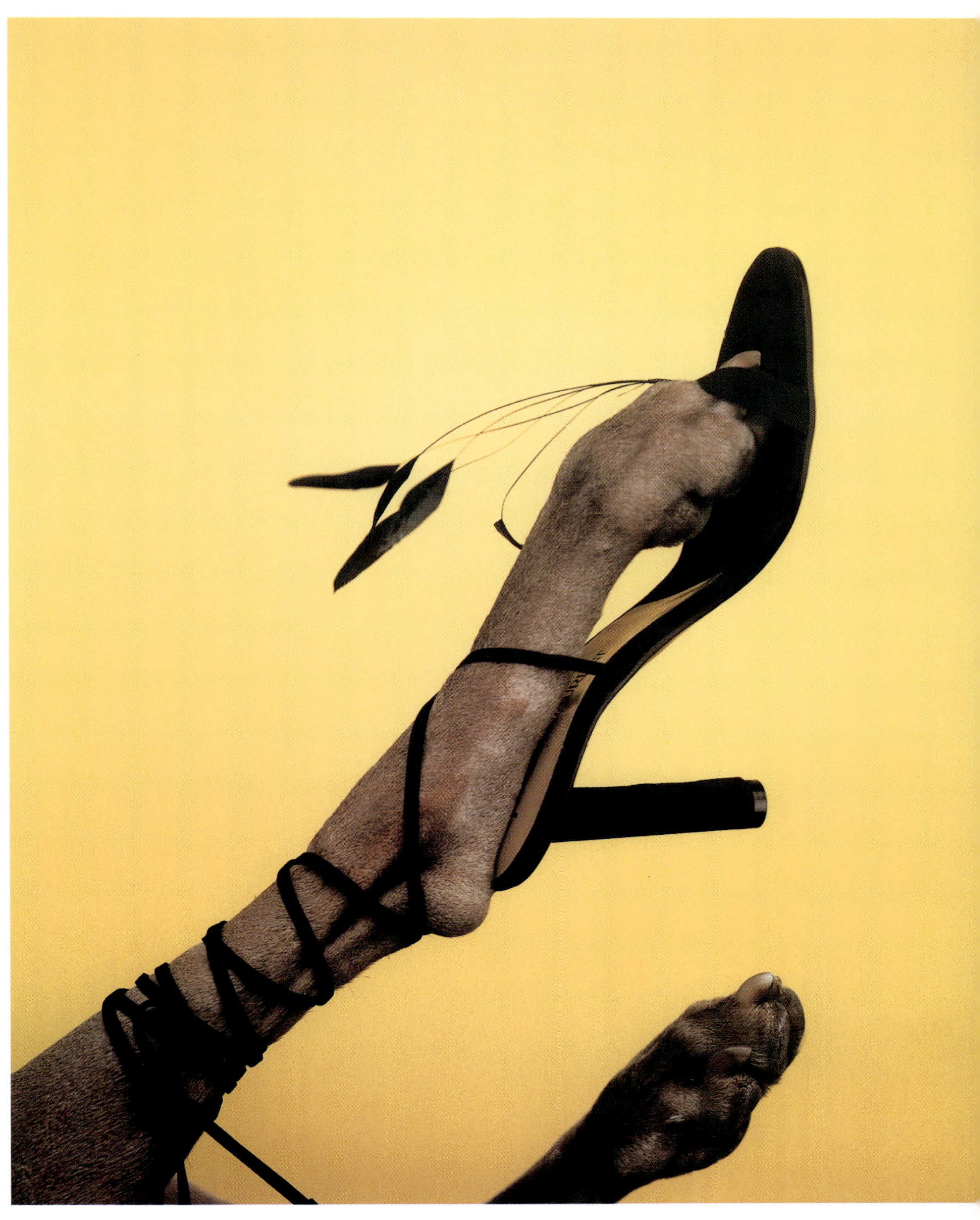

House of Miyake, 1999

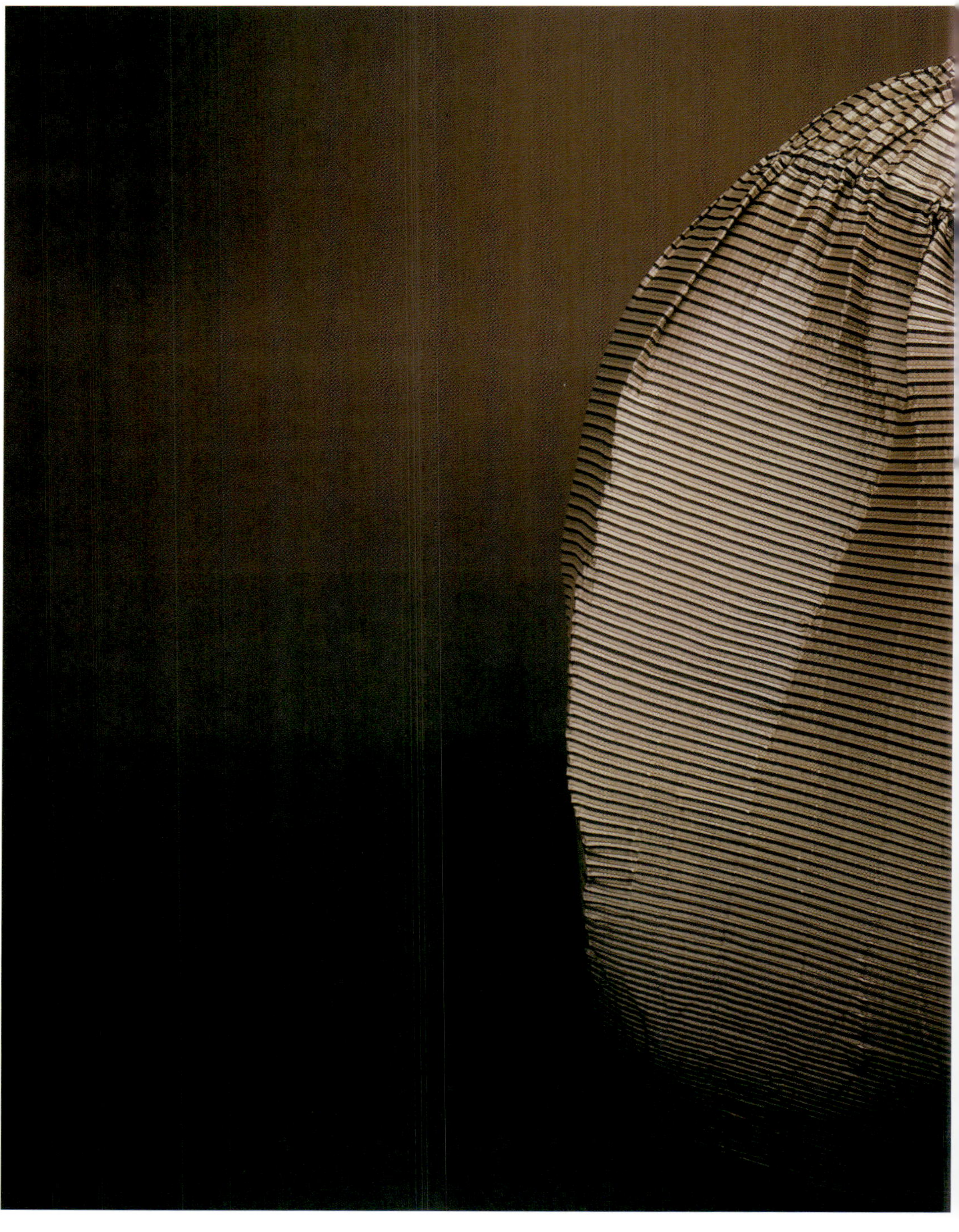

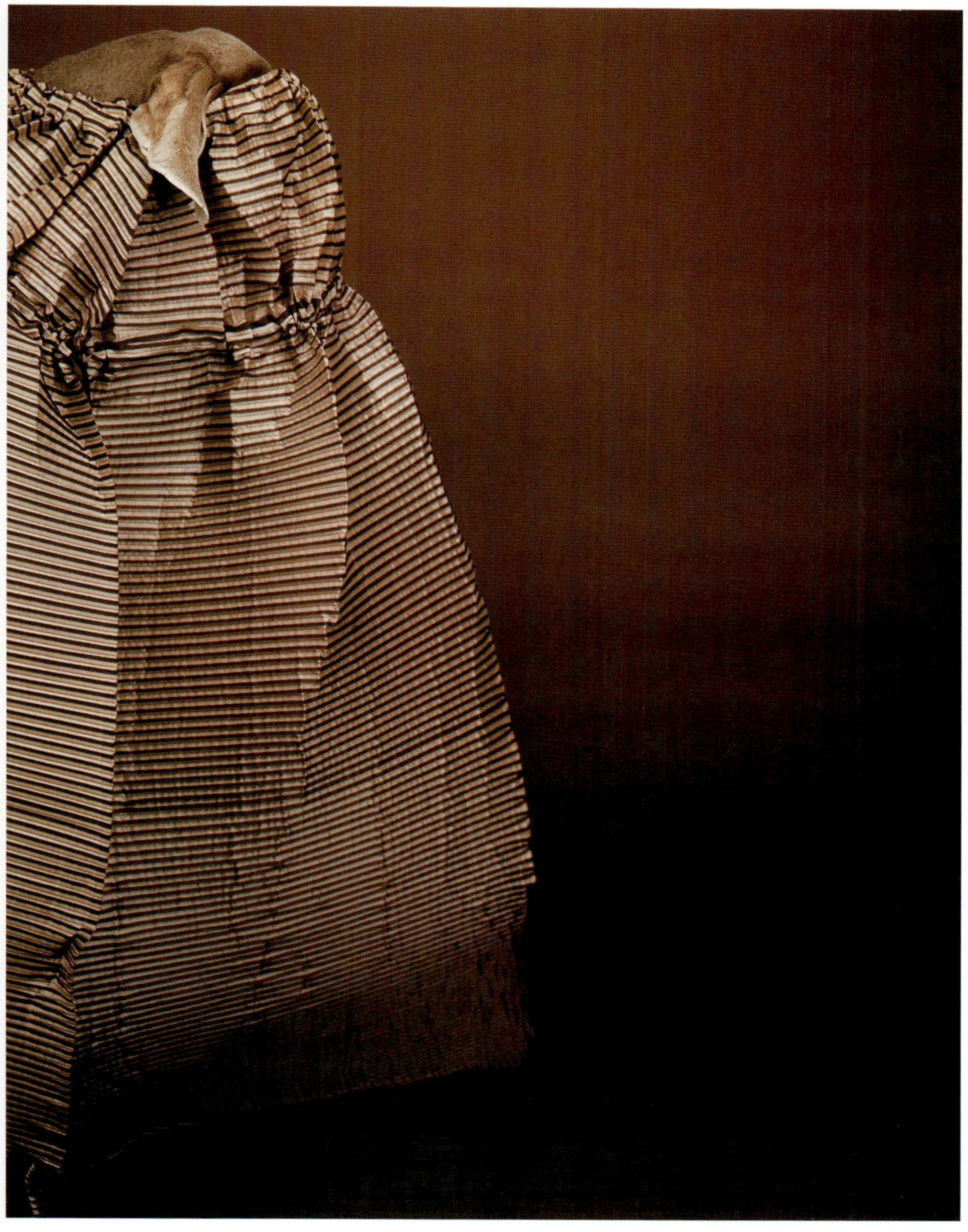

Easter, 2000

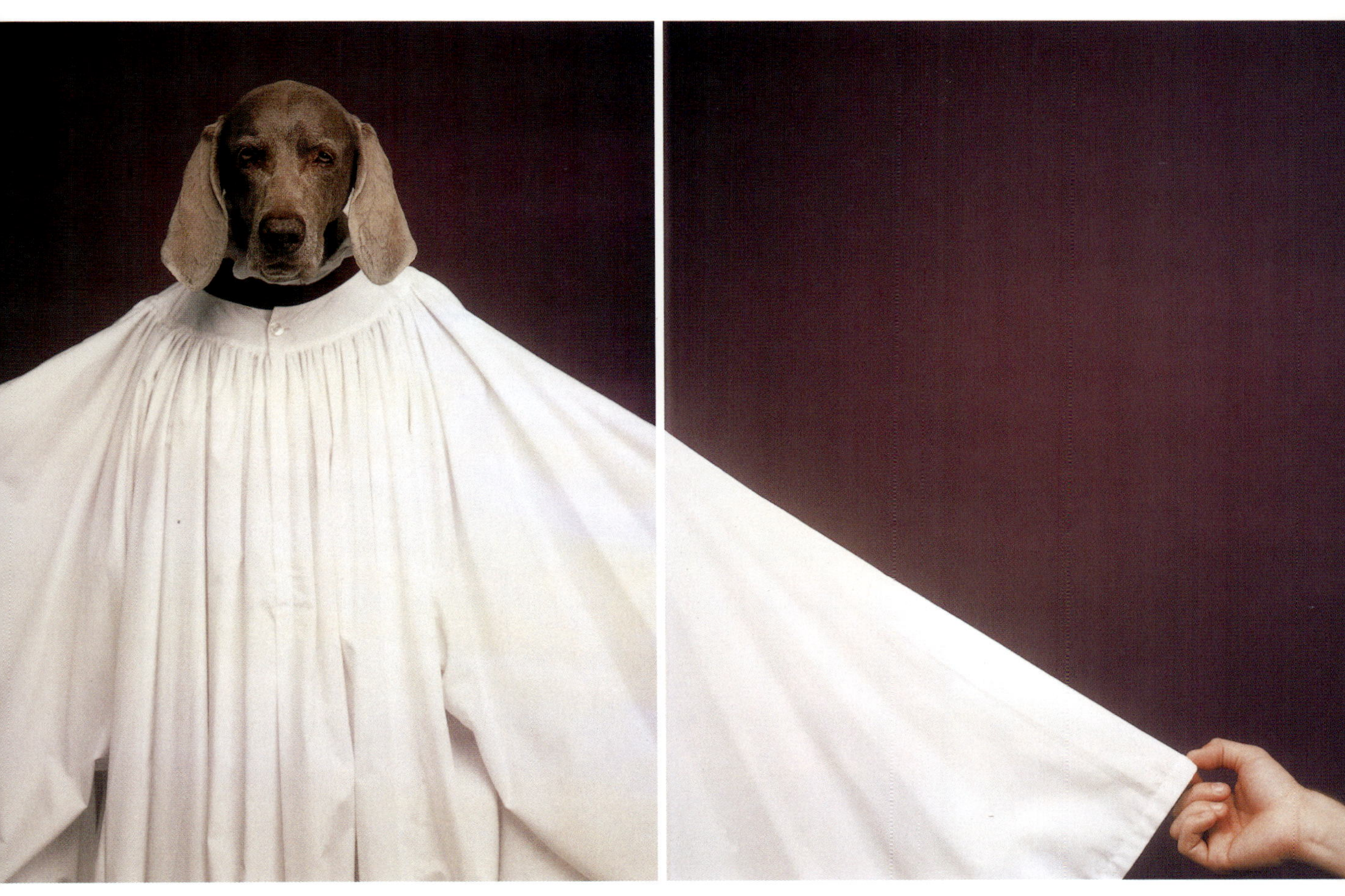

Second Choristers, 2000

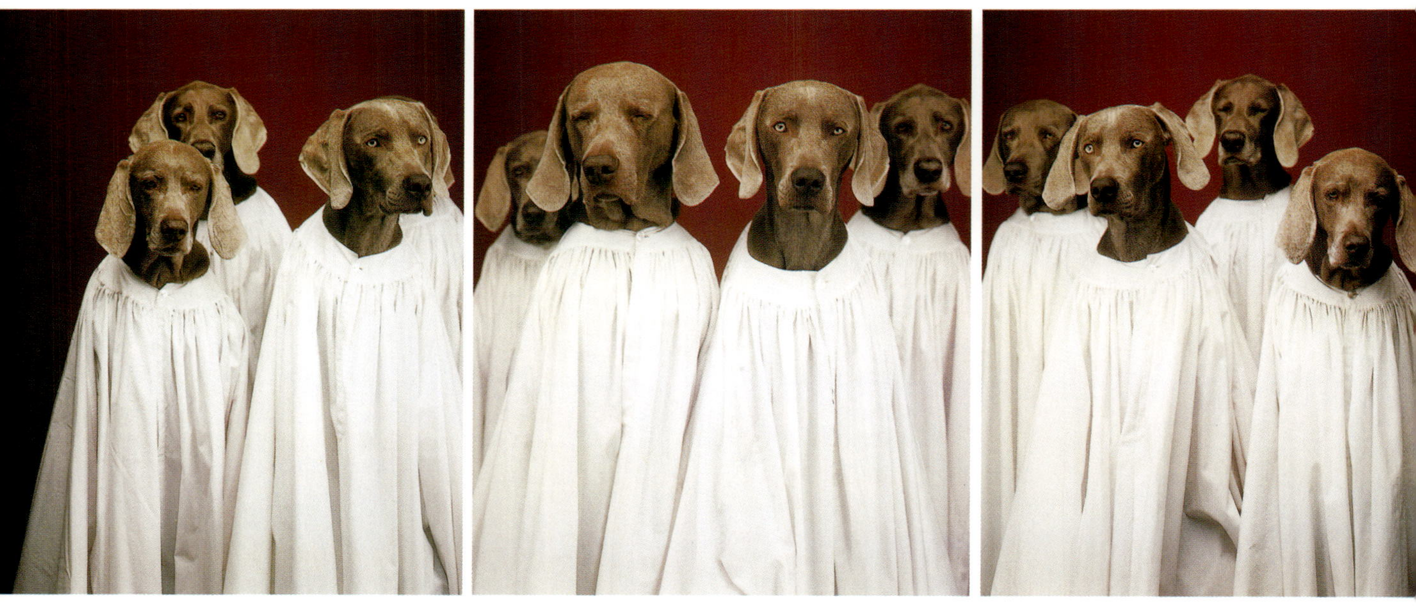

Left: ***Canon Aside*, 2000**
Right: ***Canon Back*, 2000**

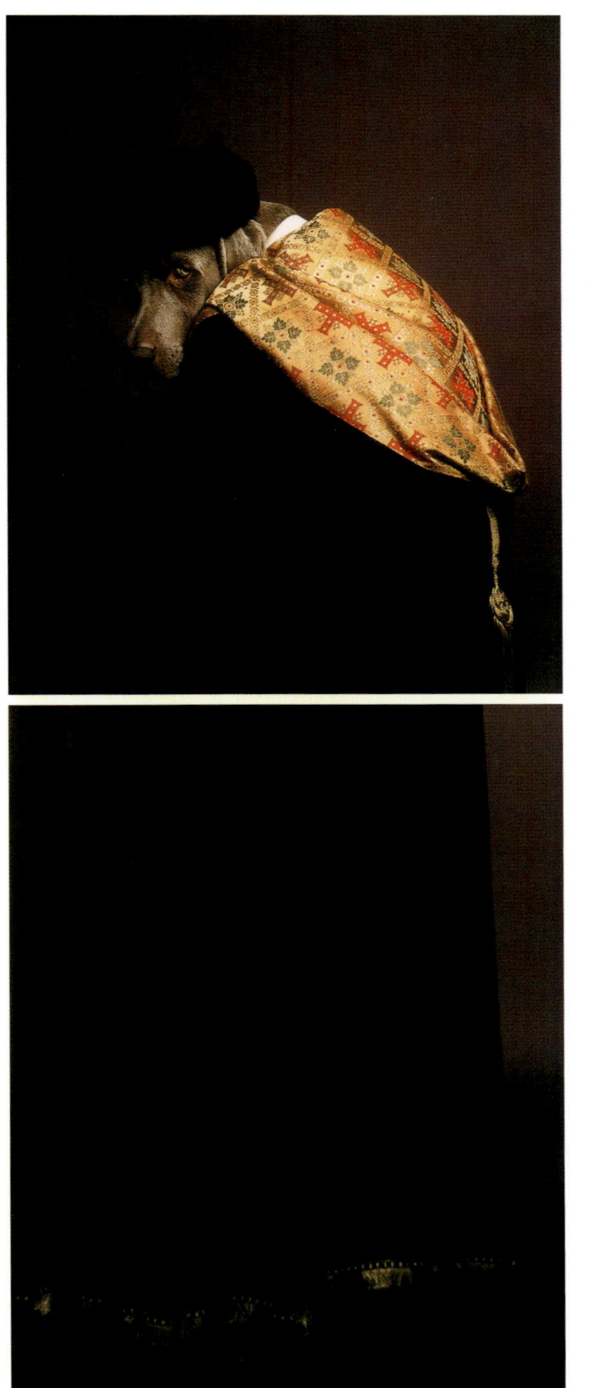

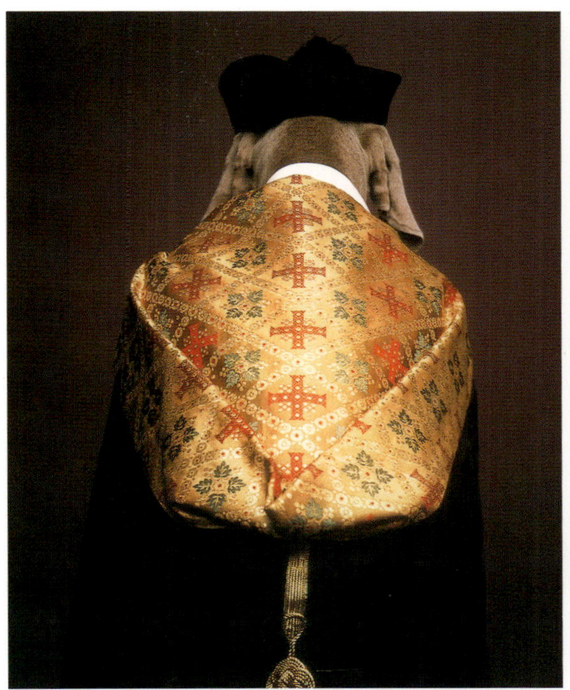

Mephisto, 1996

There were four males in Batty's litter in May 1995: Chip, Chester, Hector, and Dr. Greene.

I knew right away that Chip was the pup I would keep. In July, we packed up the puppies and moved to Maine for the summer as usual. One day the pen containing the puppies blew over and they escaped into the woods, causing us quite a fright. All except for Chip, who remained on the porch next to the pen. He knew too.

As a puppy Chip was astonishingly easy to work with. He was three days old as the sleeping infant in *Mother and Son*. When he was old enough to open his eyes, he gazed at me with stealthy non-anticipation. At the rascally age of six months, when most puppies are at their most fidgety, I called on him to perform with his mother Batty and uncle Chundo in a series of poster-like pictures for the Houston Grand Opera, and he donned hats, wigs, and costumes of great heft and bulk with sublime obliviousness. Chip maintained his calm personality throughout, maturing into a gentle, masculine, self-assured adult, combining Fay's sculptural physique with Batty's dreamy serenity.

Chip's personality led to the evolution of a new character in my anthropomorphic series: the adolescent boy-wanderer. When dressed in his signature maroon shirt with yellow polka dots, sporty jacket, and green cords, Chip looks quite like a young lad on a journey. Unlike Man Ray and Chundo before him, Chip has a camera presence that is eternally youthful. He is a particularly good foil for Batty's, Crooky's, and Chundo's adult characters.

With an expanded cast of four weimaraners now sitting up and begging for roles, my interest in telling stories was piqued. For this work, much of which needed to be shot on location, the 20x24 was too slow and so I returned to the smaller, quicker 120mm format of the Hasselblad. Meanwhile, the direction I should take was becoming clearer to me—in the future, when I went to the studio, I would bring the dogs, leave the clothes.

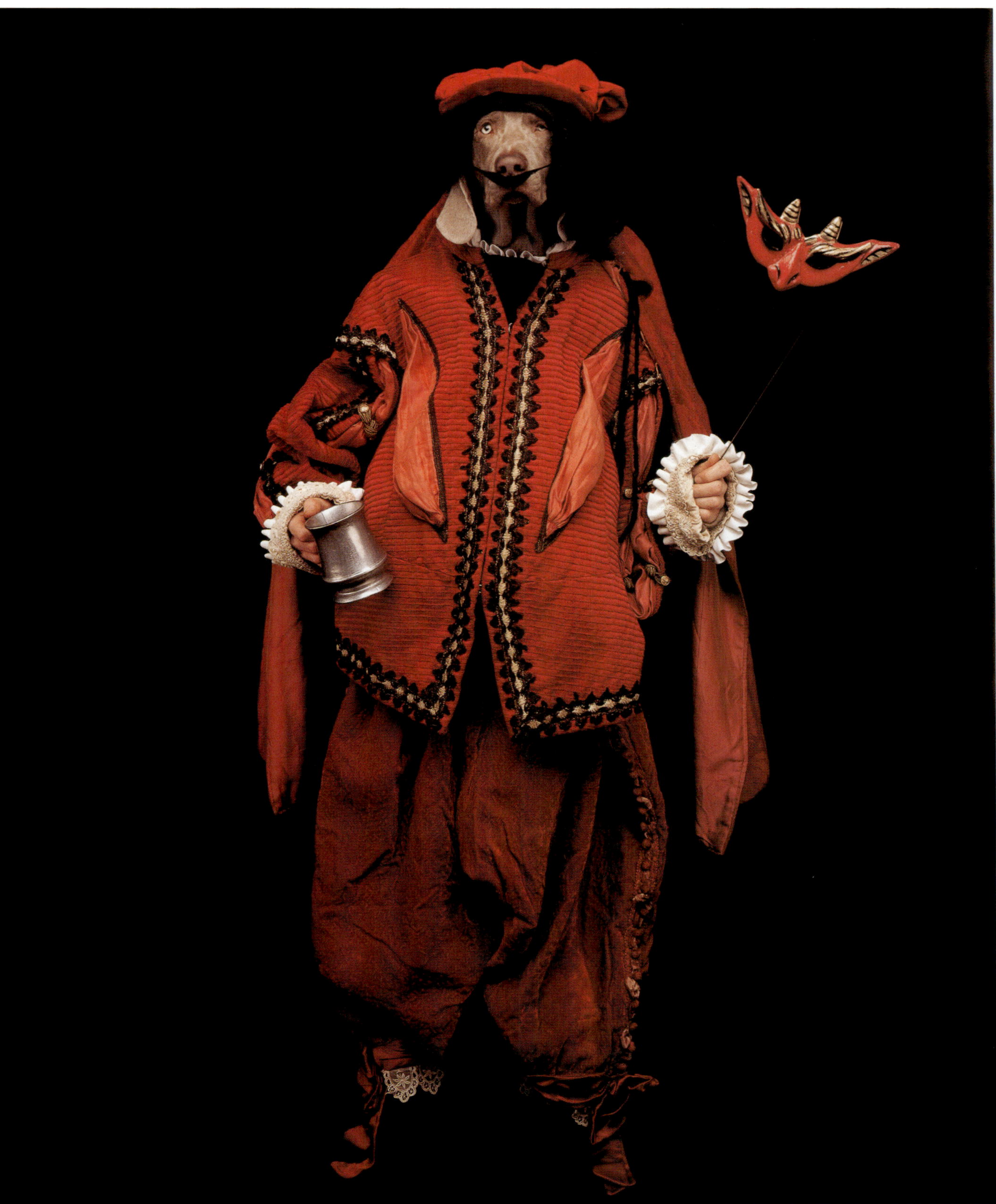

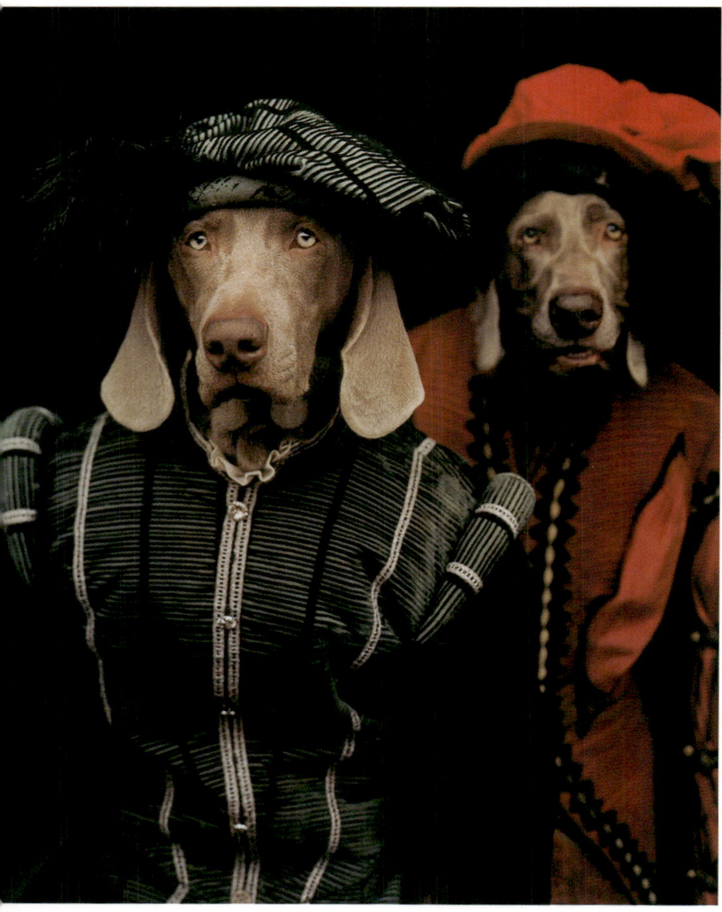

Faust, 1996

Left: ***The Magic Flute,*** **1996**
Right: ***Tosca,*** **1996**

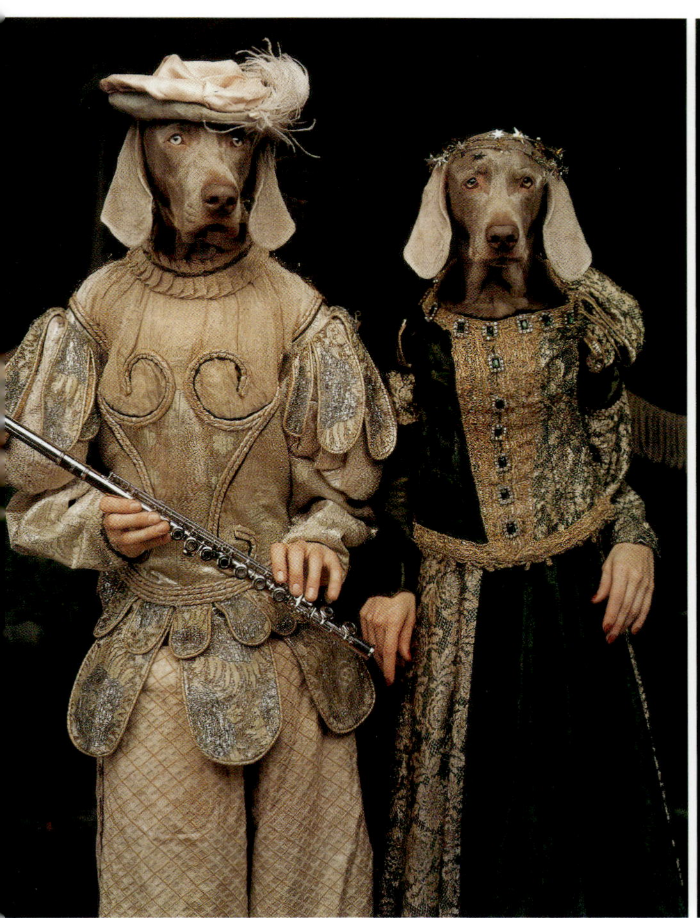

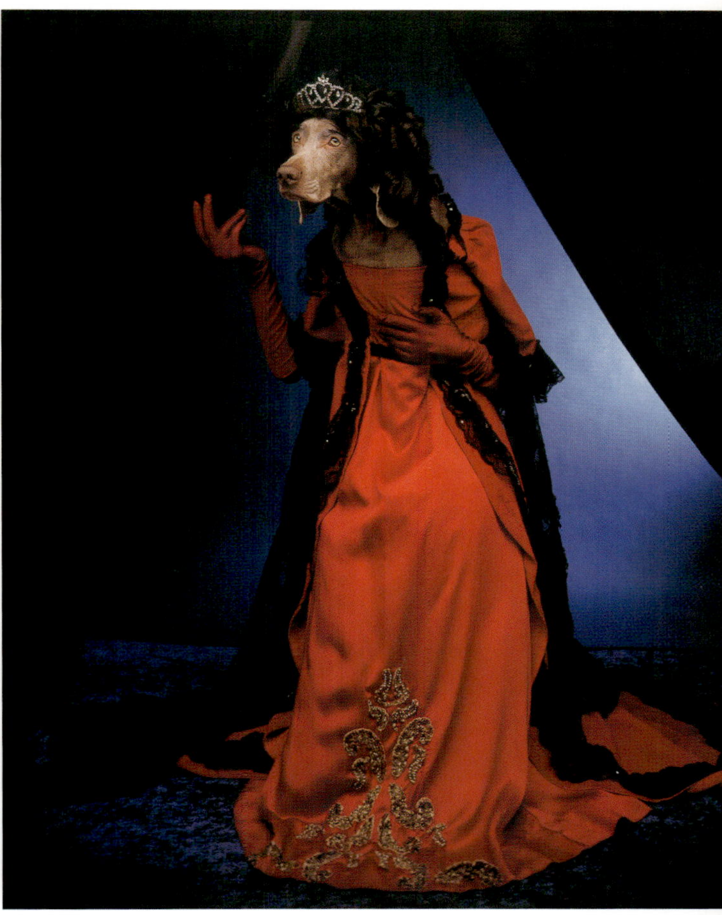

Below: *Topographical*, 1998
Opposite: *Pat*, 1997

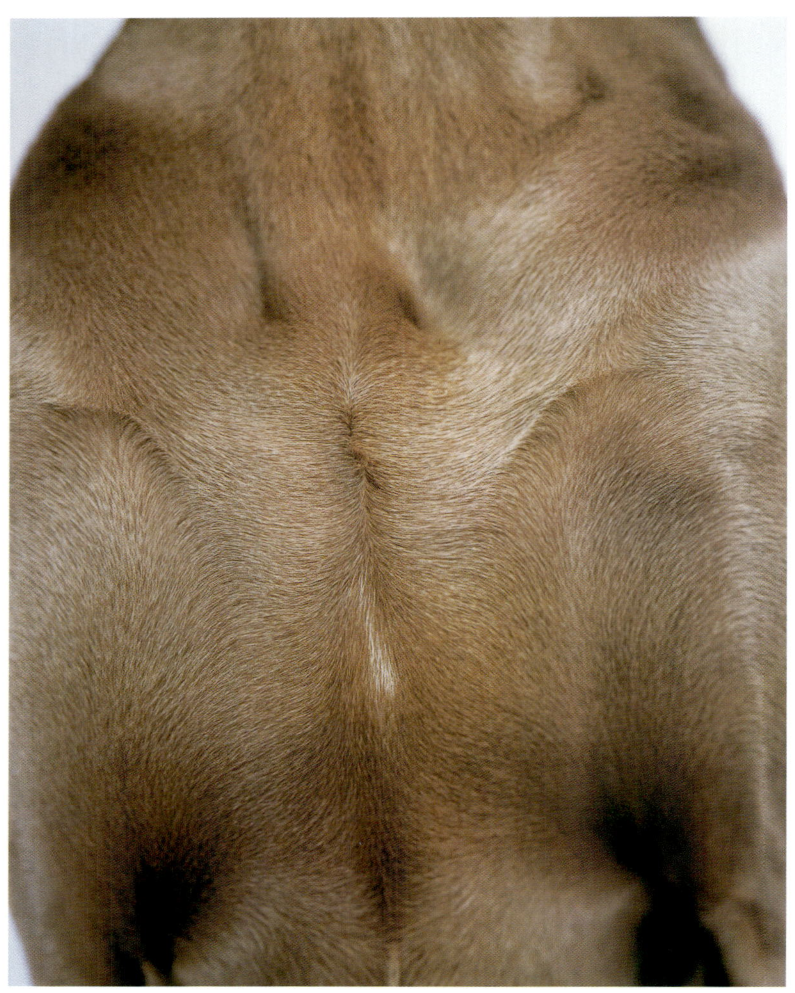

There was something very compelling about Chip's physical attributes:

the spiraling cowlick at the base of his head; the sensuous twirl at the back of his ears; his shapely head, neck, and dynamic torso. I began to look deeply into the fur, bringing the lens closer and closer to him as I had with Man Ray at the end of his life. Chip was new, and his surface planes radiated warmth and abstract beauty. Compared to Chip, the other dogs seemed worn.

He is the dog with the beautiful head.

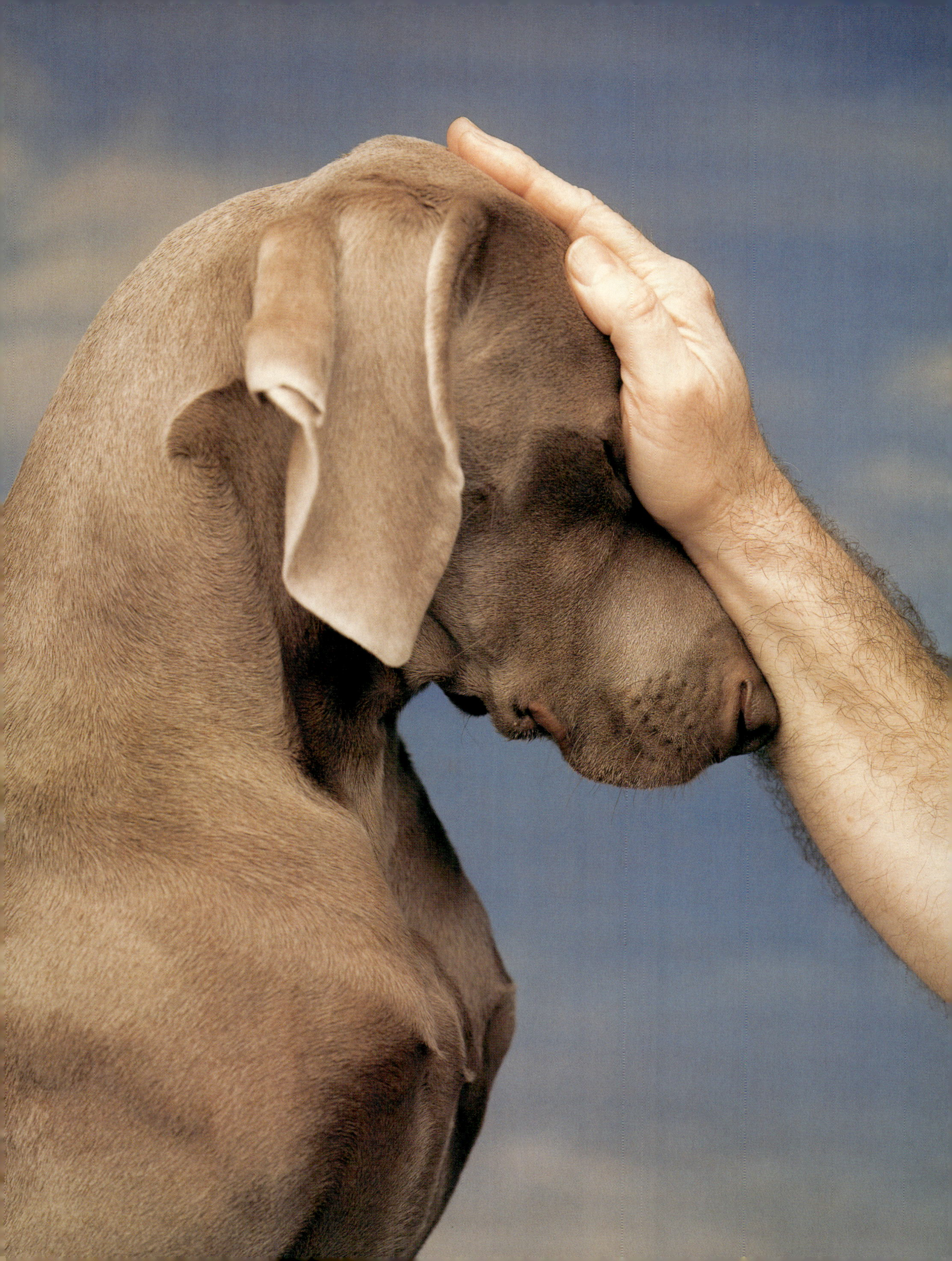

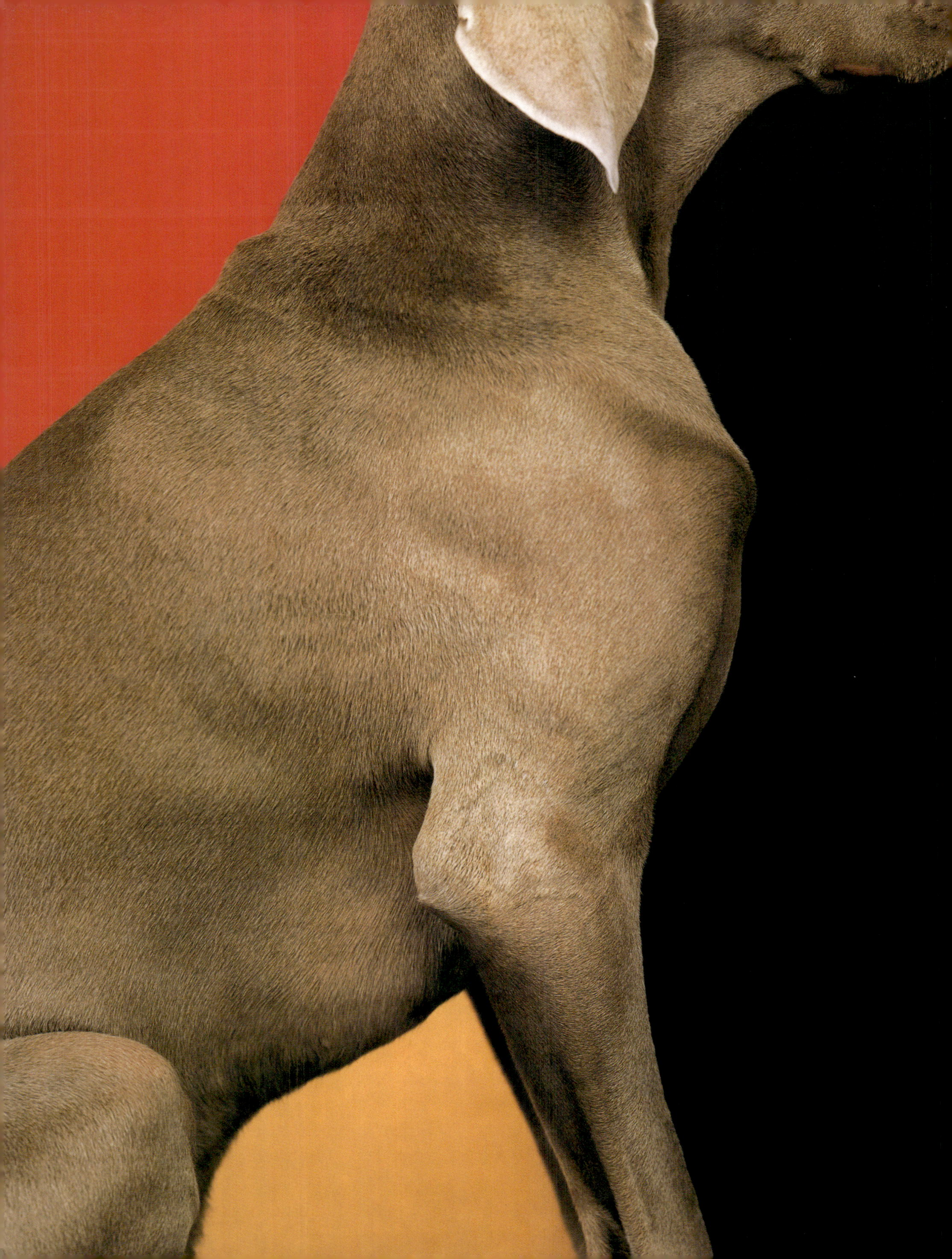

Opposite: ***Léger,* 1998**
Below: ***Red Wine,* 1998**

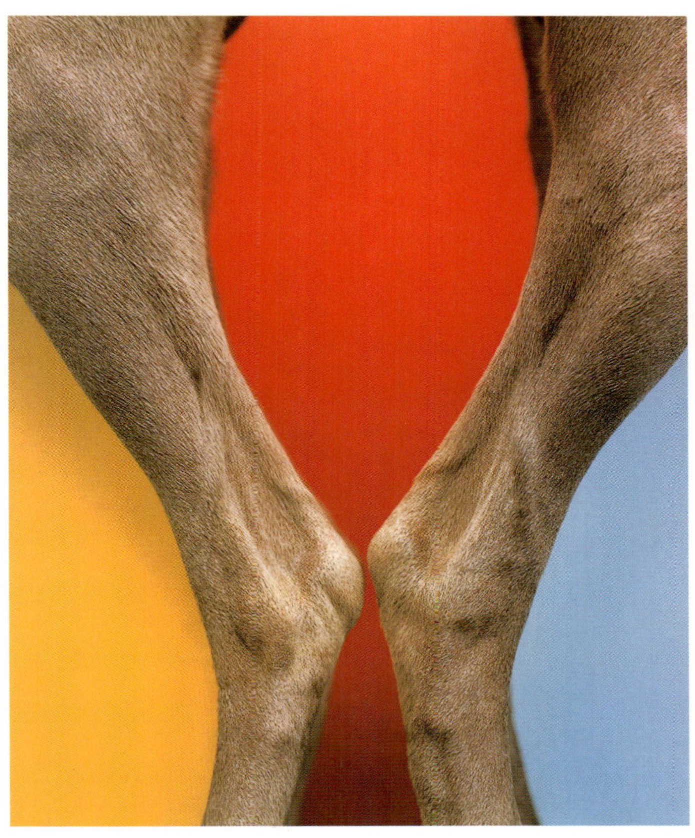

The simplest works can be the most maddeningly difficult to pull off.

Those that I sometimes think of as the game boards are at the top of my failure rate list. These formally driven works use the dogs in combination with colored panels. The panels were made by attaching colored set paper to Foamcore, then cutting it to fit in the negative areas formed by the dogs.

Léger stands out in my mind as being particularly difficult, but in the end most rewarding. I positioned Chip on the high table and composed the frame. Then I cut out three color panels, which were held in place by three assistants. This is a ridiculously crazy way to achieve the effect I wanted, but at the time I couldn't think of a better one. Everything has to be perfectly in place and stay there. If the dog moves a fraction of an inch, it's a no. The work is like a stained-glass window, where the dog acts as lead framework for panes of color. It also reminds me of a game board like Parcheesi, and of modern art—Léger perhaps.

As I was making these formal pieces, a part of me was aware that I was making Art, as distinct from the costumed characters that had begun to fill my children's books. They had wall power. Art audiences, it was hinted to me, were becoming confused and alienated by my less *pure* art, which was becoming well known—too well known—through postcards, T-shirts, calendars, and books. I predicted that these works, with their abstract orientation, would be taken more favorably by my first and in some ways most important audience, the art world. I was full of enthusiasm, with maybe just a touch of cynicism.

Front to Red Yellow, 1998

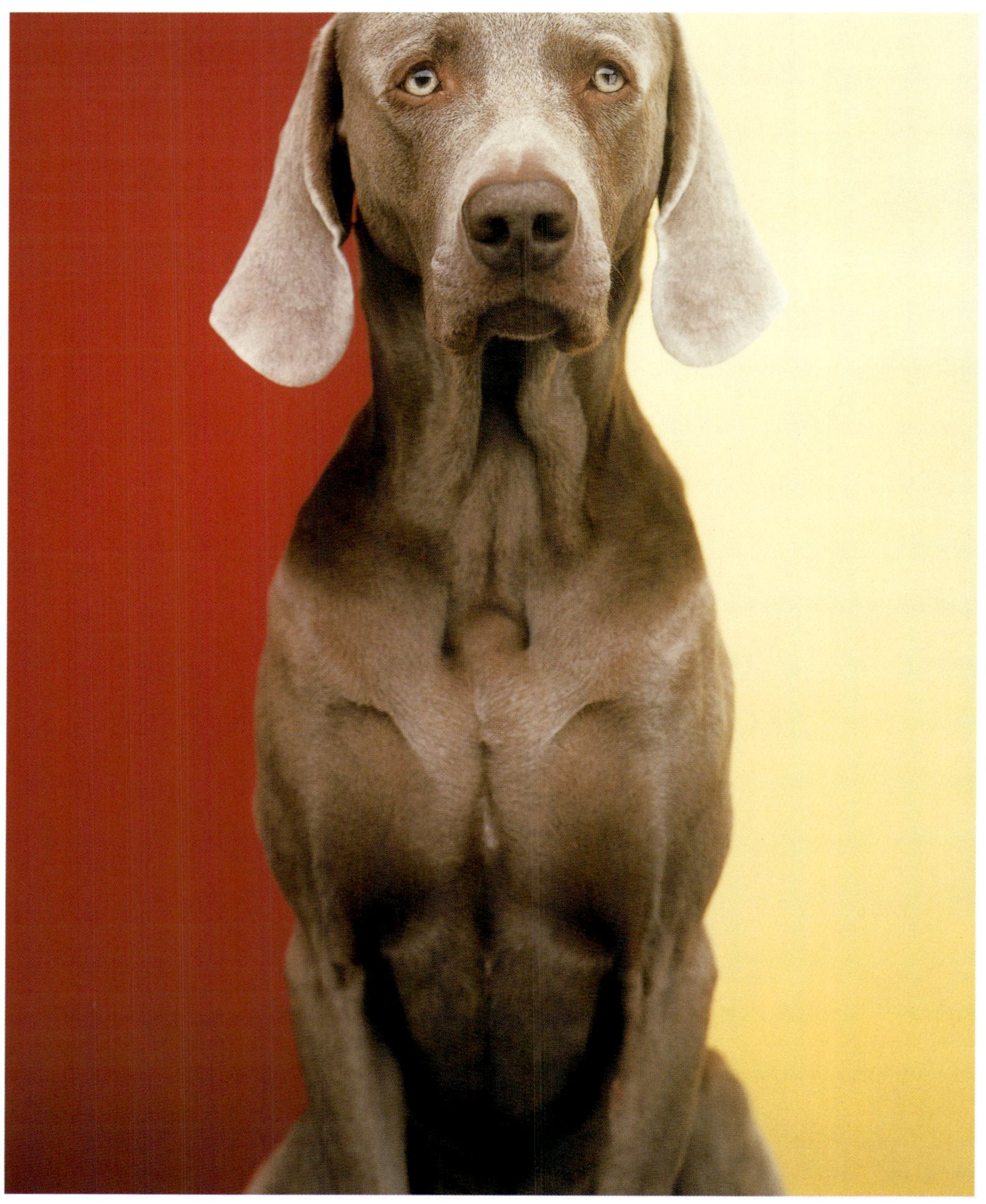

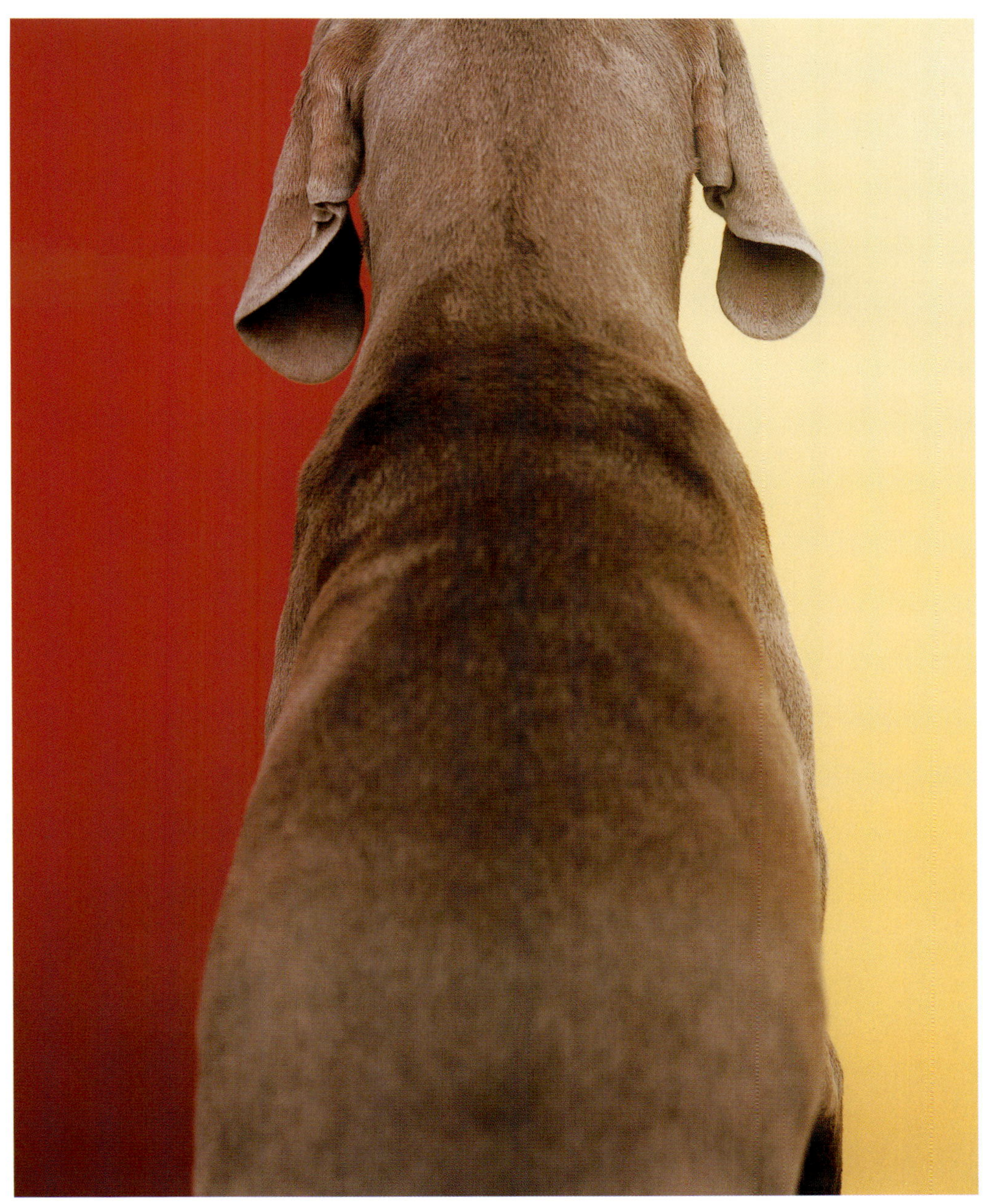

Back to Red Yellow, 1998

Munsel Abridged, 1998

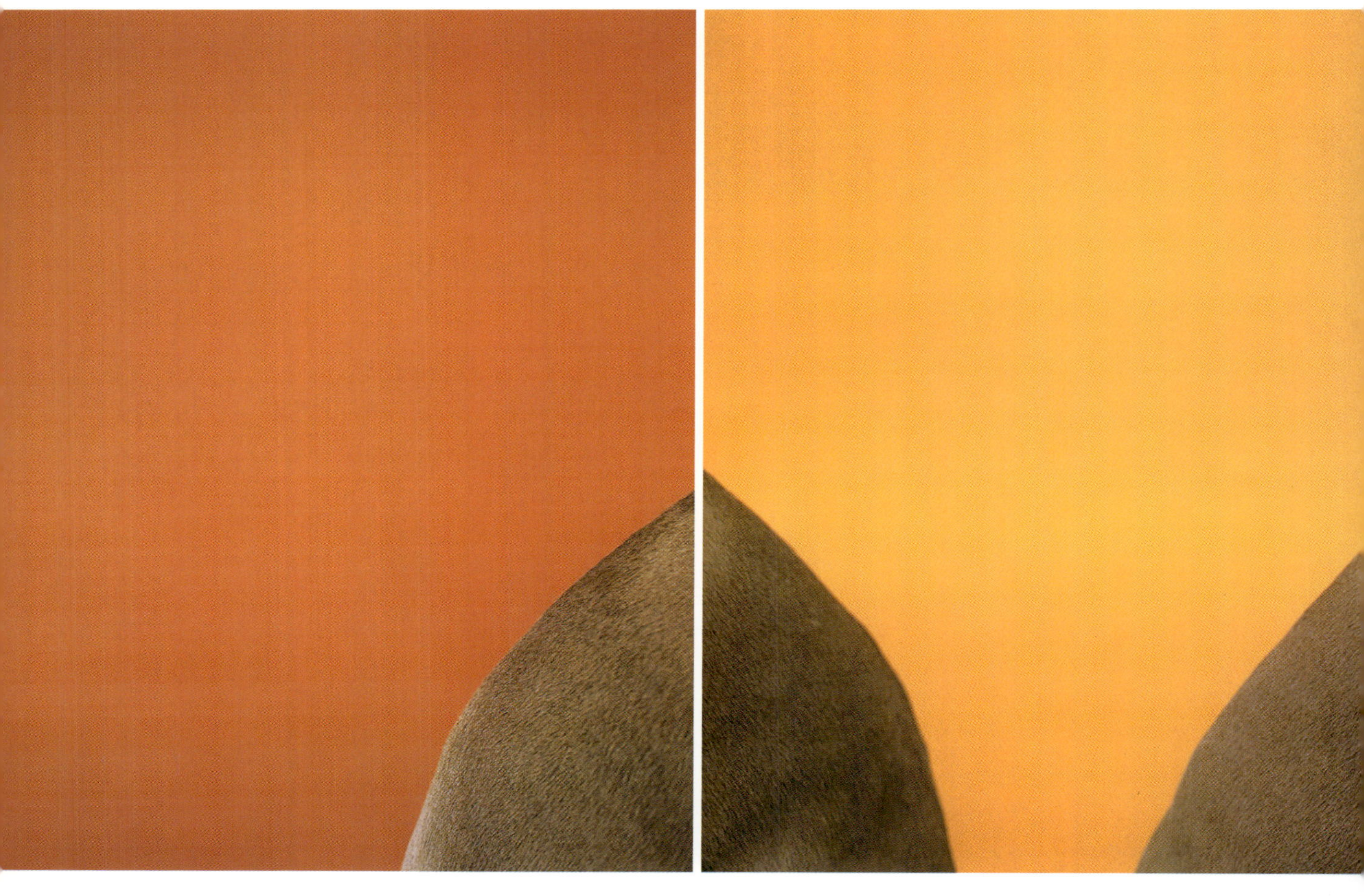

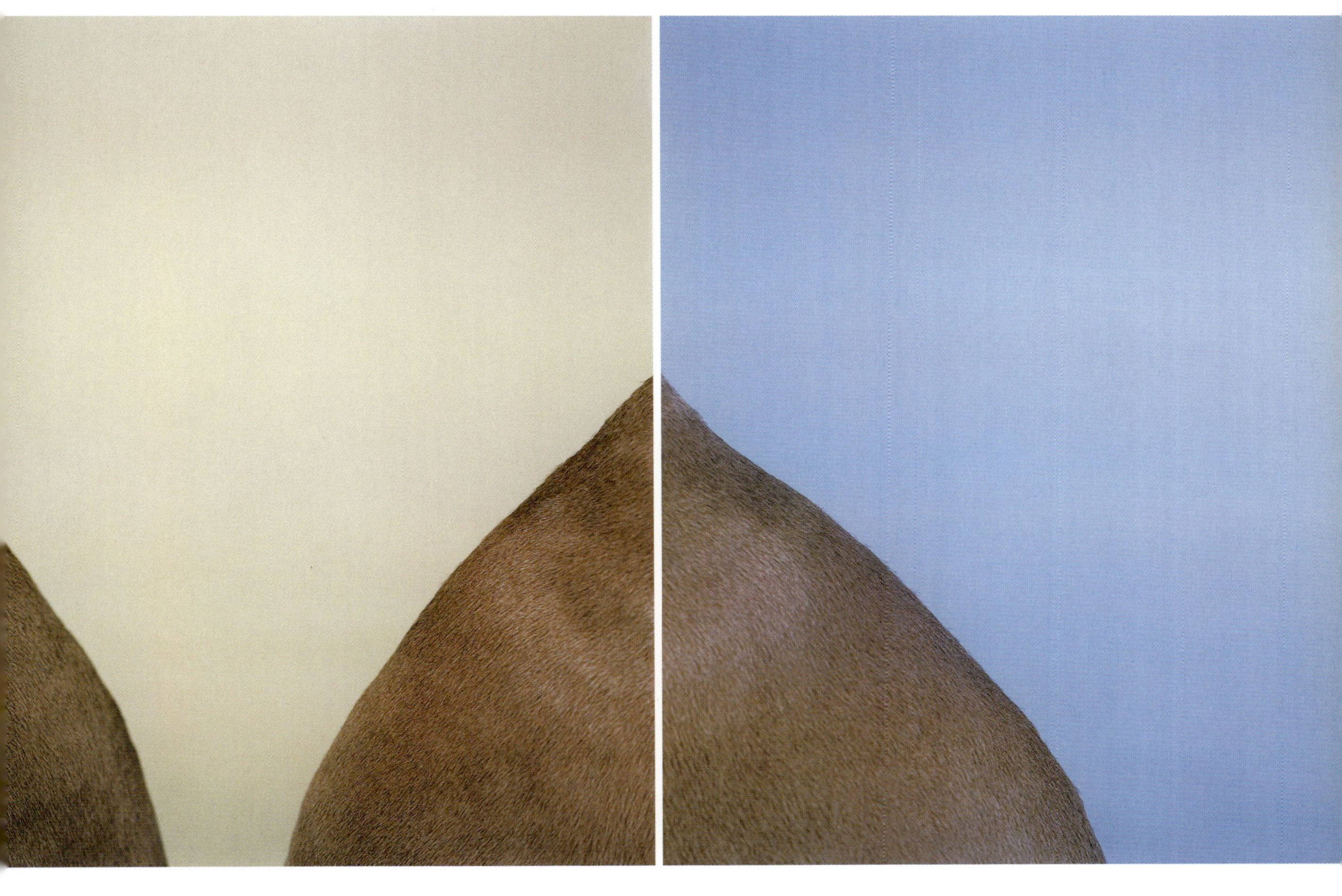

Boulder, 1997

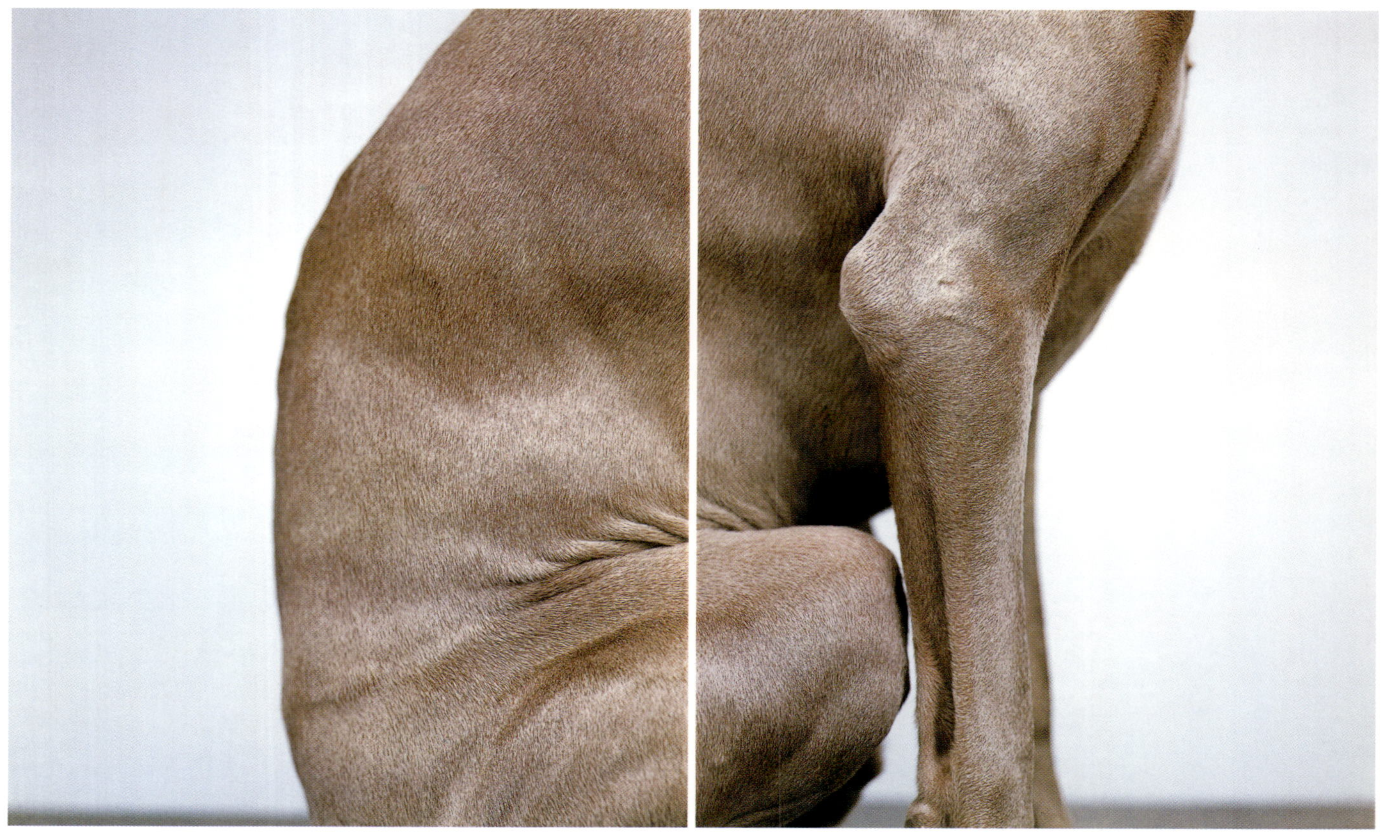

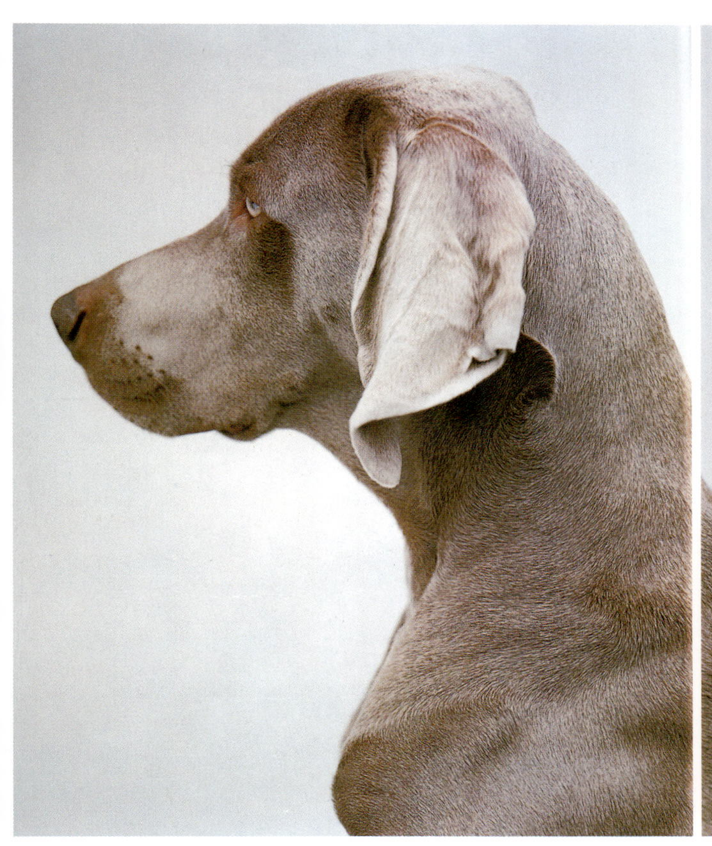

Swirl, 1997

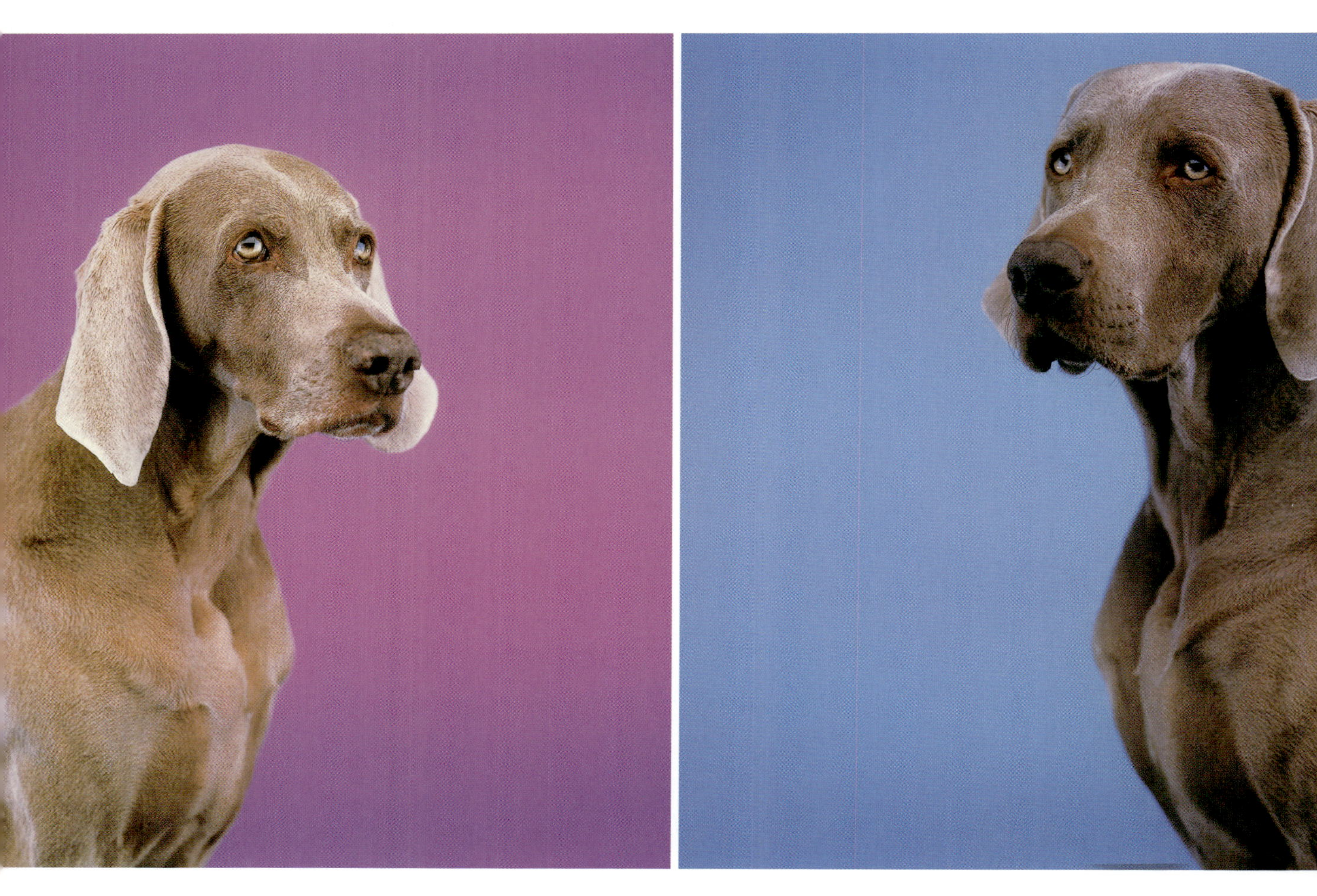

Interior Colors, 1998

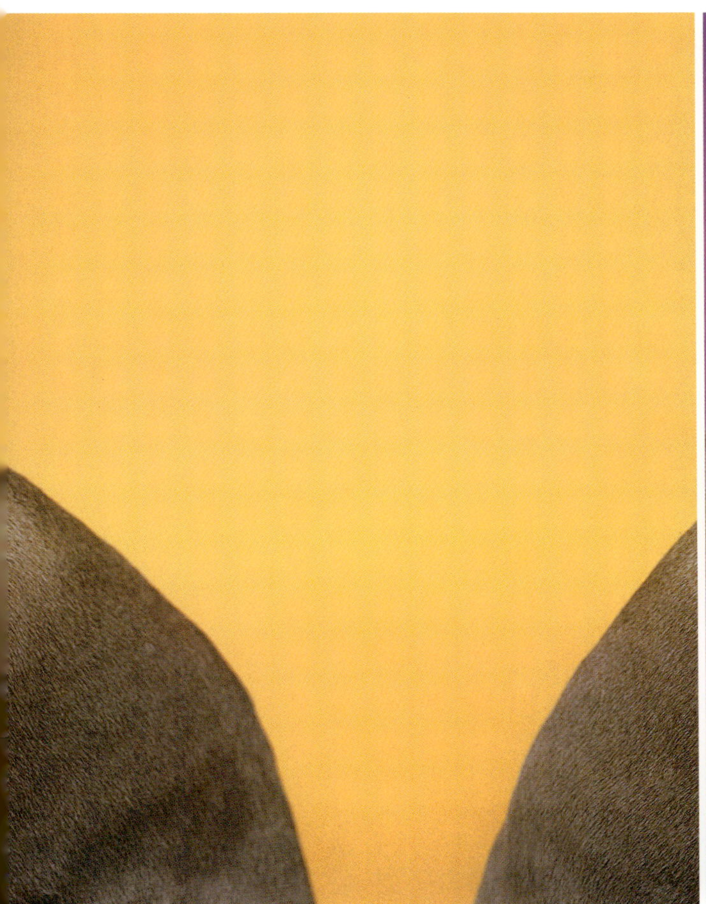

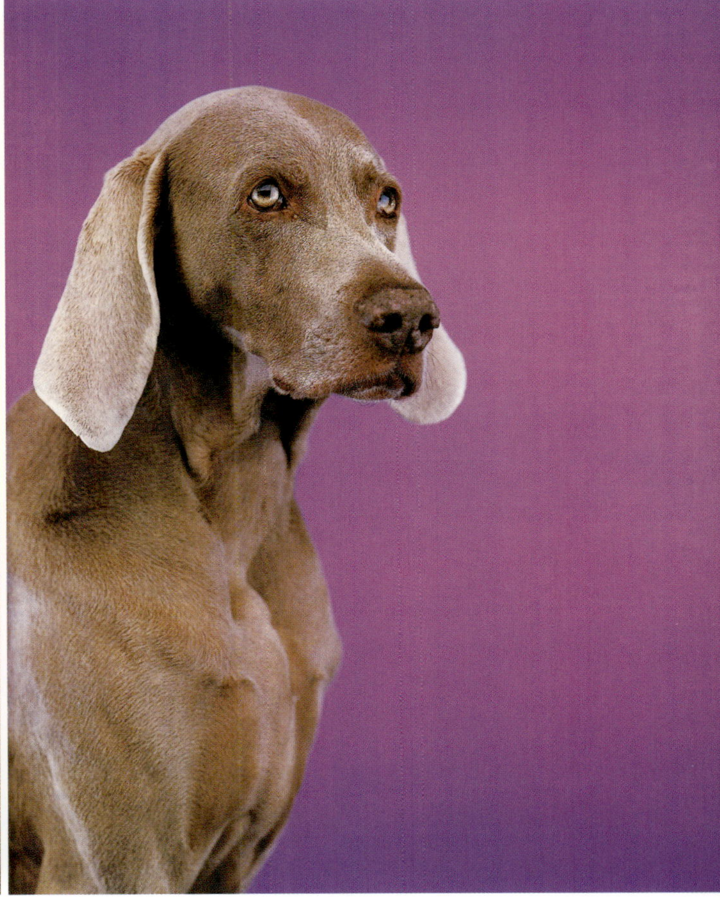

Head to Toe, 1998

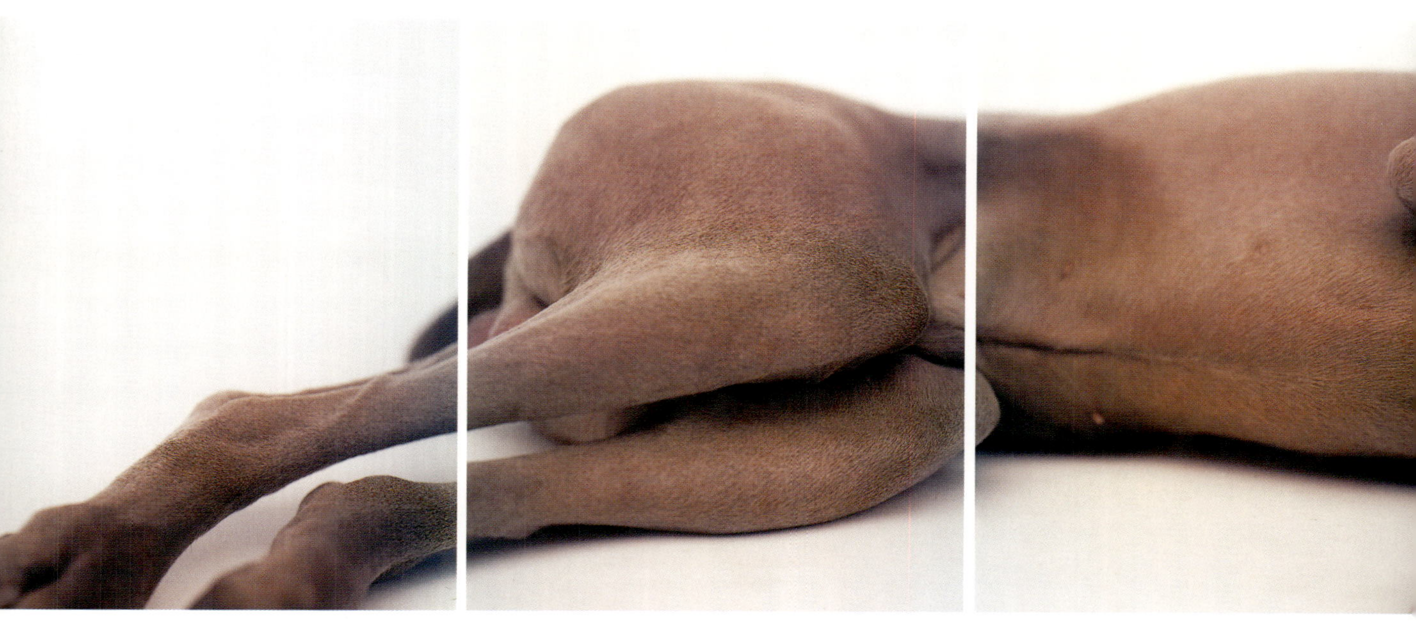

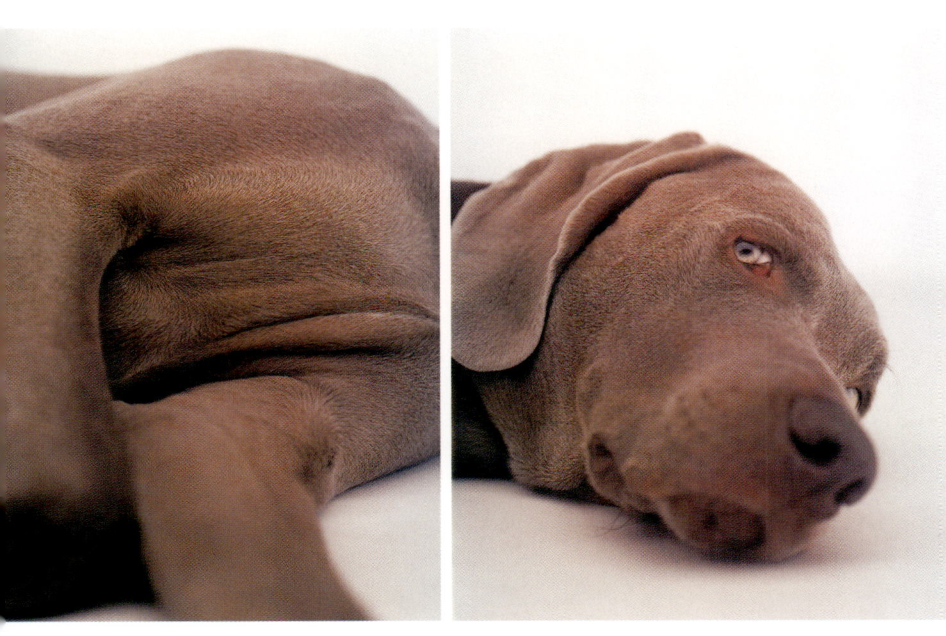

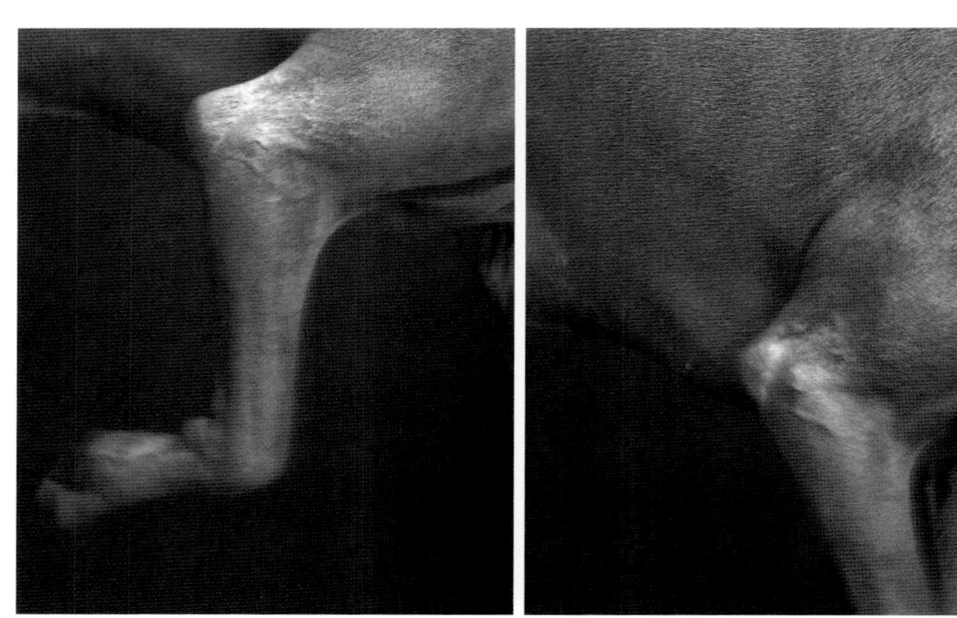

Stop Action, 1999
Overleaf: ***Headers***, 1998

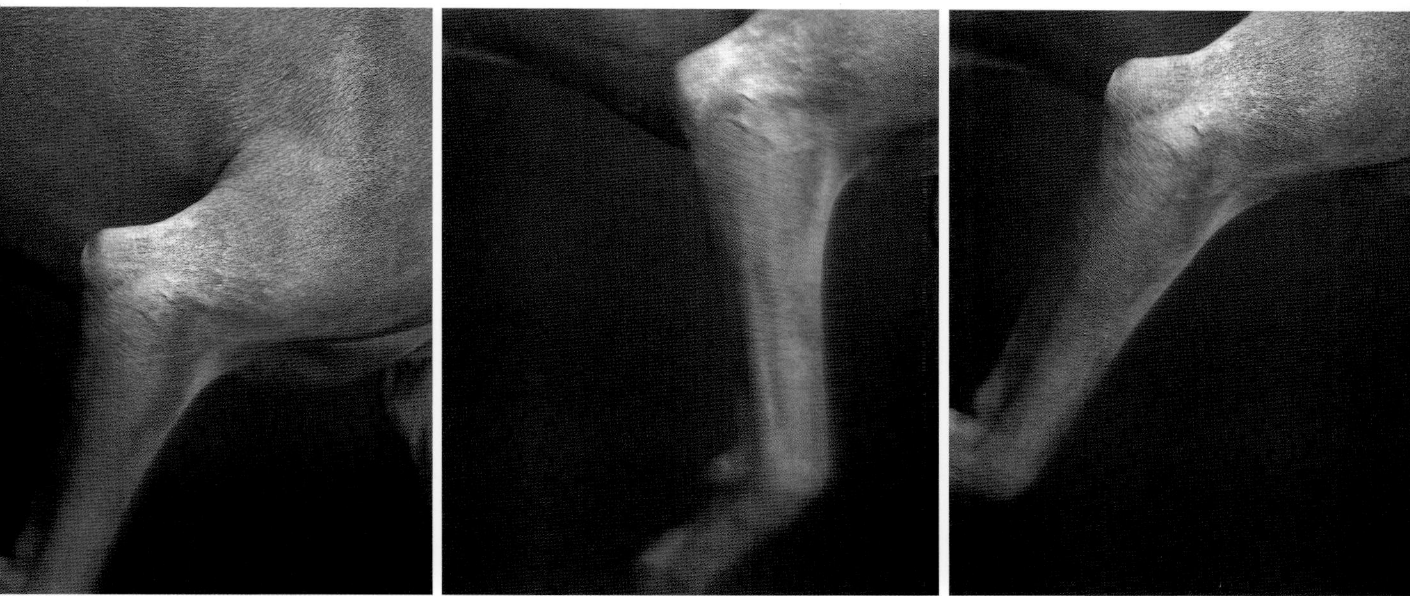

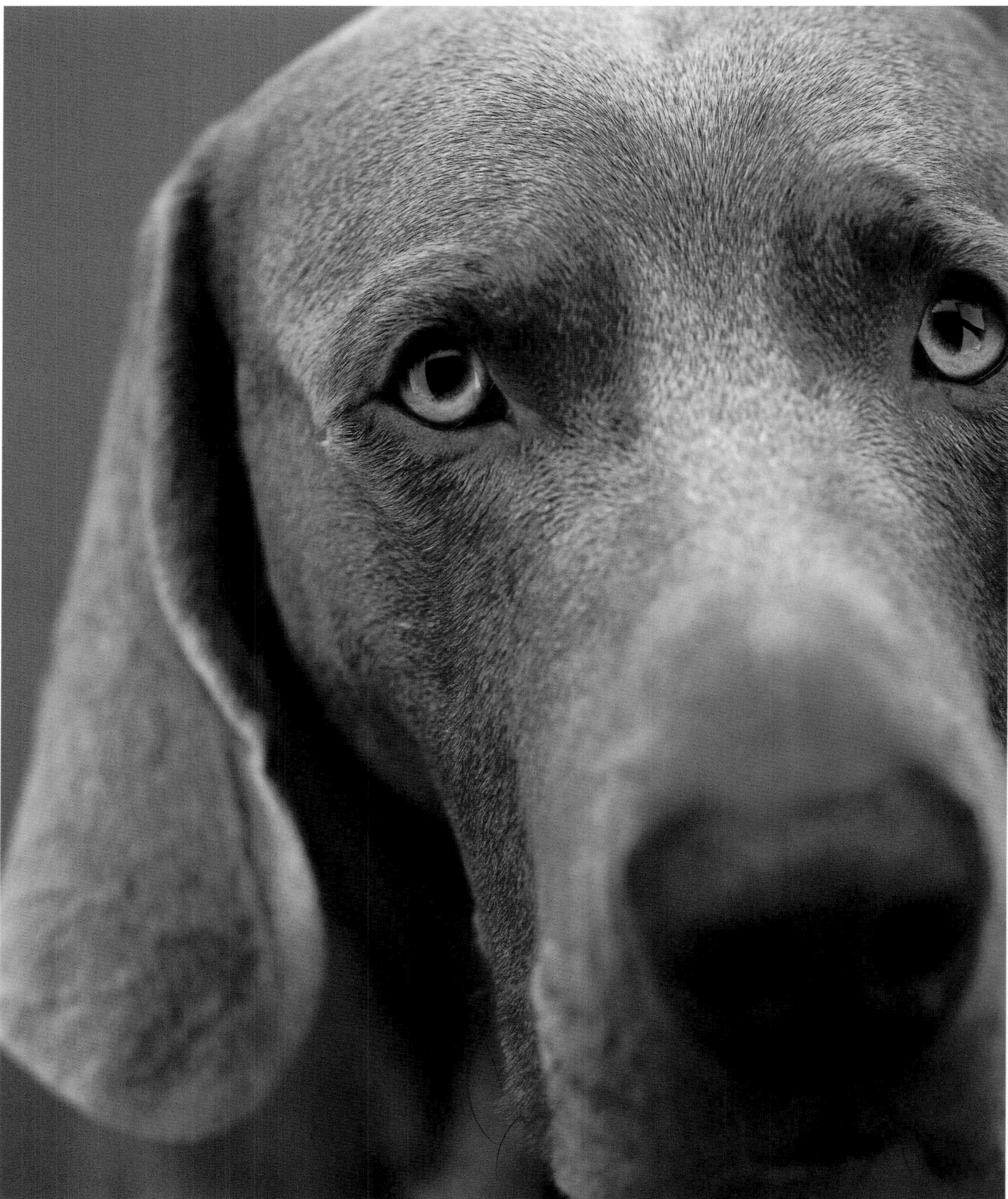

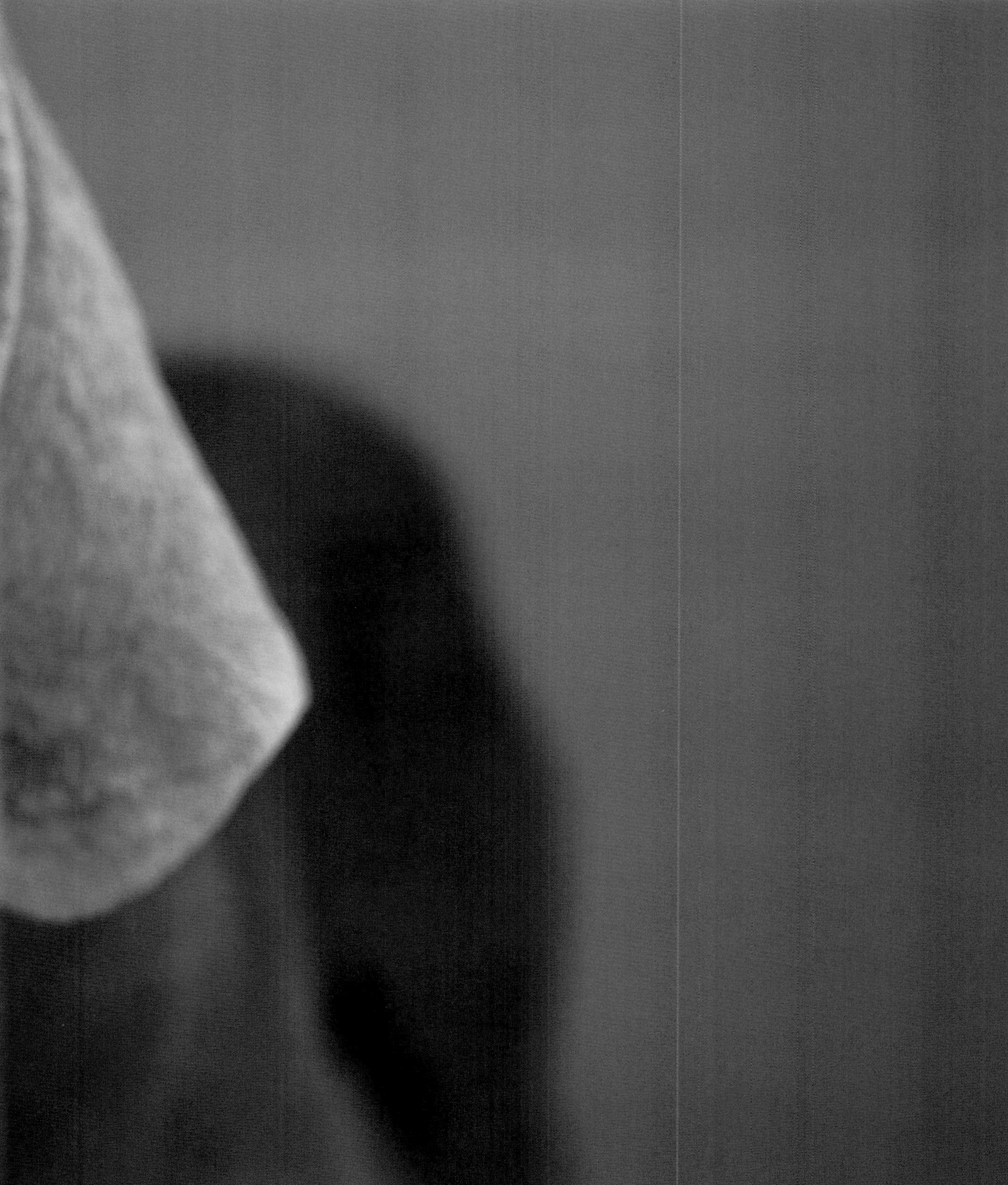

Gatefold: ***Forest,* 1998**

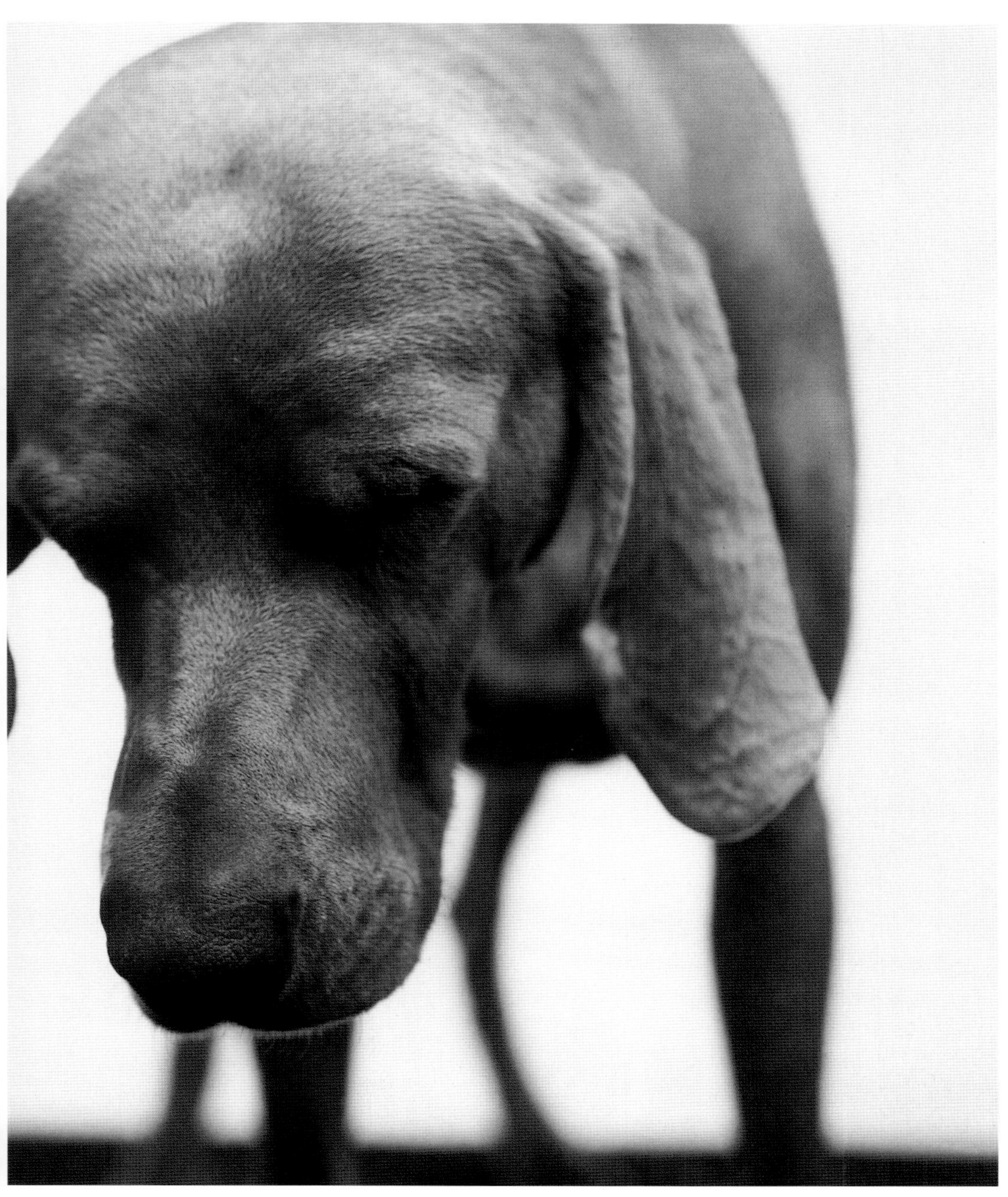

Crowd Scene, 1999

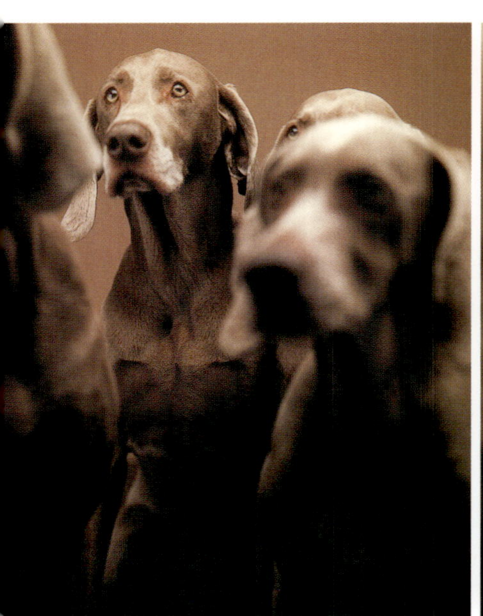
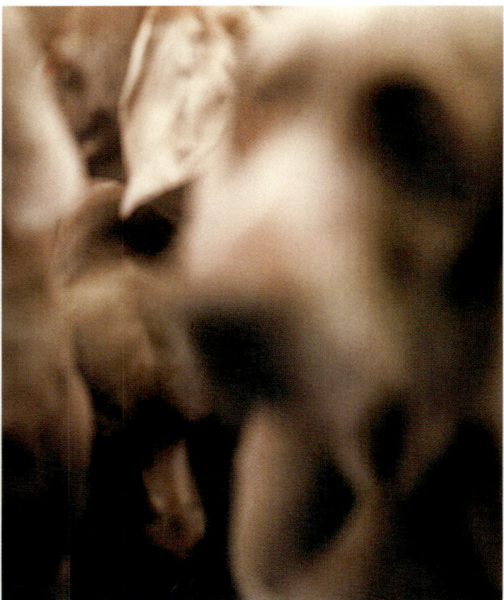
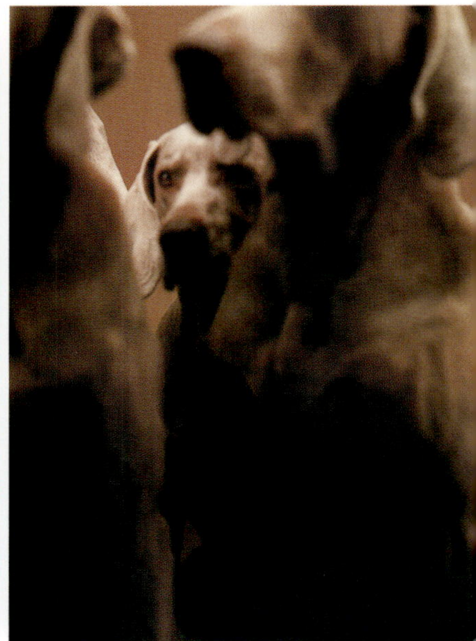

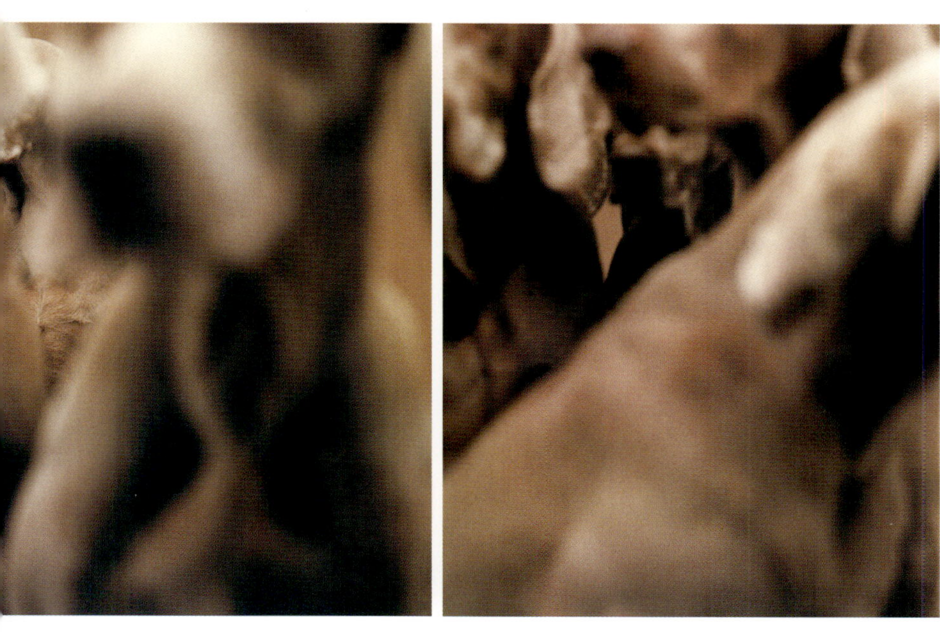

Paolo and Francesca, 2001

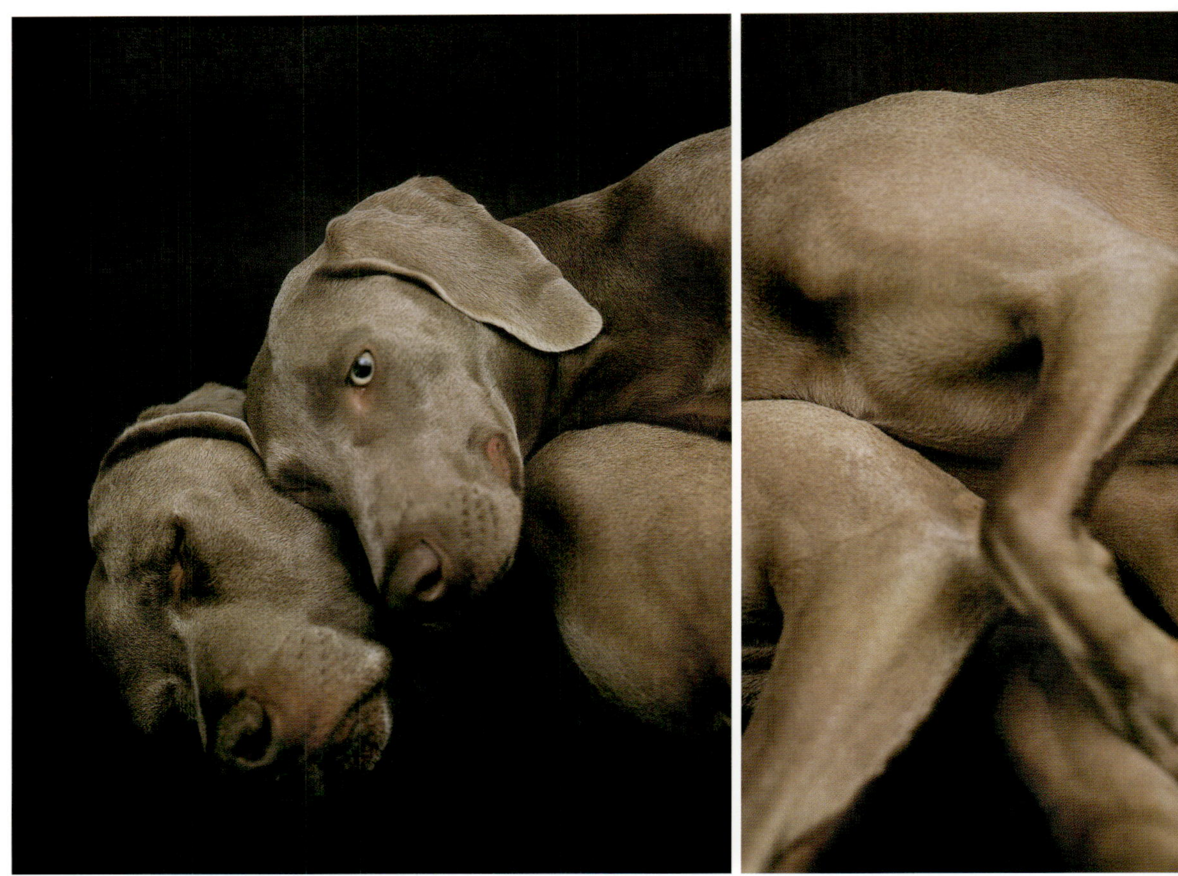

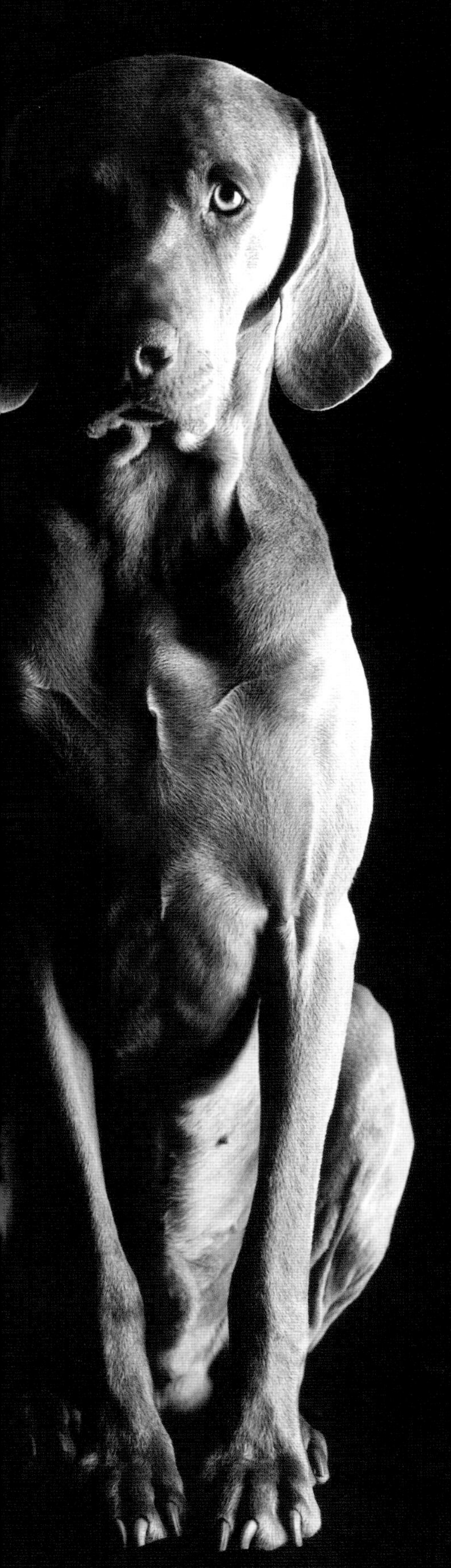

Modern Psychology, 2000

Time Garden, 2001

Not surprisingly, having four dogs in the studio brought new pictorial possibilities to the foreground.

Up close, standing, sitting, or lying naked before the eye of the big camera, all body parts become landscape, a forest of trees, a topography of hills and valleys, earth and boulders in a shoreline of endless interconnectivity. Bodies overlap, collide, recline, extend, appear as shadows, reflections, negative shapes.

Recalling that in the early Seventies, I had made a multiple panel work using two black Labs and Man Ray, where each dog connects to each other dog until permutationally complete, I began to re-explore the multiple panel work with renewed enthusiasm. Three new shades of gray were added to my palette. Four slumbering dogs grouped together on a long table four or five feet high, under the warmth of the Cumulite, became a vacation land.

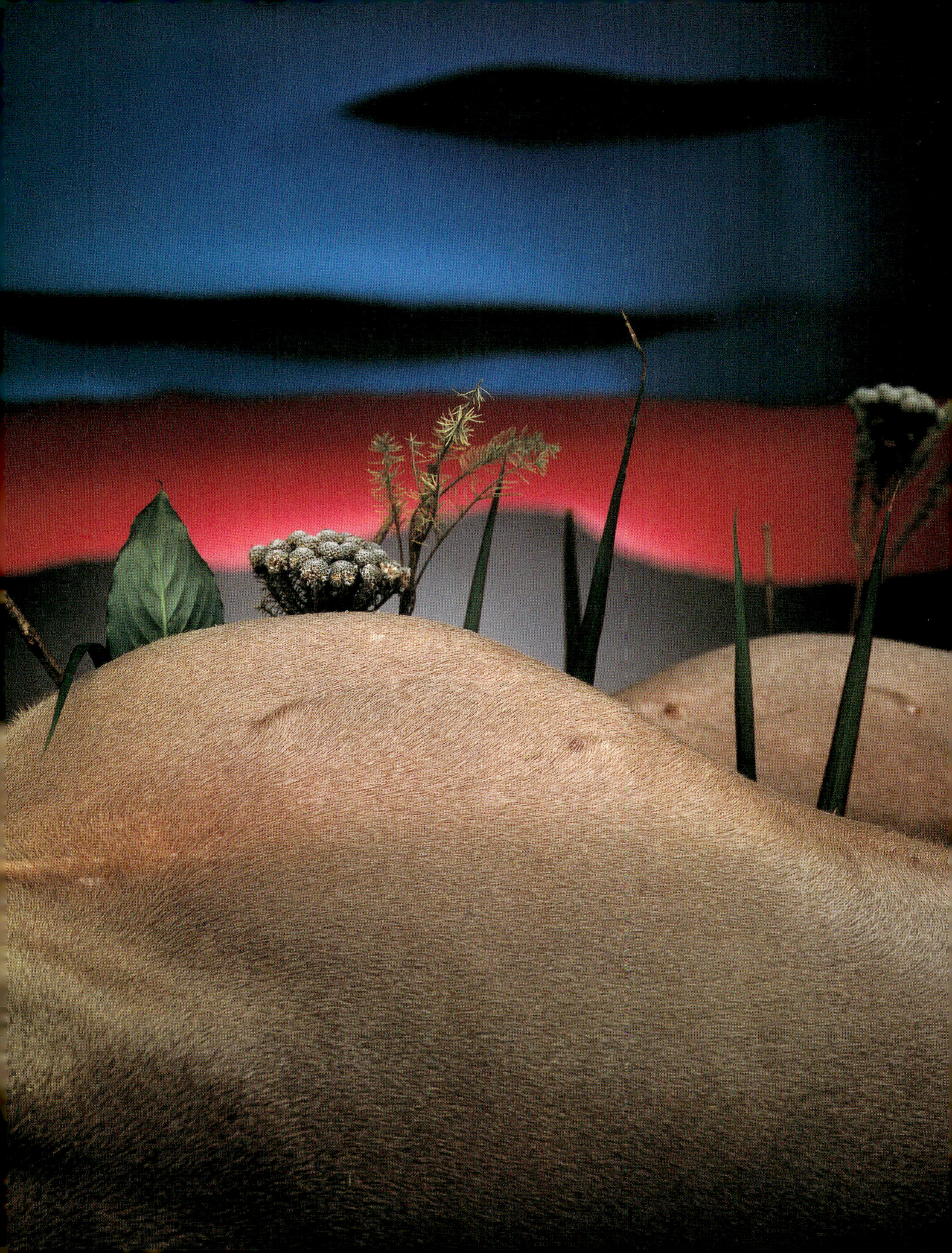

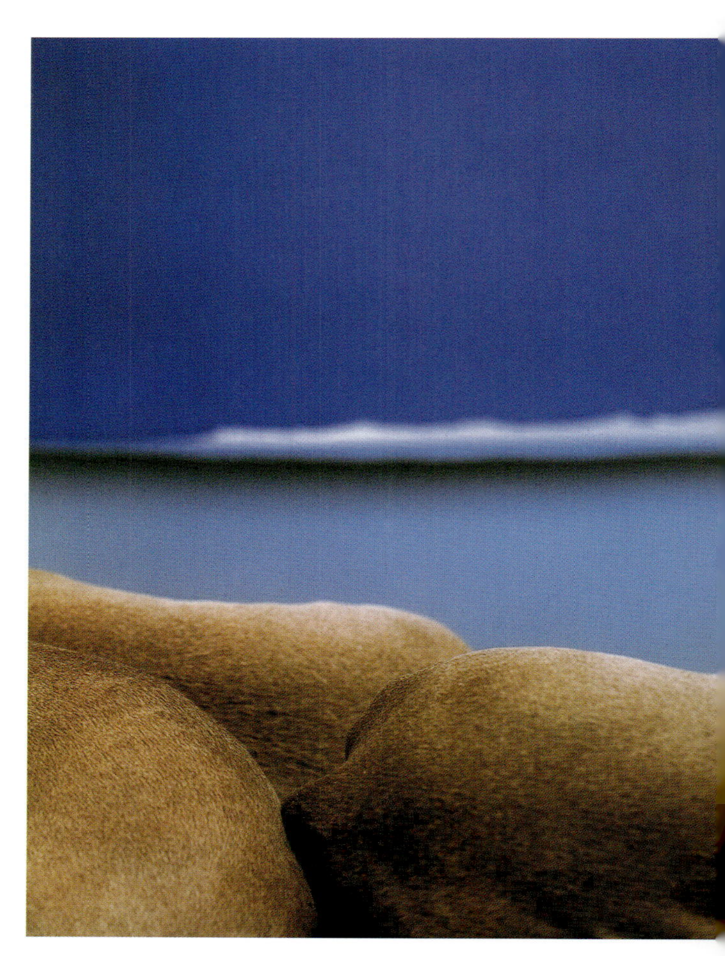

Breakers, 1999

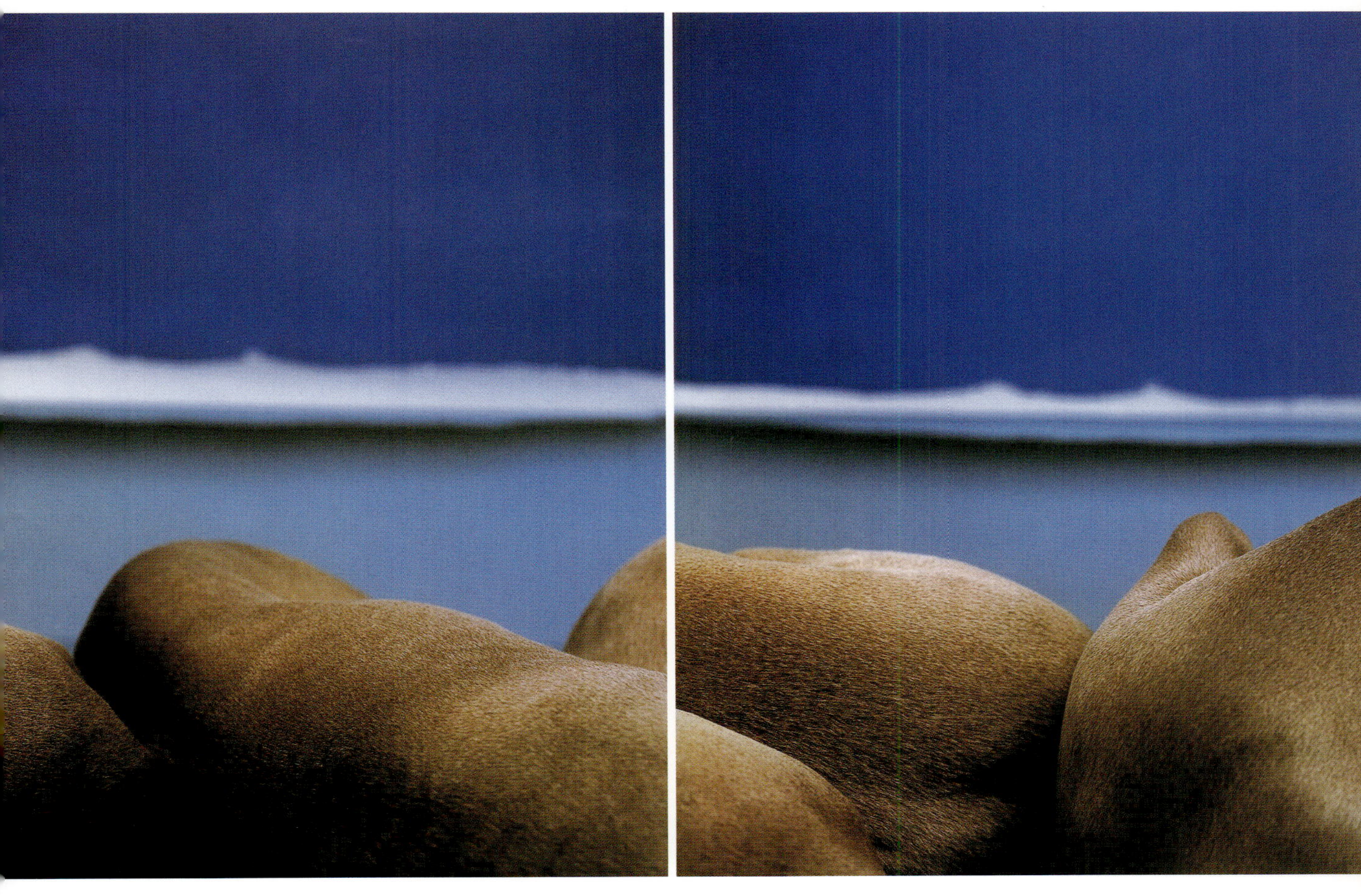

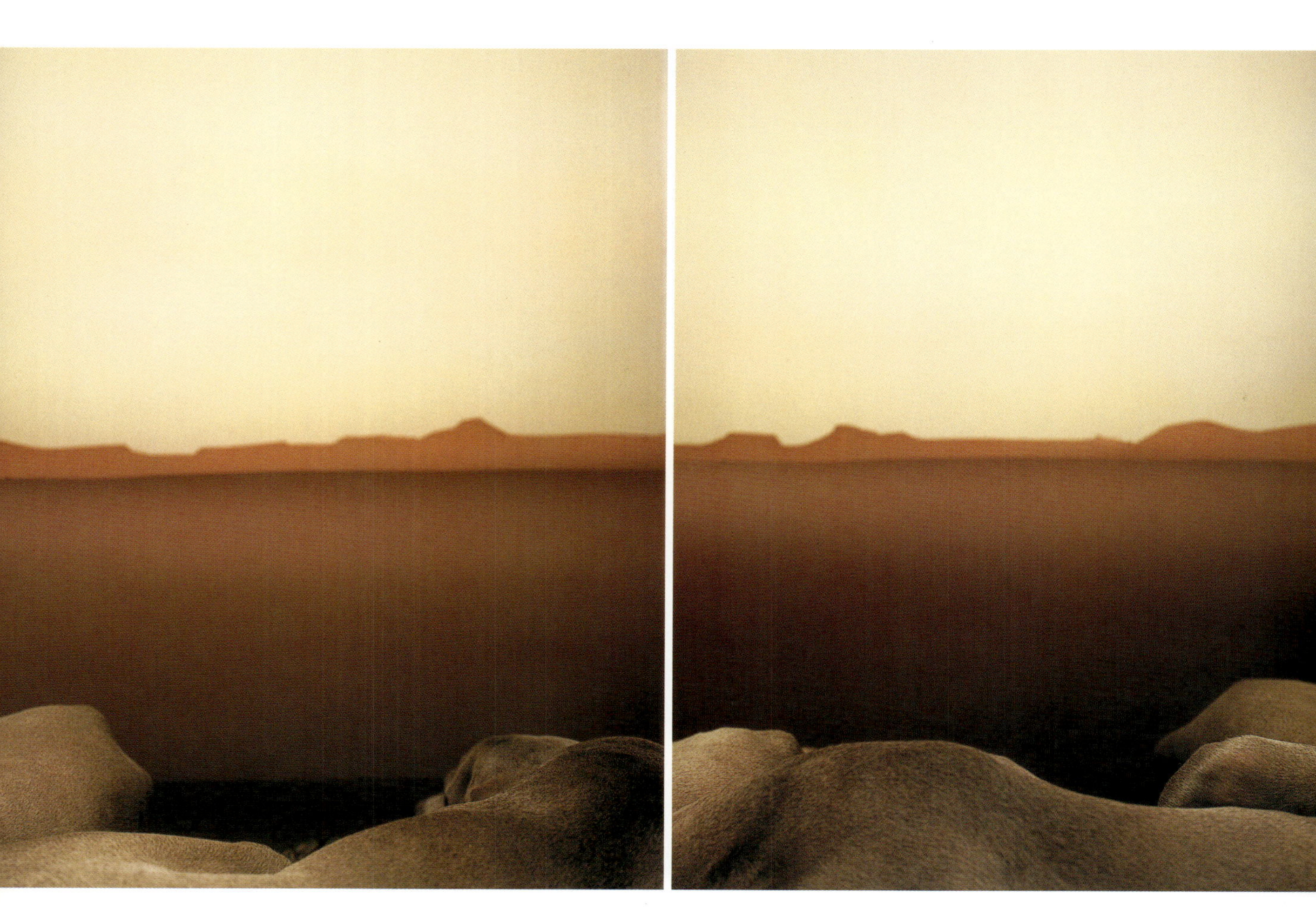

Out West, 2000

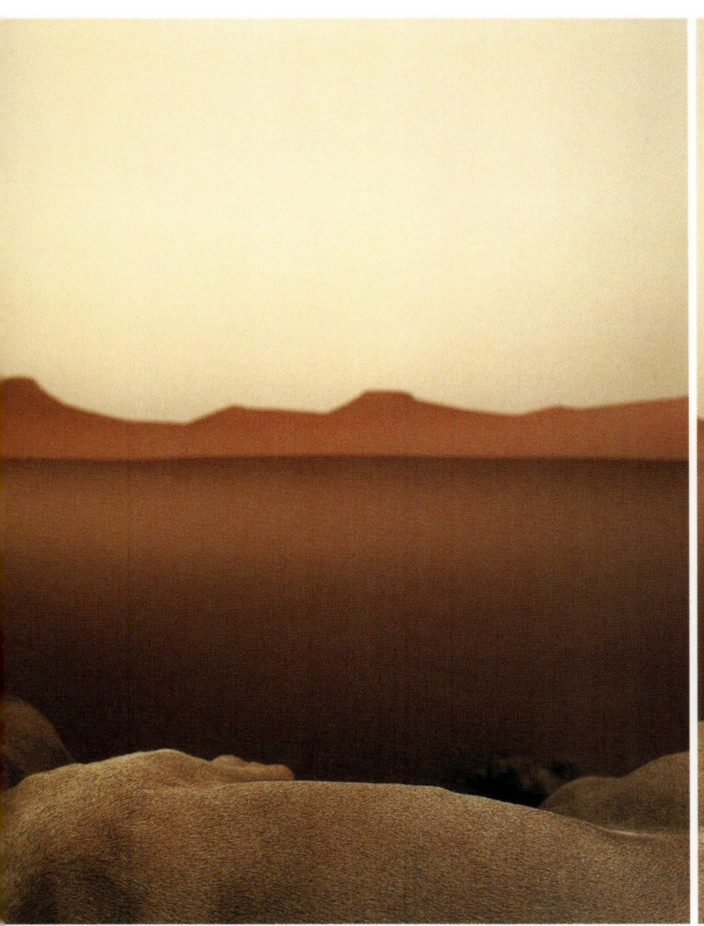

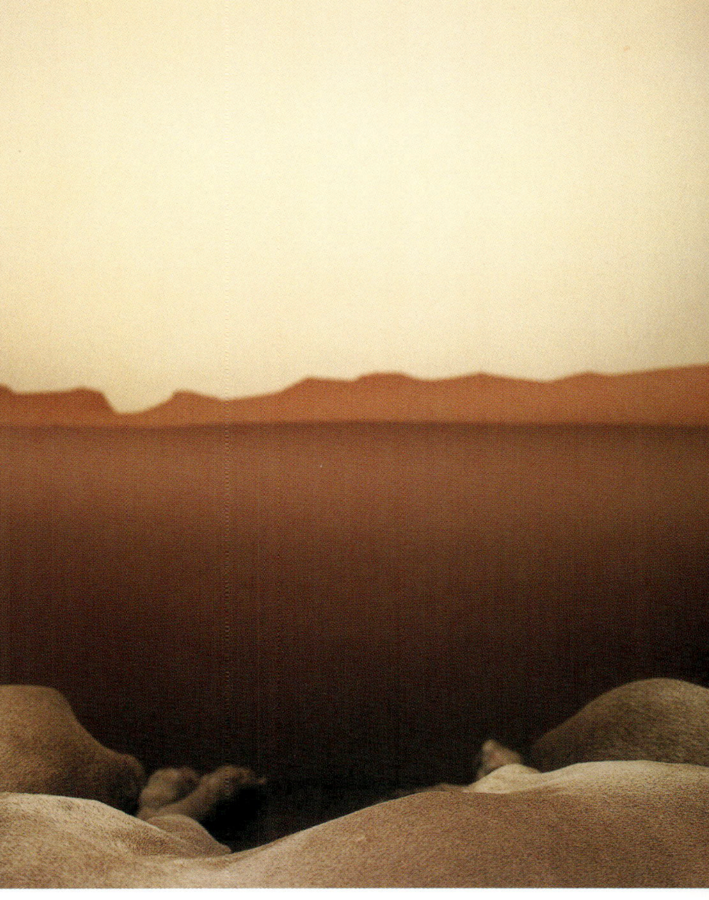

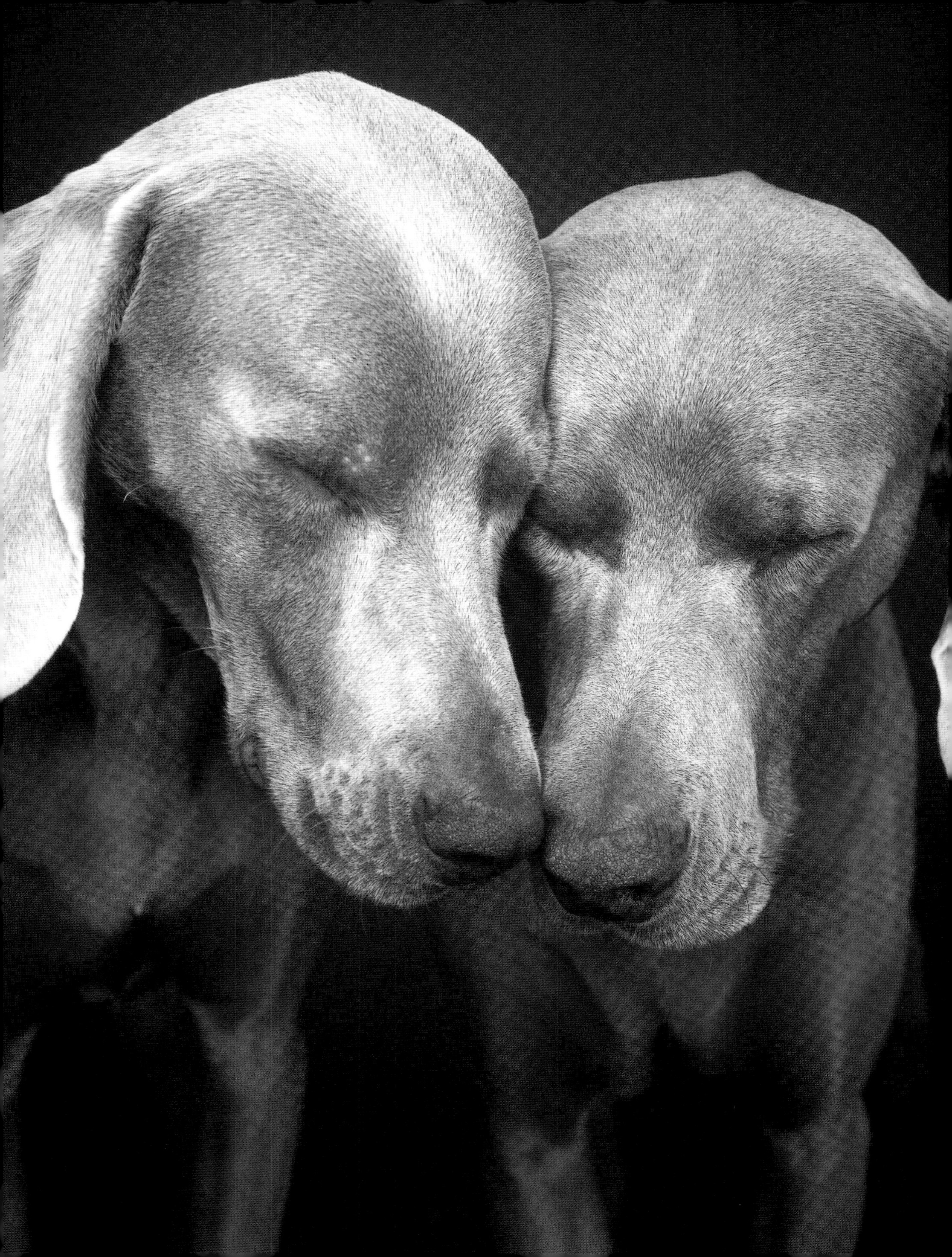

Reflectional, 2000

Mechanical, 1998

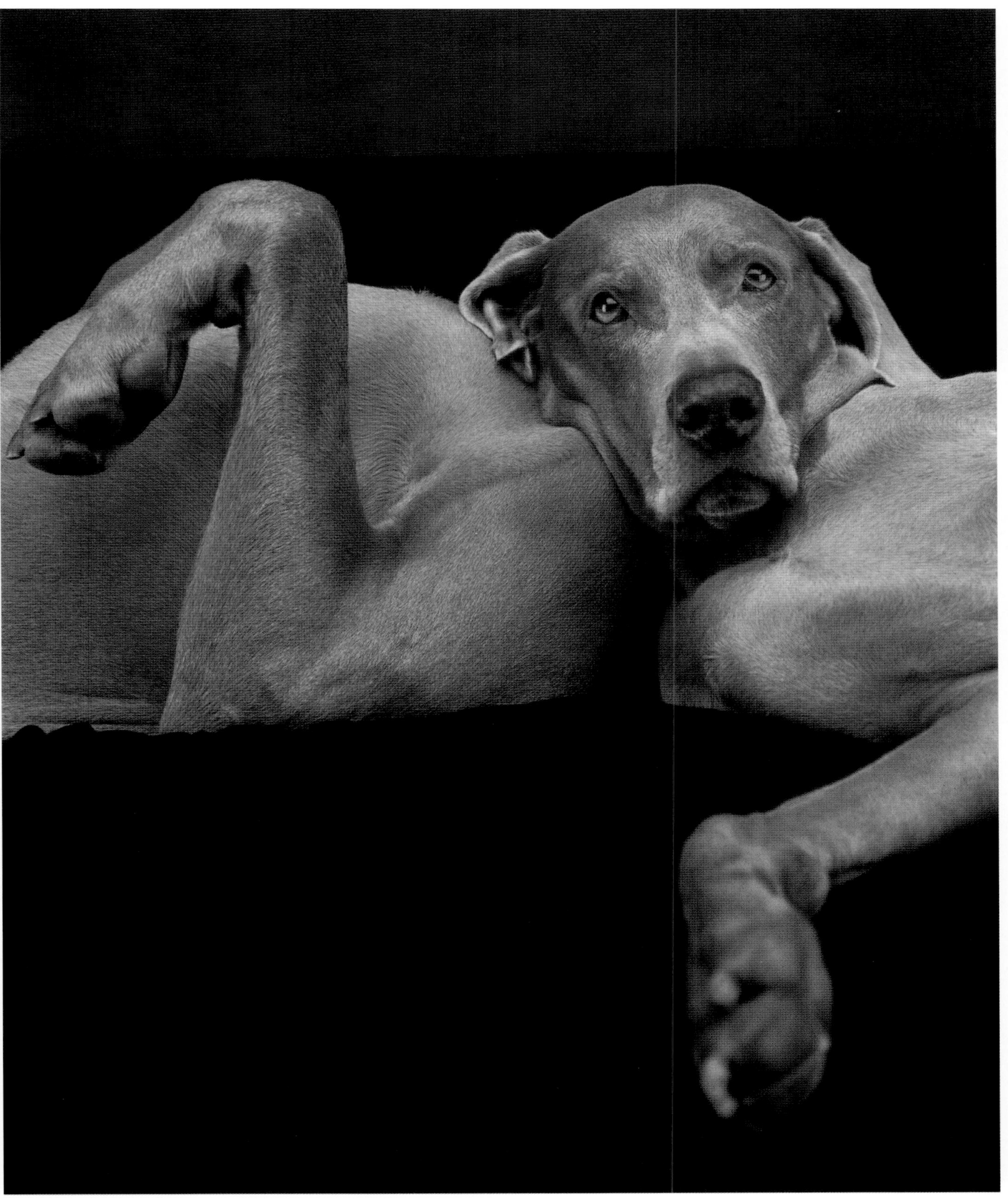

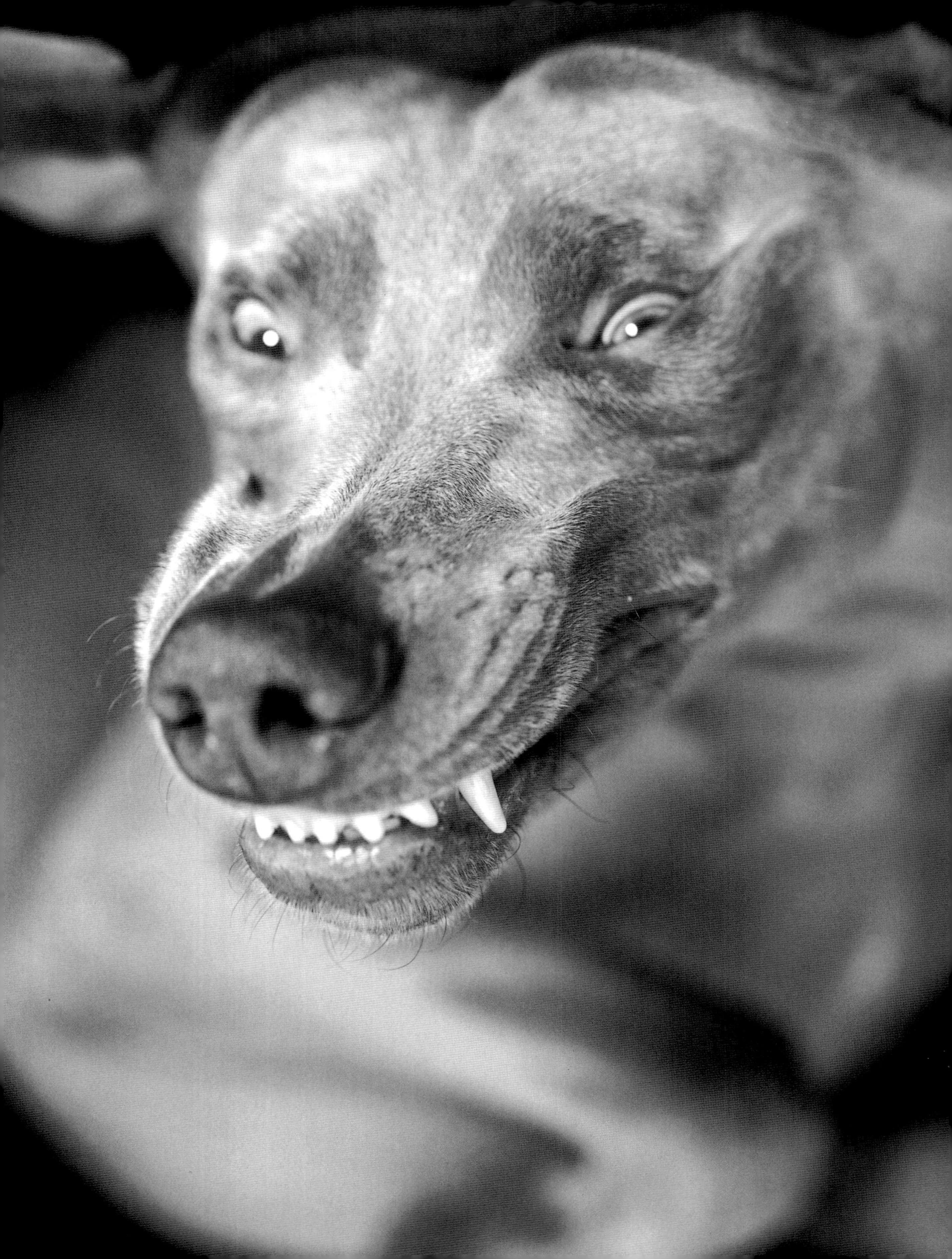

Opposite: ***Gargoyle I,*** 2000
Below: ***Smoke,*** 2001

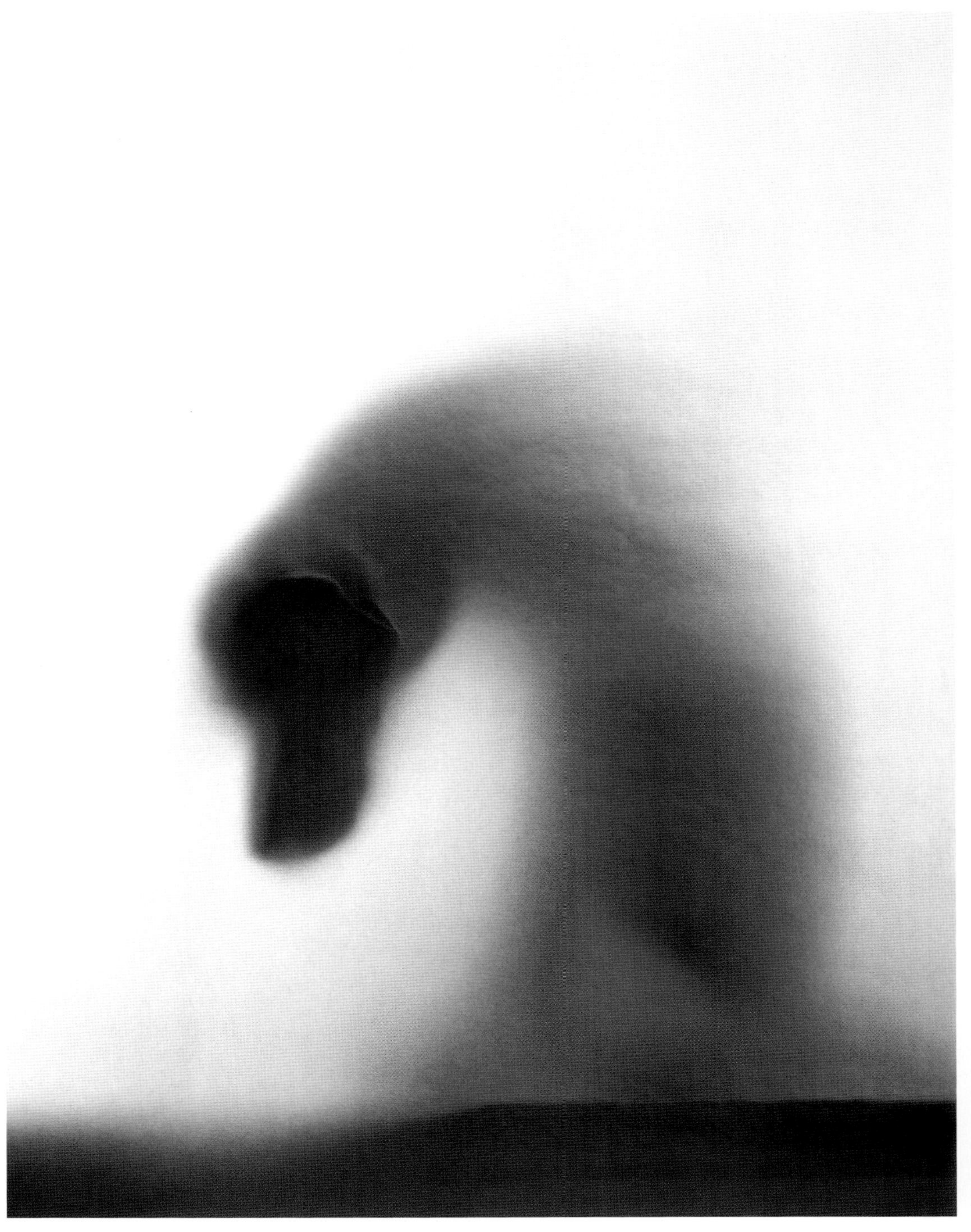

Below: ***Hair Do,*** 2001
Opposite: ***Earfold,*** 2001

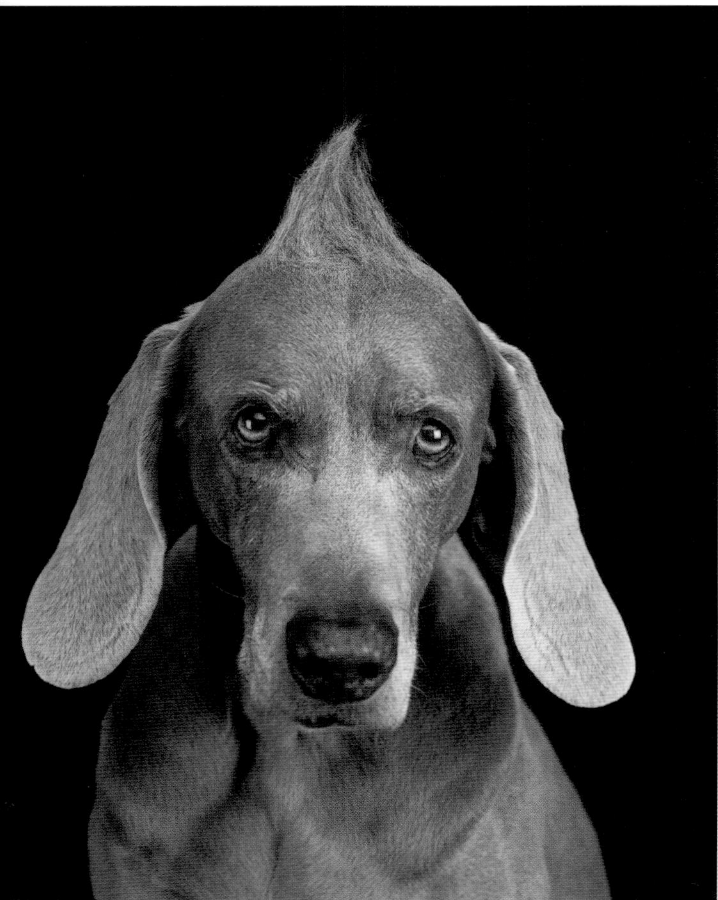

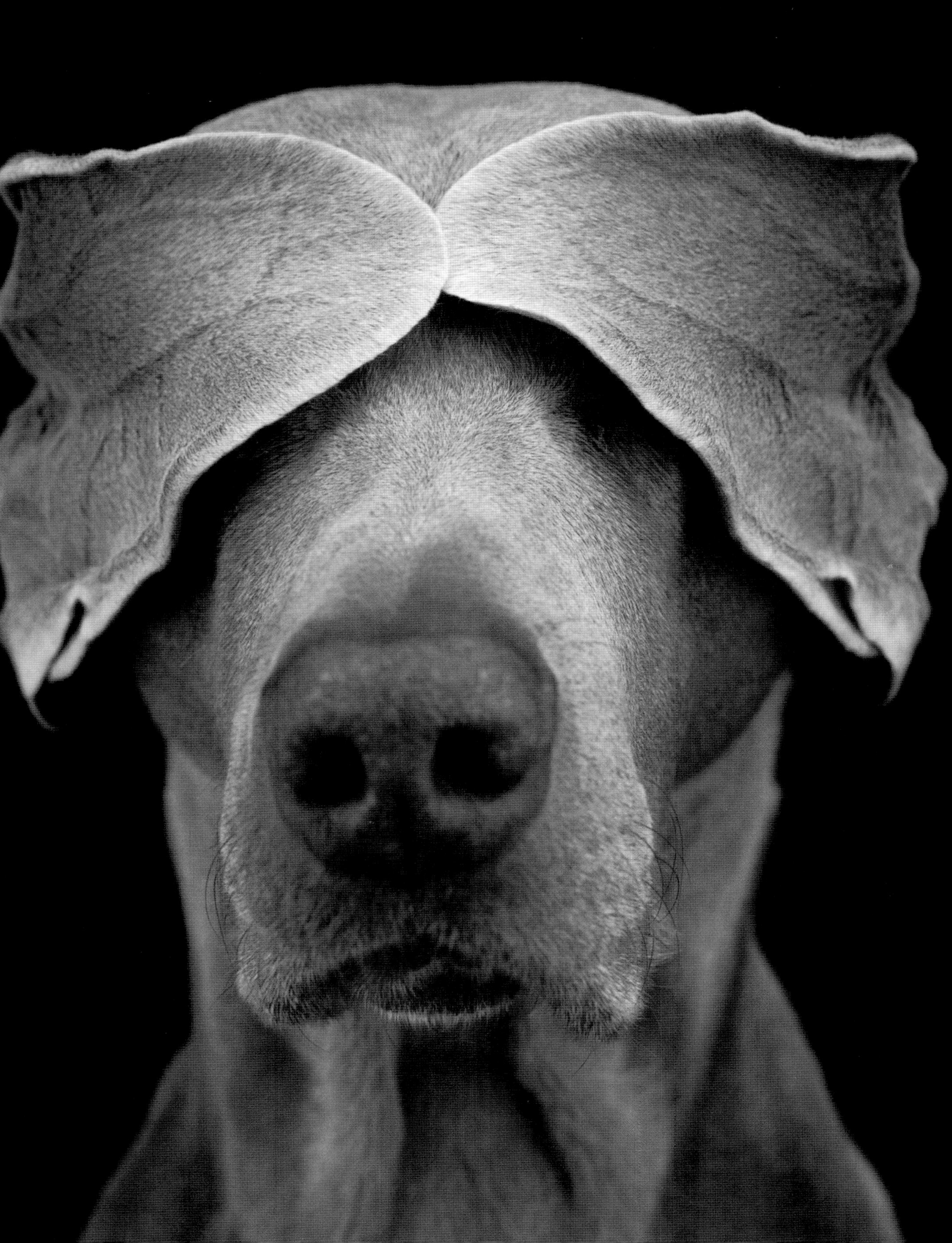

Gold Chamberlain, 2000

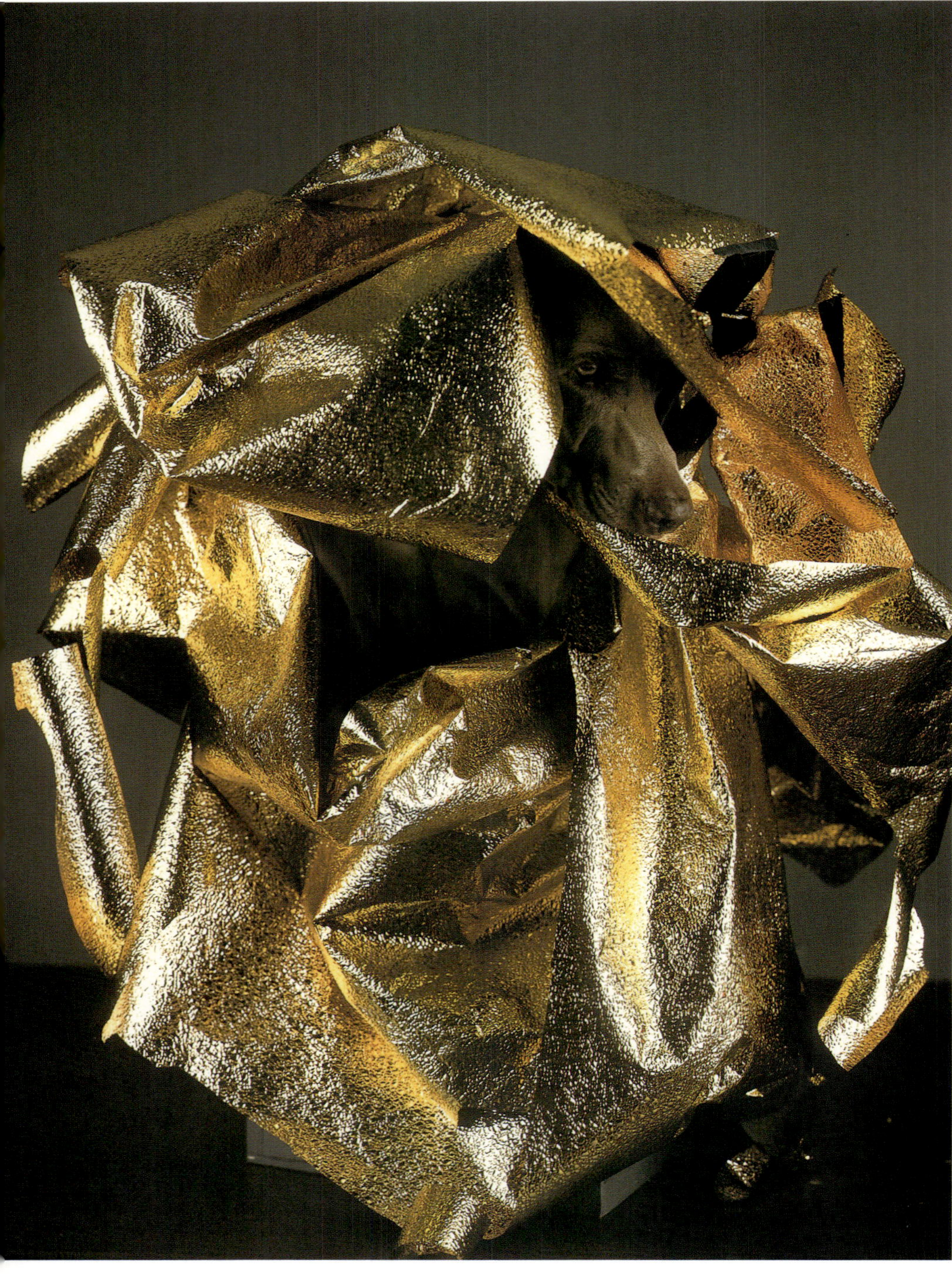

Gabo, 2001

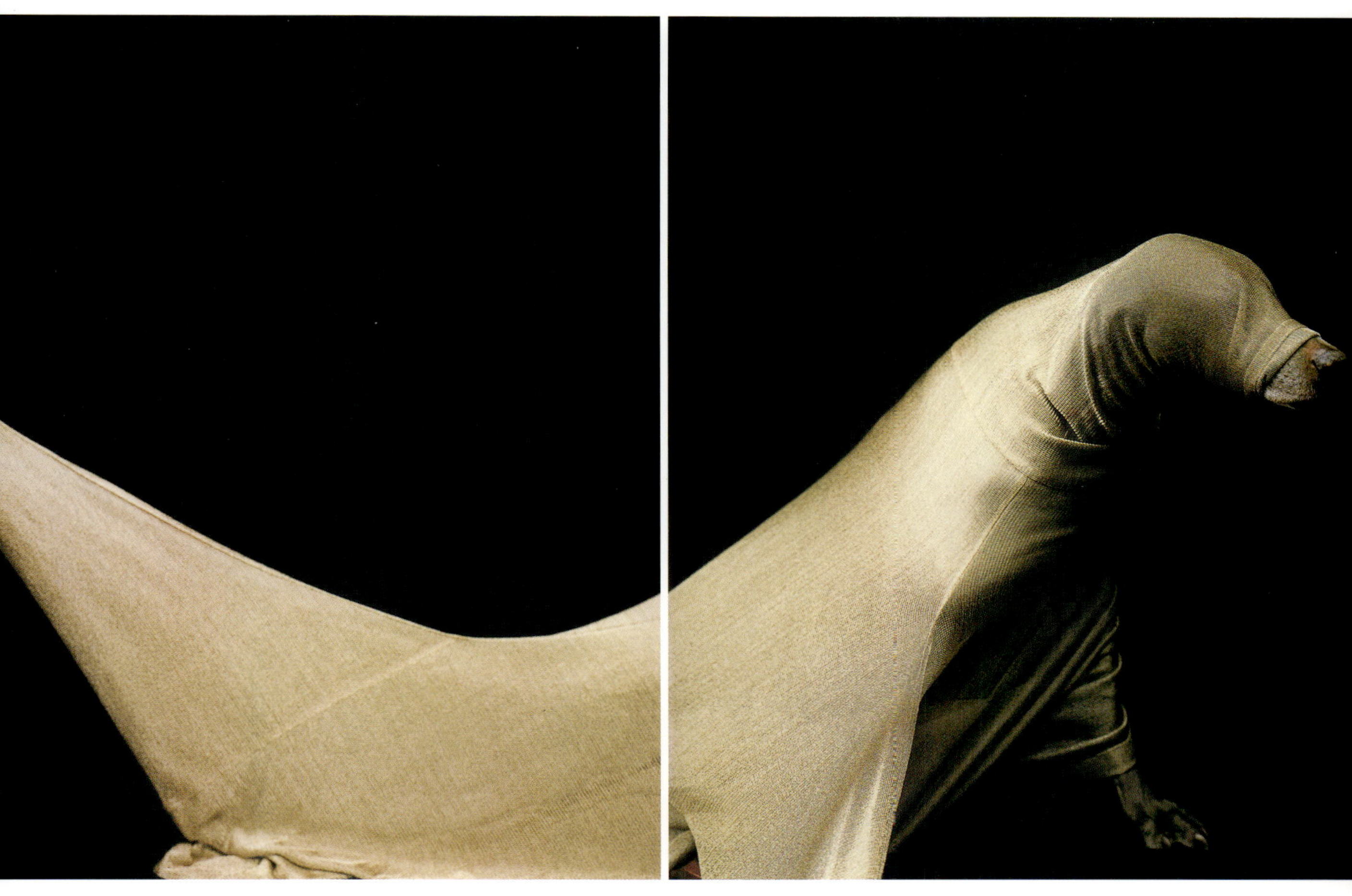

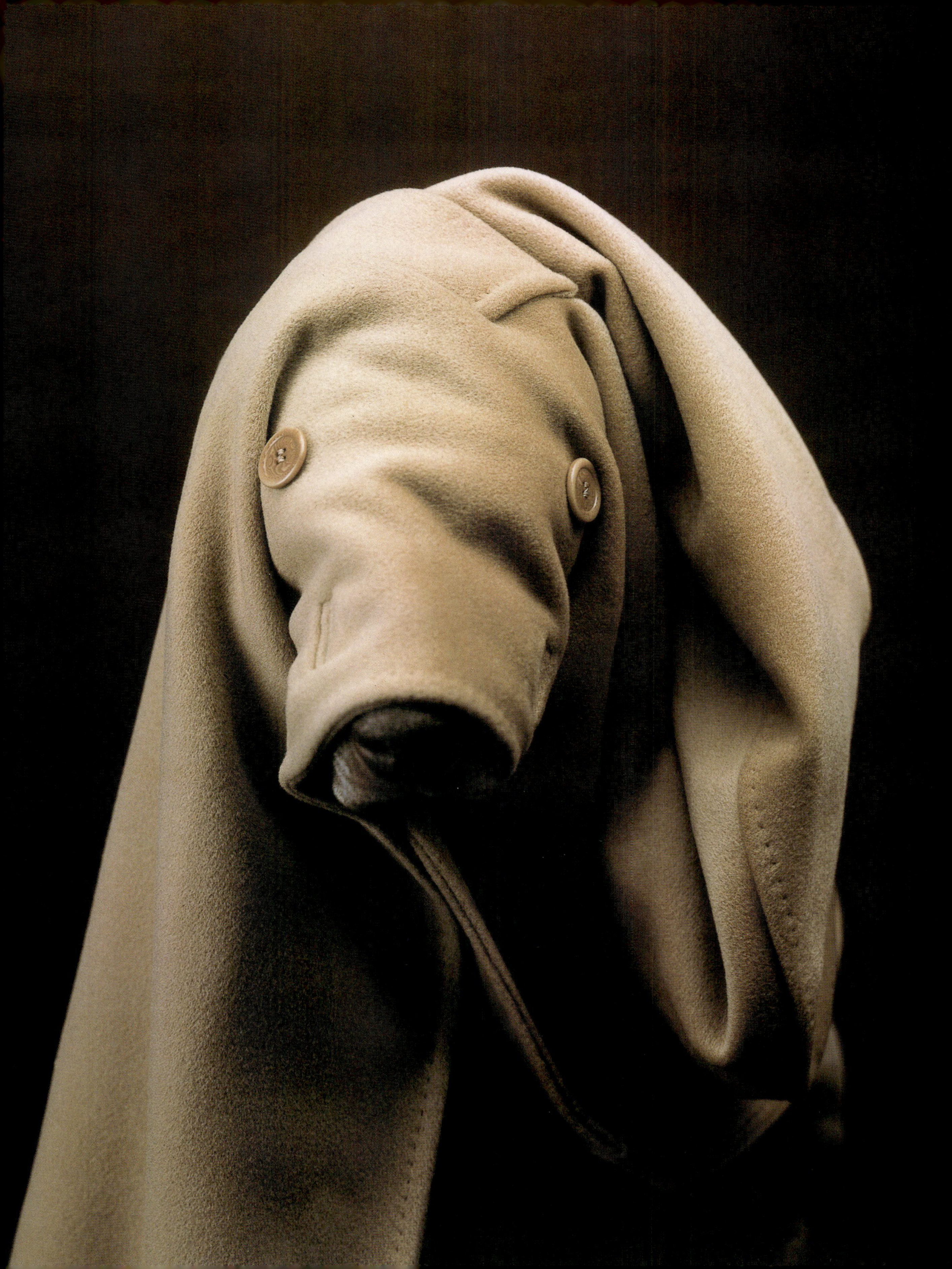

Steedette, 2001

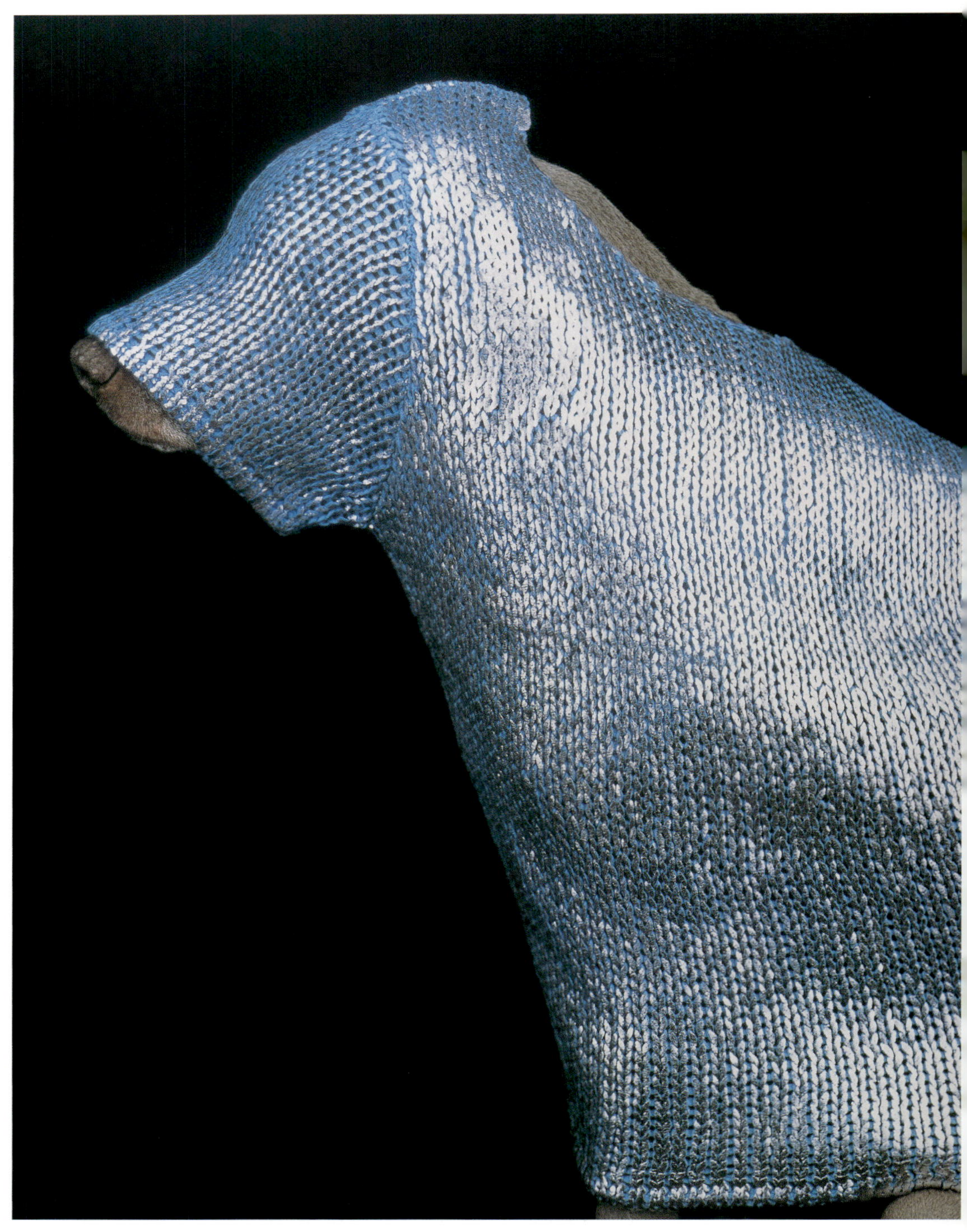

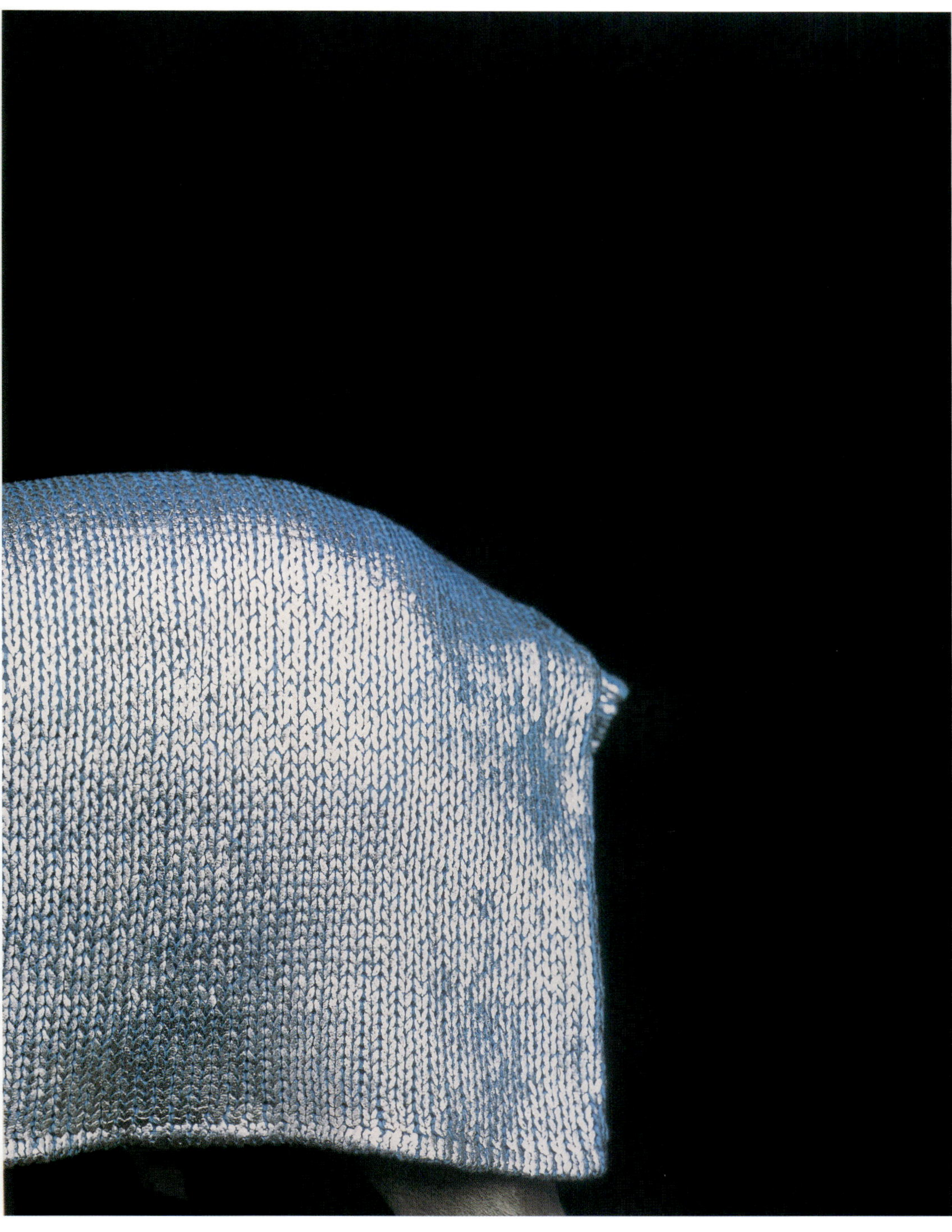

Flora to Fauna, 2001

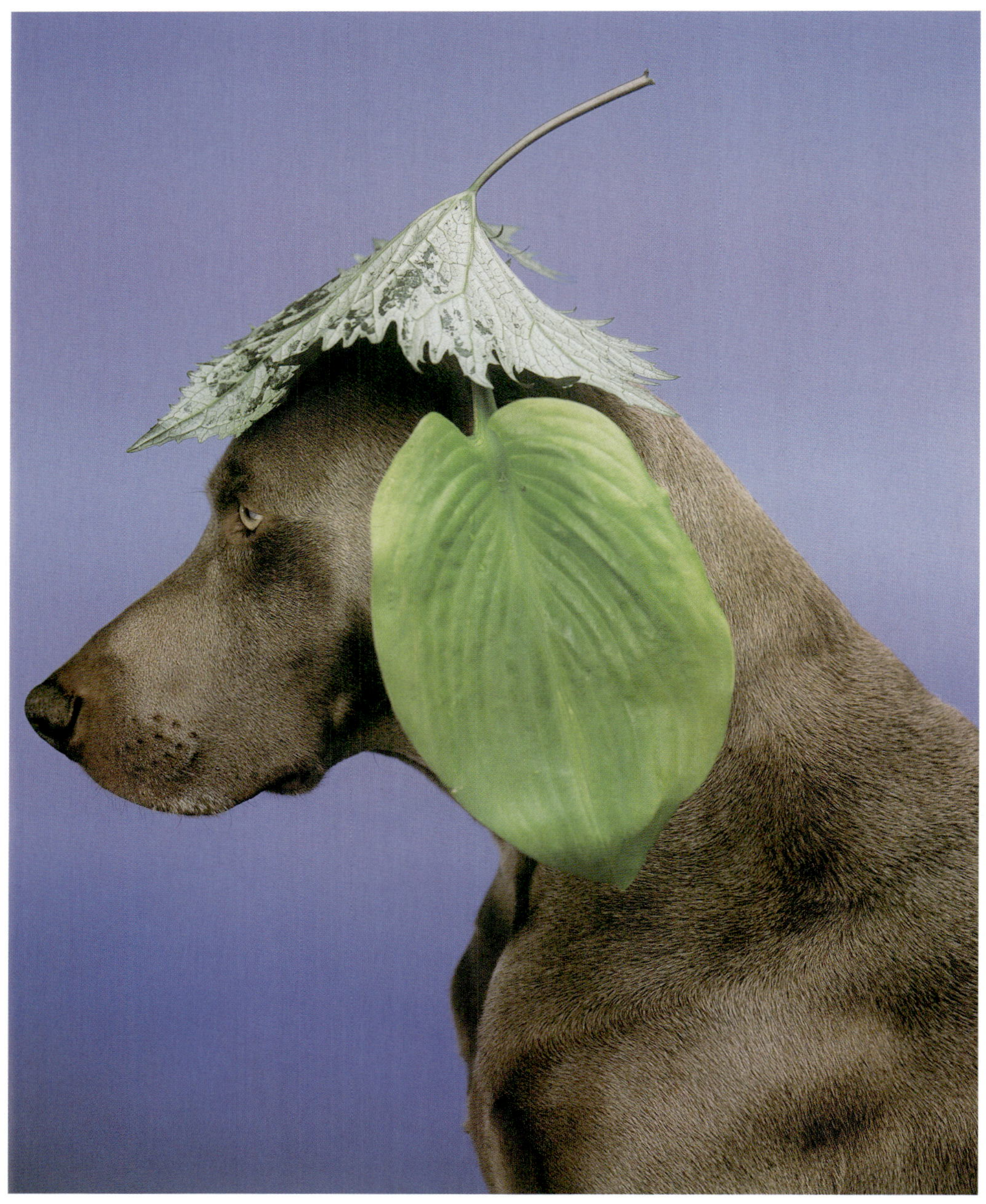

Top Left: ***Faun***, 2001
Top Right: ***Viking Vitae***, 2001
Lower Left: ***Maple Terrace***, 2001
Lower Right: ***Florastan***, 1989

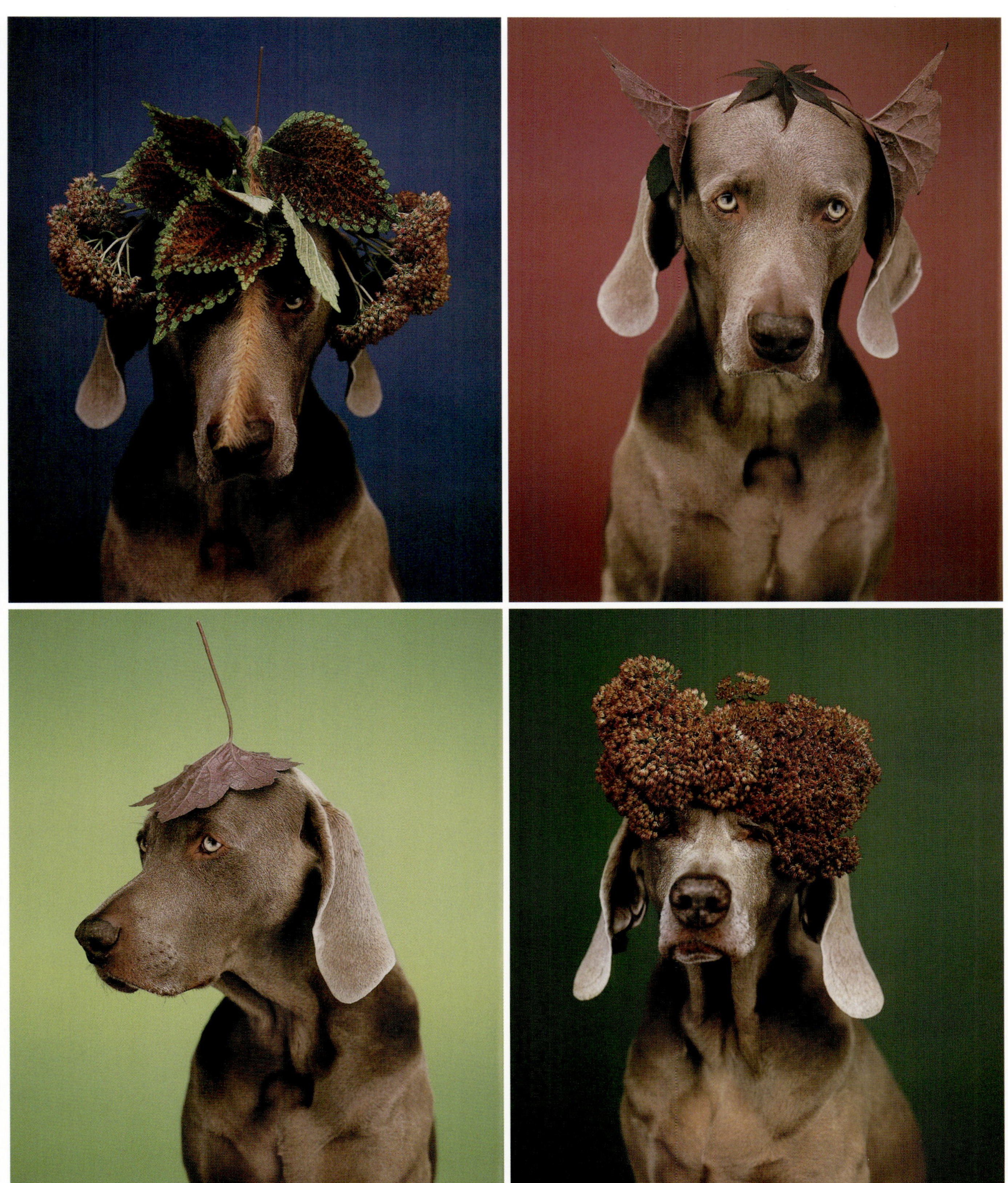

Below: ***Inner Dog*, 2000**
Opposite: ***Catty*, 2000**

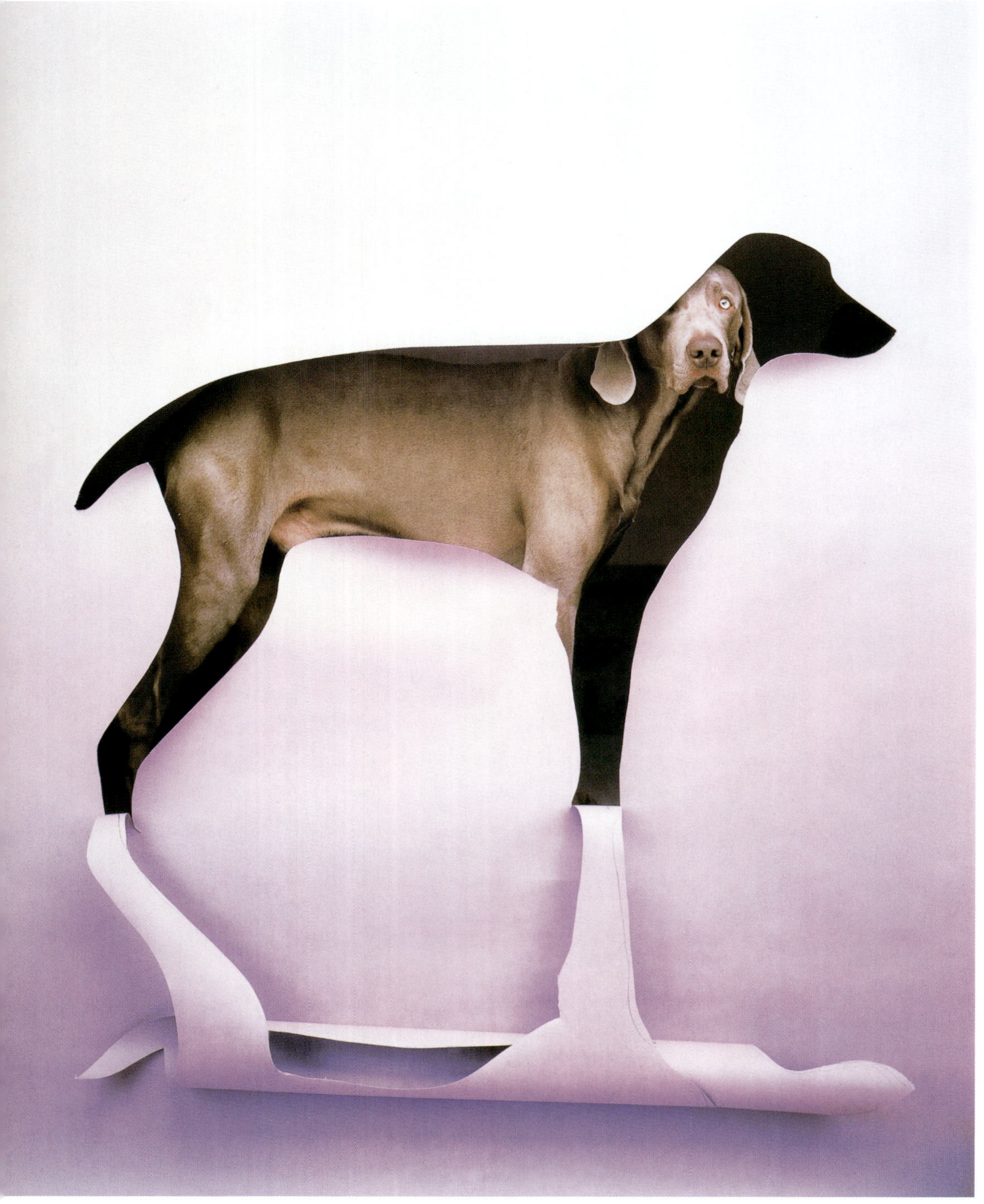

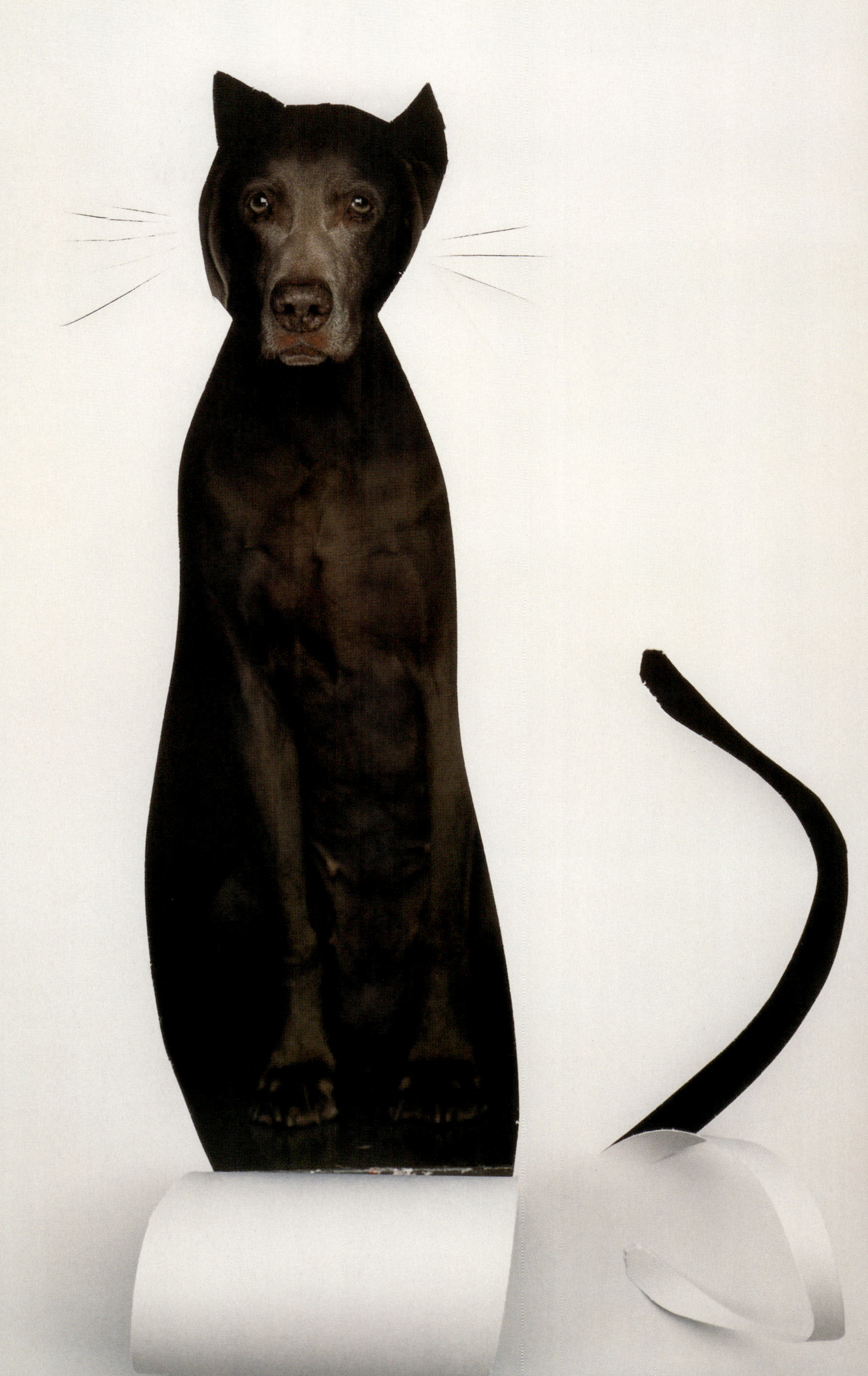

Below: ***Paper Posey,*** 2001
Opposite: ***Prototype II,*** 2001

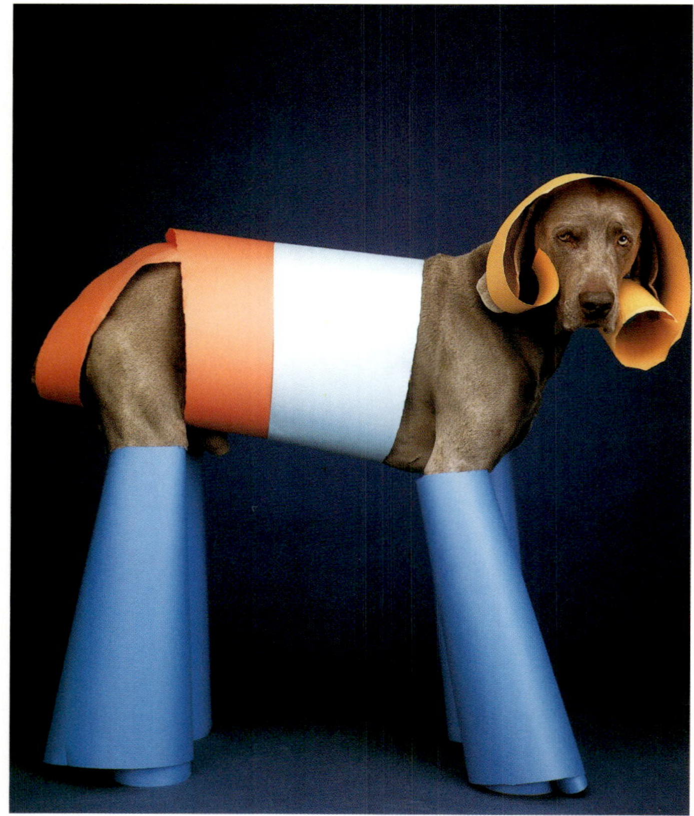

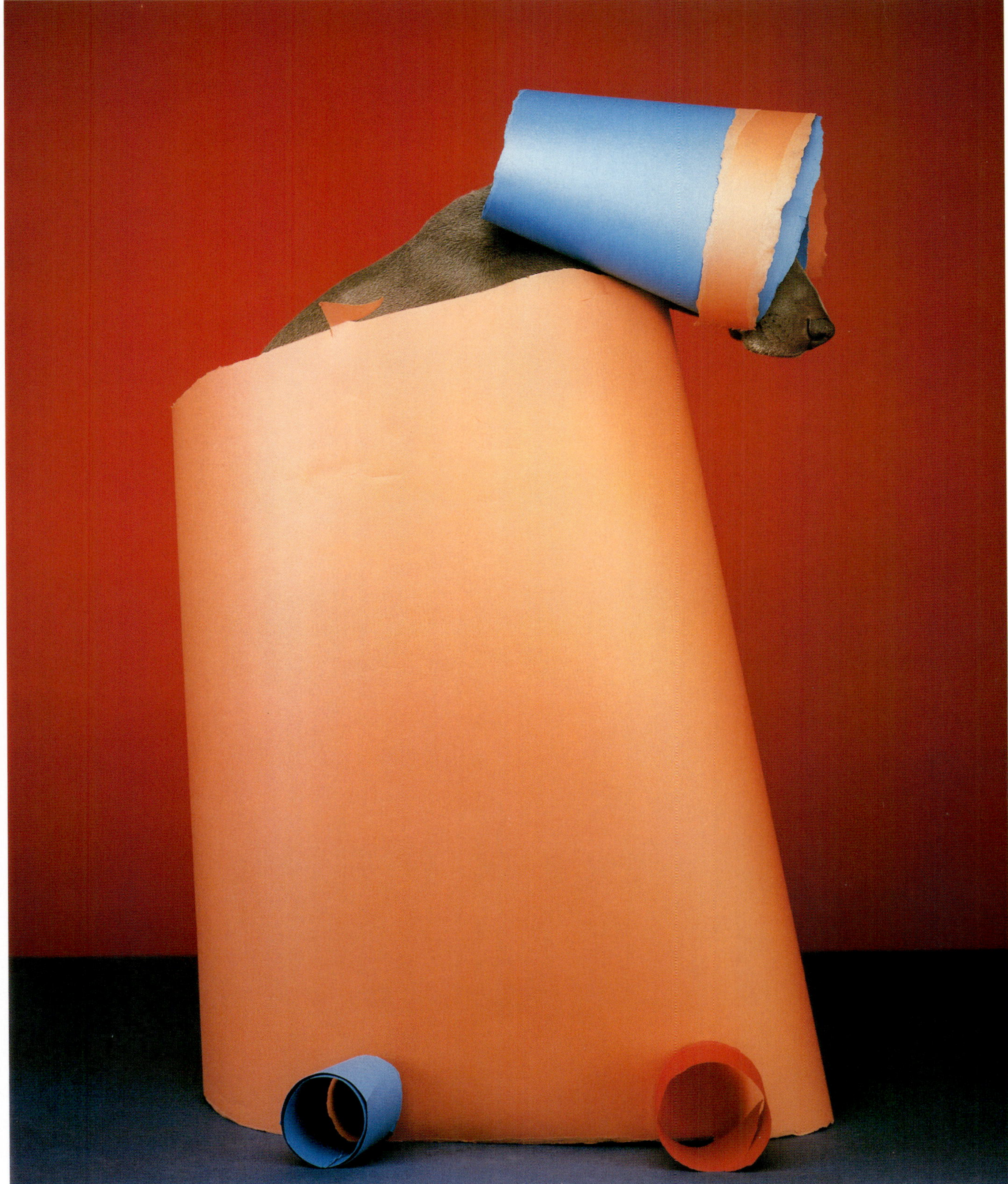

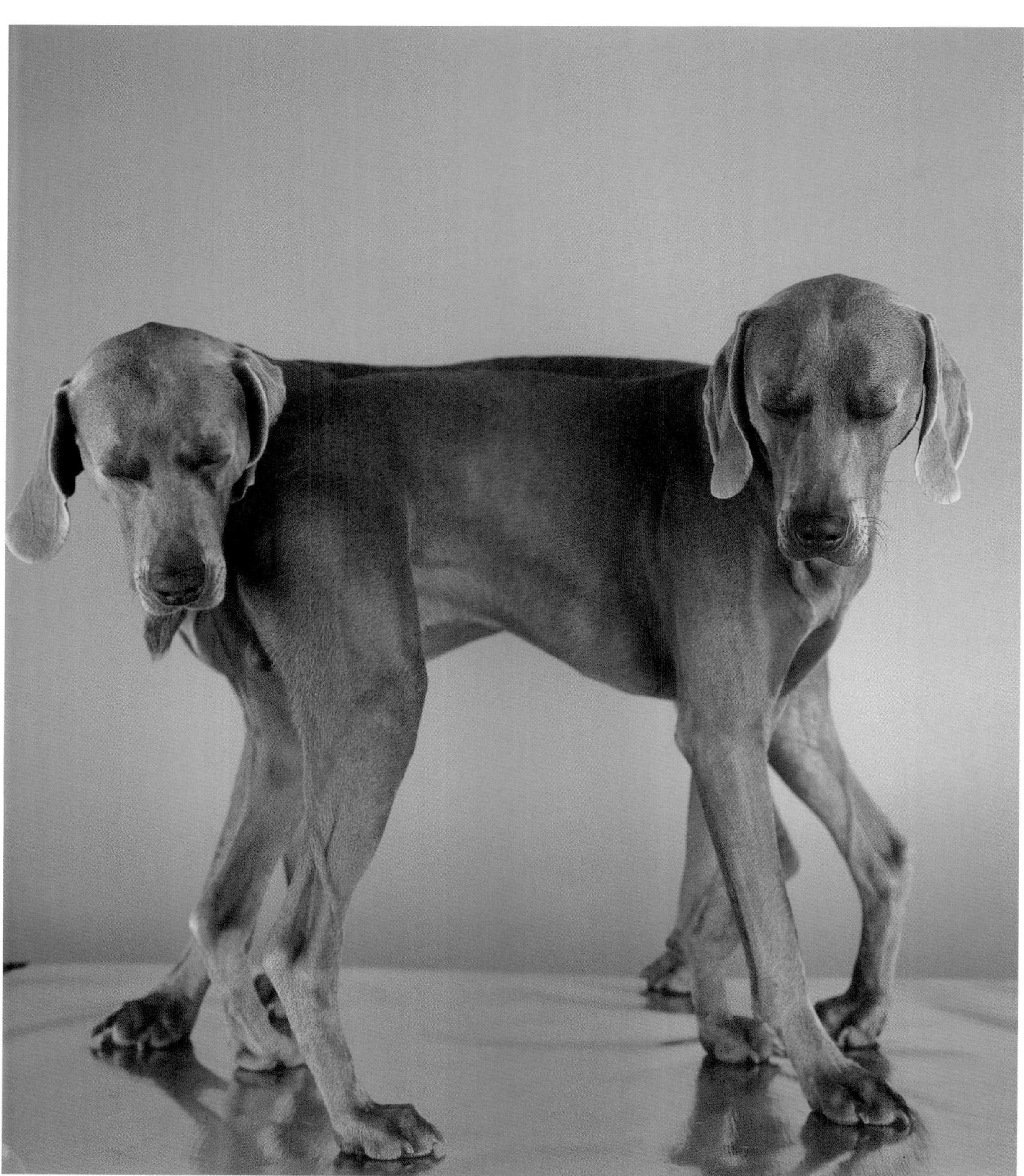

At this writing I have five related dogs: Chundo, Batty, Crooky, Chip, and Bobbin.

In 1999 Chip, mating with Midge, sired three male puppies.Pam took Bobbin (named after my droll comic heroes Bob & Ray and because she likes to sew). A good choice. Bobbin is a wonderful dog, outgoing and studly. He looks just like Chip except he's more . . . um . . . chipper. Fortunately for me, he takes after Chip in his indefatigable willingness to pose. Bright-eyed and outgoing, Bobbin brings an exuberant luminosity to the page. See if you can pick him out in *Second Choristers.* Living in Maine with Chundo and near Crooky, as well as in New York, Bobbin is falling into the mold of all my lucky dogs. Bobbin has a great future. He has the best of both worlds.

And now alongside Batty and Chip, I have Candy, a young female weimaraner bred outside Fay's line who may one day mate with . . . are you reading this, Bobbin? She is exceptionally different from all the others. Although she has become a bright star of my video work for Sesame Street, she is not so sure about photography and it shows in her expression while posing. She seems to be making progress. My last session with her was promising. With Candy, whose image closes the book, I'm left wondering.

Below: ***Ribboneal,*** **2002**
Opposite: ***Pupitto,*** **2002**

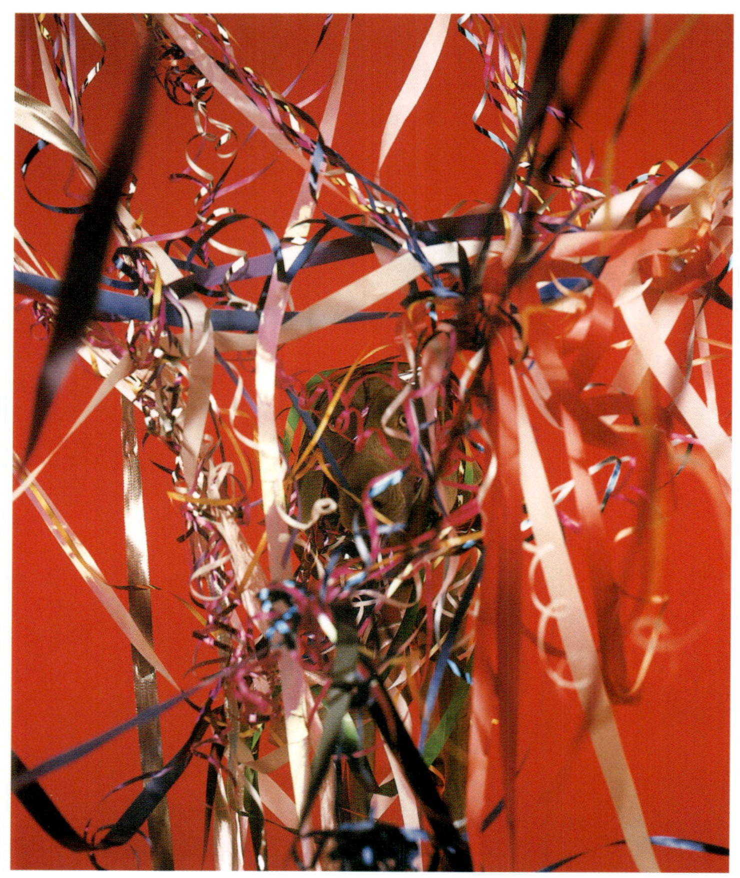

What will become of the 20x24?

I asked the same question twenty years ago when the camera was placed in storage indefinitely. The camera is fragile, a rickety homemade contraption, an experimental prototype. You can't buy one. When you run out of film, you can't run to the store and get more. Of the five that were made in the mid-Seventies, only three are still functioning. I'm surprised it's lasted as long as it has. This may be the end, but as long as it's around I'll probably use it. I'm a Polaroid 20x24 addict.

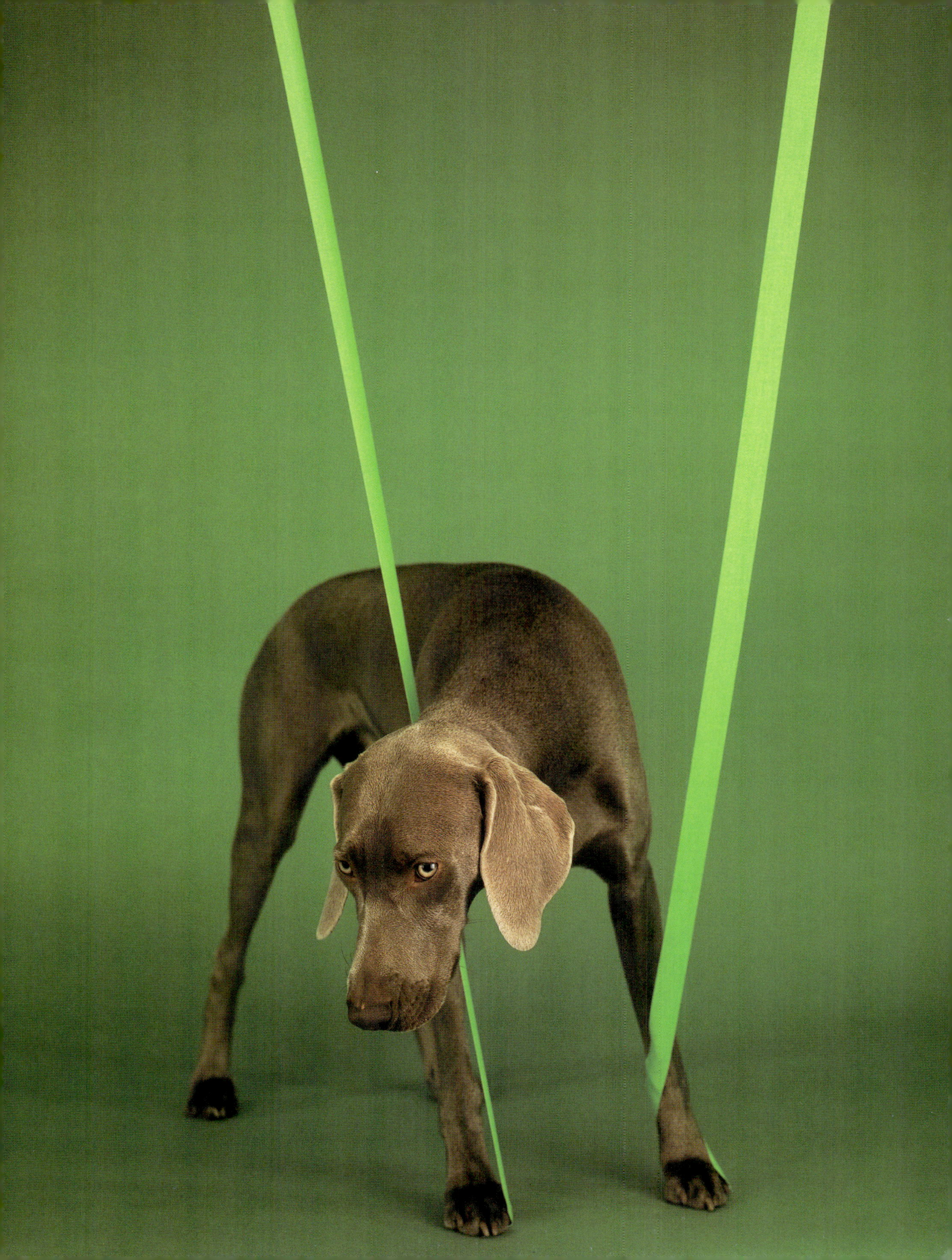

ACKNOWLEDGMENTS

For their considerable and valuable help in editing and designing this book, I would like to especially thank Christine Burgin, Gary Tooth, Eric Himmel, and Patrick O'Rourke.

I am deeply grateful and profoundly indebted to all assistants past and present for their enthusiastic willingness and talent. Without their help my work with the dogs would not be possible. Thanks to Andrea Beeman, Jason Burch, Betsy Connors, Ariel Dill, Catherine Ecclestone, Matt Garton, Arnie Hernandez, Julie Hindley, Marlo Kovach, Marion Maloney, Lisa Martin, Dave McMillan, Erick Michaud, Heather Murray, Chris Schiavo, John Slyce, Jeff Smith, Katleen Sterck, and Pam Wegman.

A very special thanks to John Reuter of the Polaroid studio, whose technical expertise and aesthetic judgement I have relied on for over twenty years. Thanks to Peter Bass, Stacey Fischer, Ben Fraser, Rogier Gregoire, Trisha Krauss, Barbara Hitchcock, Stanley Rowin, Tracy Storer, JoAnn Verburg, Eelco Wolf, Sam Yanes, and the Polaroid Corporation.

Thanks to the humans who have posed in these pictures and for lending their hands: Andrea Beeman, Jason Burch, Betsy Connors, Eve Darcy, Julie Hindley, Trisha Krauss, Hester Laddey, Lisa Martin, Heather Murray, David Ross, Lindsay Ross, Ed Ruscha, and Veronica Webb.

I would also like to thank Virginia Alexander, Jen Allison, Empire Design Studio, Mary Dinaburg, Marvin Heiferman, Houston Grand Opera, Mark Hunt, Frederica Hunter, Janklow & Nesbit Associates, Randy Johnsen, Jeff Keogh, Carole Kismaric, Peter MacGill, Massachusets College of Art, New Jersey State Council on the Arts, Pace/MacGill Gallery, Dale Rubin, Ed Ruscha, Saks Fifth Avenue, Holly Solomon, Tavi Storer, Jeanette Ward, Canon Jay Wegman, and the Cathedral of Saint John the Divine.

—William Wegman

Editor: Eric Himmel
Designer: Gary Tooth, Empire Design Studio, NYC
Production Director: Hope Koturo

Page 2: *Artist Contemplating*, 1994
Page 4: *Towel*, 1998
Page 6: *Evergreen*, 2001

Library of Congress Cataloging-in-Publication Data

Wegman, William.
William Wegman polaroids / William Wegman.
p. cm.
ISBN 0–8109–3480–9 (cloth) / 0–8109–9242–6 (pbk)
1. Photography of dogs. 2. Instant photography. 3. Wegman, William.
I. Title.
TR729.D6 W435 2002
779'.329772—dc21
2002006197

Copyright © 2002 William Wegman

Paperback edition published in 2005 by Harry N. Abrams, Incorporated, New York. All rights reserved. No part of the contents of this book may be reproduced without the written permission of the publisher

Clothbound edition published in 2002 by Harry N. Abrams, Inc.

Printed and bound in Japan
10 9 8 7 6 5 4 3 2 1

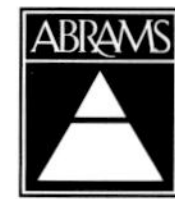

Harry N. Abrams, Inc.
100 Fifth Avenue
New York, N.Y. 10011
www.abramsbooks.com

Abrams is a subsidiary of LA MARTINIÈRE GROUPE